Tear out this answer
mask to use when an-
swering questions in the
programmed comple-
tion exercises (see Pref-
ace for further direc-
tions).

Tear out this answer
mask to use when an-
swering questions in the
programmed comple-
tion exercises (see Pref-
ace for further direc-
tions).

# UNDERSTANDING MARKETING

# UNDERSTANDING MARKETING

Study Guide for

## Marketing: Basic Concepts and Decisions

SECOND EDITION

**WILLIAM M. PRIDE**

Texas A & M University

**O. C. FERRELL**

Illinois State University

**Houghton Mifflin Company   Boston**

Dallas   Geneva, Illinois

Hopewell, New Jersey   Palo Alto   London

To
Jack and Grace Burkett
Henry and Alene Zey

Printed in the U.S.A.
ISBN: 0-395-28163-6

# Contents

# To the Student

*Understanding Marketing* has been designed to be used with *Marketing: Basic Concepts and Decisions* (Second Edition) by William M. Pride and O. C. Ferrell. We have developed this study guide (1) to assist you in learning the definitions, concepts, and relationships presented in our textbook and (2) to help you evaluate your knowledge and understanding of these materials.

For each chapter in *Marketing: Basic Concepts and Decisions* this guide contains five parts:

1. Chapter summary
2. True or false statements
3. Multiple-choice questions
4. Programmed completion exercises
5. Answers to objective questions

Each chapter summary provides an overall perspective on the content in the text chapter. We suggest that you read this chapter summary before reading the chapter in the textbook because the summary can act as a preview and make you aware of the major topics and relationships presented in the chapter. This awareness will help you to grasp the chapter material more easily. Before you attempt to complete the questions and exercises for a specific chapter, we suggest that you reread the study guide summary to refresh your memory about the contents of the text chapter.

The true or false statements and the multiple-choice questions are presented to aid you in testing your understanding of marketing terminology, concepts, and relationships. Some of these exercises deal with definitions and details, while others focus on the broader aspects of marketing decisions and activities.

The programmed completion exercises offer a method for both learning and testing your knowledge. Like the other exercises, the programmed completion exercises pertain to your understanding of both specific details and more general relationships. When working with the programmed completion exercises, you should use the perforated cardboard mask, which can be torn out from inside the front cover of this book. This mask is used to cover the correct response word(s) which complete each question. To begin, cover the answers in the left-hand column. After answering a question, move the mask down so that the answer is exposed. Thus, you can evaluate your answers immediately. When working through the programmed completion exercises, do not be overly concerned if your answers are not exactly the same as those suggested. The purpose of these exercises is to improve and evaluate your understanding of marketing topics and relationships rather than to encourage you to memorize.

The last part of each chapter supplies the answers to the true or false statements and to the multiple-choice questions. These answers are provided to help you evaluate your understanding of the material in the textbook chapter. To achieve this purpose, you should refer to these answers only after you have completed the questions.

*Understanding Marketing* is a "self-help" tool. It can help you to learn and evaluate your knowledge only to the extent that you use it correctly and regularly.

The authors both acknowledge and appreciate the assistance of Flavia Krone, Don Garrett, and Kris Miller in the development of materials for this study guide.

William M. Pride
O. C. Ferrell

# UNDERSTANDING MARKETING

# CHAPTER 1

# Marketing: An Overview

## Chapter Summary

The study of marketing is relevant for many reasons. Marketing costs consume about one-half of a buyer's dollar. Therefore, buyers should know how their money is used. Second, marketing activities are used in many organizations, and many people earn a living by engaging in these activities, which include personal selling, advertising, packaging, transportation, storage, marketing research, product development, wholesaling, and retailing. Third, marketing activities are important to business organizations and to the economy. Such activities help businesses to create and sell products and to generate profits. Finally, by studying marketing, an individual should be in a better position to weigh the costs, benefits, and flaws of marketing activities.

Marketing is broadly defined as a set of individual and organizational activities aimed at facilitating and expediting exchanges within a set of dynamic environmental forces. Marketing activities are performed by individuals and organizations. An individual who owns a store or who wants to sell a car must perform marketing activities to facilitate an exchange. Many organizations other than business organizations carry out marketing activities as a way to facilitate exchanges. Four conditions must exist for an exchange situation to arise. First, exchange requires participation by two or more individuals, groups, or organizations. Second, each party must possess "something of value" that the other party desires. Third, each must be willing to give up its "something of value" in order to receive the

1

"something of value" held by the other individual, group, or organization. Fourth, the parties to the exchange must be able to communicate with each other in order to make their "something of value" available. The "somethings of value" that are held by the two exchange parties are usually products and/or financial resources such as cash or credit. Products can be goods, services, or ideas.

The marketing concept is a philosophy that a business organization should try to satisfy customers' needs through a coordinated set of activities that at the same time allows the organization to achieve its goals. Providing customer satisfaction is the major thrust of the marketing concept. However, an organization must alter, adapt, and change current product offerings to keep pace with changes in consumers' desires and preferences, as well as to provide satisfying new products. The philosophy of the marketing concept calls for the coordination of a firm's activities—including production, finance, accounting, personnel management, and marketing—in order to provide customer satisfaction. The marketing concept, however, has not always been accepted. The marketing concept evolved through three eras in the history of U.S. business: the production era, the sales era, and the marketing era.

To implement the marketing concept, several factors are required. Top management in the organization must implement it. The high-level executives must accept the marketing concept as one of their personal philosophies of business management to the extent that it becomes the basis for all the decisions and goals they set for the firm. Management must establish an information system to learn about customers' needs and must be willing to commit necessary resources to develop and maintain such a system; in some cases the firm may have to be reorganized.

Several problems arise when attempting to implement the marketing concept. First, there is a limit to which a firm can satisfy customers' needs for a particular product class. Second, management must be able to determine customers' product needs. Third, in attempting to satisfy its customers' needs, a firm may contribute to the dissatisfaction of other societal segments. Fourth, a restructuring of the organization may be required, which may lead to morale problems. The evidence indicates that adoption of the marketing concept has been more prevalent among larger organizations. However, we can expect more organizations to adopt the philosophy of the marketing concept in the future.

The marketing mix consists of four major variables: product, price, distribution, and promotion. The marketing mix is built around buyers. To provide consumer satisfaction, a marketing manager must create and maintain a marketing mix that fits consumers' needs for that general type of product. Even though marketing mix variables can be altered, they are not totally controllable; marketing managers are limited in the degree to which they can change the mix variables. The marketing mix variables are affected in three general ways by the marketing environment. First, the marketing environment affects consumers' lifestyles, standards of living, and preferences and needs for products. Second, forces in the marketing environment directly affect a marketing manager's ability to perform certain marketing activities. Third, forces in the marketing environment influence the way consumers react to a firm's marketing mix. The marketing environment includes political forces, legal and regulatory forces, societal forces, consumer movement forces, and economic and technological forces. To create and maintain an effective marketing mix, marketers must recognize and analyze the effects of the marketing environment on marketing decisions and activities. They must be able to adjust the marketing mix to major changes in the marketing environment.

# True or False Statements

(T)  F      1. A sizable proportion of individuals who work for nonbusiness organizations are involved in marketing activities.

(T)  F      2. An organization's marketing activities are aimed directly or indirectly at helping to sell the organization's products.

T  (F)      3. According to the authors, marketing is defined as selling and advertising.

T  (F)      4. Marketing begins after goods and services have been produced.

(T)  F      5. All kinds of organizations such as churches, schools, and hospitals perform marketing activities.

(T)  F      6. The consummation of a specific exchange between two parties does not in itself determine whether or not marketing activities have occurred.

(T)  F      7. Products can be goods, services, or ideas.

(T)  F      8. A good is a tangible object possessing physical features.

T  (F)      9. The marketing concept should be viewed as a philosophy aimed at satisfying consumers, even though it may cost the firm long-run survival.

T  (F)      10. The customer orientation of the marketing concept means that business activities start within a firm and end with the consumers.

(T)  F      11. To satisfy customers, management should try to satisfy short-run needs as well as long-run desires.

(T)  F      12. The philosophy of the marketing concept calls for the coordination of a firm's activities.

(T)  F      13. Since the marketing concept is a management philosophy that affects all types of business activities, it must be implemented by top management in the organization.

T  (F)      14. Marketers are under very little pressure to provide high living standards and ideal lifestyles through socially responsible decisions and activities.

T  (F)      15. When implementing the marketing concept, the business organization should strive to build products to fit the needs of each consumer.

(T)  F      16. Many consumer product companies spend considerable amounts of time and money to research consumers' needs.

(T)  F      17. When a firm satisfies one segment of society, it may also contribute to the dissatisfaction of another segment.

(T)  F      18. Research findings generally indicate that the marketing concept has been adopted more by larger organizations than by smaller ones.

T  (F)    19. Marketing mix variables are totally controllable.

T  (F)    20. Marketing activities are associated with two general kinds of marketing variables—marketing mix variables and consumer variables.

(T)  F    21. One primary goal of a marketing manager is to create and maintain a marketing mix that satisfies consumers' needs for a type of product.

(T)  F    22. Through the marketing mix variables a marketing manager can develop and change marketing decisions and activities.

(T)  F    23. Marketing mix variables are often viewed as "controllable" variables because the marketing manager can change them.

T  (F)    24. The forces in the marketing environment do not directly affect the ability of a marketing manager to perform certain marketing activities.

(T)  F    25. The forces in the environment are sometimes called "uncontrollable" variables because the marketing manager cannot directly control them, although the manager can influence them.

T  (F)    26. Firms should not be concerned about how they are viewed by political officials.

(T)  F    27. To a large extent, economic forces determine the competitive atmosphere within which a firm operates.

(T)  F    28. Technology affects people's everyday lives.

T  (F)    29. Technology affects people's lifestyles and their standards of living but does not have a direct impact on the creation of a marketing mix.

# Multiple-Choice Questions

  1. Approximately what percentage of a buyer's dollar is used for paying the costs of marketing activities?
   a. 50 percent
   b. 60 percent
   c. 45 percent
   d. 40 percent
   e. 25 percent

_C_  2. Approximately what percentage of U.S. civilian workers employed by business organizations perform marketing activities?
   a. 30 to 35 percent
   b. 50 to 55 percent
   c. 25 to 33 percent

d. 33 to 38 percent

e. 50 percent

**B**

3. An organization's marketing activities are
    a. an essential part of all organizational activities.
    b. aimed directly or indirectly at helping to sell the organization's products.
    c. developed for the sole purpose of producing profits through exchanges.
    d. the lifeblood of an organization.
    e. utilized by the firm only in the event of a profitable exchange.

**C**

4. To survive in a capitalistic economy, a firm must
    a. grow.
    b. generate immediate profits.
    c. generate long-run profits.
    d. attract more capital.
    e. produce more products.

**E**

5. Which of the following is *not* considered a marketing activity?
    a. Promotion
    b. Storage
    c. Product development
    d. Wholesaling
    e. Production

**C**

6. Which of the following statements most completely defines the term *marketing*?
    a. Marketing is the transportation of goods from the manufacturer to the retailers so that goods are available when and where consumers want them.
    b. Marketing occurs when consumers go shopping and make purchases.
    c. Marketing consists of individual and organizational activities aimed at facilitating and expediting exchanges.
    d. Marketing is the efficient organization of the firm's activities into a single customer-oriented entity.
    e. Marketing includes all those activities involved in the production, transportation, and ultimate sale of products.

**B**

7. Even universities are involved in marketing activities. Which of the following is *least* likely to be considered a marketing activity?
    a. Addition of a new course of study requested by many students
    b. Application to the state government for building funds
    c. Expansion of the school cafeteria to include fast-order foods
    d. Fine arts series sponsored on campus
    e. Extension of free-time hours in athletic facilities to meet demand overflow

A    8. The intangible "something of value" that is provided by applying human and mechanical efforts to people or objects is called a
    a. service.
    b. product.
    c. good.
    d. market variable.
    e. exchange variable.

B    9. Concerning marketing activities, which statement is most correct?
    a. Most of the approaches, concepts, and activities are used by business organizations.
    b. Many marketing activities are performed to support exchanges even though some situations do not result in exchanges.
    c. The consummation of a specific exchange must occur for marketing activities to occur.
    d. Marketing activities must be performed by individuals, not by organizations.
    e. Marketing activities can be justified only if an exchange occurs and if profit results from the exchange process.

e    10. The customer orientation of the marketing concept stresses the importance of the customer. The main thrust of this statement is that organizations should
    a. create new products whenever possible.
    b. provide products that will satisfy short-term needs.
    c. avoid duplication of products already on the market.
    d. get the products into the hands of consumers.
    e. provide customer satisfaction.

B    11. To provide customer satisfaction, marketing activities must begin with
    a. the creation of high-quality products.
    b. a focus on customers in order to determine what will satisfy them.
    c. concentration on putting the product in the hands of consumers.
    d. attempts to alter product offerings to keep prices as low as possible.
    e. attempts to satisfy existing customers' needs.

C    12. In attempting to satisfy customers, businesses must consider not only short-run, immediate needs but also
    a. economic conditions.
    b. short-run consumers' wants.
    c. broad, long-run desires.
    d. current customer dissatisfaction.
    e. short-run effects of attempts to achieve customer satisfaction.

B   13. Marketing activities start and end with the
       a. firm.
       b. consumer or client.
       c. long-run objectives of the firm.
       d. exchange situation.
       e. middlemen.

E   14. The marketing concept developed out of a sequence of three
       eras. Identify the correct sequence.
       a. Sales era, production era, marketing era
       b. Sales era, marketing era, production era
       c. Marketing era, sales era, production era
       d. Production era, marketing era, sales era
       e. Production era, sales era, marketing era

D   15. Which of the following statements is identified most closely with
       the marketing era?
       a. Businesses realized that products would have to be promoted
          through much personal selling and advertising.
       b. The emphasis on marketing was accented by a strong con-
          sumer demand for manufactured goods.
       c. The marketing era was facilitated by the scientific manage-
          ment movement to increase organizational efficiency.
       d. Businesses discovered that they first must determine what
          consumers want and then produce it.
       e. Businesses began to view sales as the major vehicle for in-
          creased profits, which led to the development of marketing
          activities.

e   16. Which of the following is not a likely occurrence when imple-
       menting the marketing concept?
       a. There is a limit to which a firm can satisfy customers' needs
          for a particular product.
       b. The marketing concept affects all types of business activities,
          not just marketing activities.
       c. To provide customer satisfaction, management must be able
          to determine customers' product needs.
       d. Managers sometimes find that by satisfying one segment of
          society, they may dissatisfy another segment.
       e. Management will have to spend little time orienting person-
          nel to the philosophy.

A   17. Concerning the adoption of the marketing concept, research
       findings indicate that
       a. the marketing concept has been adopted by a number of
          business organizations.
       b. the adoption of the marketing concept has been more prev-
          alent among smaller firms than among larger ones.

c. there are few businesses that have not attempted to implement the marketing concept.

d. almost all firms that have adopted the marketing concept have become more successful.

e. the philosophy of the marketing concept is a dominant force in the organization of businesses today.

*e*

18. A marketing manager must decide what combination of variables is needed to satisfy consumers' needs for a general type of product. What are the essential variables that the marketing manager combines?

a. Product variables, price variables, consumer variables, promotion variables

b. Marketing environment variables

c. Product variables and promotion variables

d. Product variables, price variables, and consumer variables

e. Product variables, price variables, promotion variables, and distribution variables

*A*

19. Some of the variables in the marketing environment are:

a. Political forces, legal forces, consumer movement forces, economic forces

b. Social forces, technological forces, political forces, economic forces, production, consumers

c. Promotion, product, price, distribution

d. Consumers, producers, wholesalers

e. Consumers, product, economic forces, social forces

*D*

20. Concerning marketing mix variables, which of the following statements is most accurate?

a. Marketing mix variables often are viewed as uncontrollable because marketing managers cannot change them.

b. Marketing mix variables cannot be altered by marketing managers.

c. Marketing mix variables can be altered but cannot be controlled by marketing managers.

d. Marketing managers can control marketing mix variables to a limited degree.

e. Marketing mix variables can be altered and controlled by marketing managers.

*e*

21. The marketing mix ingredient that is most controllable is

a. product.

b. consumers.

c. promotion.

d. price.

e. not the same for all situations.

*e* 22. Which of the following statements about marketing environment variables is most correct?
   a. Marketing managers have more control over these variables than over most marketing variables.
   b. The strength of the variables in the marketing environment is relatively stable as compared with that of other variables in the market.
   c. Marketing environment variables affect consumers, but they do not affect the marketing mix.
   d. The forces in the marketing environment influence marketing managers but do not directly affect their ability to perform certain activities.
   e. These forces influence consumers' reactions toward the firm's marketing mixes.

*e* 23. Which forces in the marketing environment are concerned primarily with the three general areas of product safety, information disclosure, and protection of the environment?
   a. Political forces
   b. Legal forces
   c. Regulatory forces
   d. Economic forces
   e. Consumer movement forces

*e* 24. The marketing environment forces that primarily determine the size and strength of demand for products are
   a. consumer movement forces.
   b. technological forces.
   c. societal forces.
   d. promotion forces.
   e. economic forces.

*A* 25. Concerning technological forces, which of the following statements is most correct?
   a. Technological developments have a direct impact on creating and maintaining a marketing mix.
   b. Technological developments have their greatest impact on the pricing of products.
   c. Technology does not influence people's desires for products but does affect their reactions to a business organization's marketing mix.
   d. Technological developments have their greatest impact on the distribution of products.
   e. The real impact of technology in this country depends solely on consumers' acceptance.

# Programmed Completion Exercises

activities,
facilitating,
expediting

1. Marketing is a set of _____ that are aimed at _____ and _____ exchanges.

somethings of
value, products

2. The _____ _____ _____ that are held by two exchange parties are usually _____ and/or financial resources such as money or credit.

human,
mechanical

3. Services result from the application of _____ and _____ efforts to people or objects.

concepts,
philosophies,
images, issues

4. Products in the form of ideas include _____, _____, _____, and _____.

marketing
concept,
customers',
clients',
coordinated

5. The _____ _____ is a philosophy that a business organization should try to satisfy _____ or _____ needs through a _____ set of activities that allows the organization to achieve its goals.

alter, adapt

6. To be customer oriented, a firm must _____ and _____ current product offerings to keep pace with changes in consumers' desires and preferences.

customer
satisfaction,
coordinated
activities

7. The marketing concept stresses the point that a business organization can achieve its goals by providing _____ _____ through _____ _____.

coordinated,
coordination,
dissatisfaction

8. If the firm's activities are not effectively _____, the lack of _____ not only may lead to less customer satisfaction but also may cause severe customer _____.

production,
sales, marketing

9. The marketing concept developed out of a sequence of three eras: _____, _____, and _____.

philosophy,
activities, top
management

10. Since the marketing concept is a management _____ that affects all types of business activities rather than just marketing _____, it must be implemented by _____ _____ in the organization.

information
system,
satisfying
products

11. Management must establish an _____ _____ that allows the firm to obtain information about customers' needs and to use that information internally to create _____ _____ .

top
management,
individuals,
organization

12. In order to be implemented, the marketing concept philosophy must receive the support not only of _____ _____ but of all the other _____ in the _____ .

management,
product needs

13. To provide customer satisfaction, _____ must be able to determine customers' _____ _____ .

departments,
restructuring

14. To properly coordinate the actions of _____ in a business organization, a _____ of the organization may be required.

controllable,
mix variables

15. Even though marketing mix variables can be altered, they are not totally _____ because marketing managers are limited in the degree to which they can change the _____ _____ .

pricing policies,
product prices

16. In dealing with the price variable, marketing managers usually are concerned with establishing _____ _____ and determining _____ _____ .

quantities,
inventory,
transportation,
storage

17. When dealing with the distribution variable, marketing managers attempt to make products available in the _____ desired, to as many customers as possible, and to keep total _____ , _____ , and _____ costs as low as possible.

informing,
organization,
products

18. The promotion variable in the marketing mix is directed toward _____ one or more groups of people about an _____ and its _____ .

partially,
environment
variables,
consumers'
reactions

19. The outcomes of a marketing manager's decisions and actions may be determined _____ by marketing _____ _____ because these forces influence _____ _____ toward the firm's marketing mixes.

product safety,
information
disclosure,
protection,
environment

20. The numerous issues that are of major concern to consumer forces can be categorized into three general areas: (a) _____ _____, (b) _____ _____, and (c) _____ of our _____.

consumer
organizations,
consumer laws,
consumer
education

21. The major forces in the consumer movement are _____ _____, _____ _____, _____ _____, and individual consumer advocates.

product, prices,
distribution,
promotion

22. Technological developments have a direct impact on creating and maintaining a marketing mix because they affect products and _____ development, _____, _____ systems, and methods of _____.

legislation,
interpretation of
laws, regulatory

23. Legal and regulatory forces in the environment arise from _____, the _____ _____ _____, and _____ units.

marketers,
courts

24. The real effects of legal provisions on the marketing mix variables depend largely upon how _____ and the _____ interpret them.

variables,
buyer,
marketing mix

25. The marketing environment consists of several _____ and surrounds both the _____ and the _____ _____.

# Answers to Objective Questions

| *True or False* | | *Multiple-Choice* | |
|---|---|---|---|
| 1. T | 16. T | 1. a | 14. e |
| 2. T | 17. T | 2. c | 15. d |
| 3. F | 18. T | 3. b | 16. e |
| 4. F | 19. F | 4. c | 17. a |
| 5. T | 20. F | 5. e | 18. e |
| 6. T | 21. T | 6. c | 19. a |
| 7. T | 22. T | 7. b | 20. d |
| 8. T | 23. T | 8. a | 21. e |
| 9. F | 24. F | 9. b | 22. e |
| 10. F | 25. T | 10. e | 23. e |
| 11. T | 26. F | 11. b | 24. e |
| 12. T | 27. T | 12. c | 25. a |
| 13. T | 28. T | 13. b | |
| 14. F | 29. F | | |
| 15. F | | | |

## CHAPTER 2

# Marketing Management

## Chapter Summary

The management of marketing activities provides purpose, direction, and coordination for marketing activities. Marketing management is the process of planning, organizing, implementing, and controlling marketing activities to facilitate and expedite exchanges. The place of marketing in a company is determined largely by the extent to which the firm is production, sales, or marketing oriented.

Marketing planning is a systematic process that involves the assessment of opportunities and organizational resources, the determination of marketing objectives and of a marketing strategy, and the development of the plan for implementation and control. Marketing planning is a continuous process that provides marketing managers with a basic framework for implementing and controlling the marketing activities of an organization. A marketing manager's plans can be short-range, covering a year or less; medium-range, which normally encompasses up to five years; or long-range, which usually lasts for over five years.

Marketing managers gain several benefits from planning. Planning forces them to formulate objectives, helps to reduce operating costs, and aids in the controlling and coordinating of marketing activities. Marketing planning has two major components—marketing objectives (which state what is to be accomplished through marketing activities) and marketing strategy (which is developed to achieve marketing objectives). When creating marketing objectives, a marketing manager must be sure that the marketing objectives are consistent with the overall objectives of the firm.

A marketing strategy is the core of a successful marketing plan, for it provides the key ideas or means for using the organization's resources and advantages. The development of a marketing strategy involves two major steps. The first step is to select and analyze a target market, that is, a group of persons for whom a firm wishes to create and maintain a marketing mix that specifically fits the needs and preferences of that group. The second step is to create and maintain a marketing mix that satisfies the needs of people in the target market.

To execute and achieve a marketing plan effectively, managers must organize marketing activities in a way that contributes to the accomplishment of a firm's overall objectives. The place of marketing within a company is determined largely by whether the firm is production, sales, or marketing oriented. The degree to which a firm's marketing management can plan and implement marketing strategies effectively depends on the manner in which the marketing unit is organized.

Marketing management must develop an organizational structure that establishes authority relationships. A marketing unit can be organized according to (1) functions, (2) products, (3) regions, or (4) types of customers. Organization of a marketing unit according to functions is fairly common and consists of grouping marketing activities by what marketing personnel are involved in doing—for example, research, advertising, customer relations. When marketing operations are organized on the basis of products, the product manager assumes full responsibility for the marketing of a particular product or product group. A business that produces and markets diverse products, for example, may wish to organize its marketing department or unit on this basis; organizing by product group gives a firm the flexibility to develop special marketing mixes for different products. On the other hand, a large company that markets products throughout the entire nation may organize its marketing activities by geographic regions. This approach is especially effective for a firm whose customers' characteristics and needs vary greatly from one region to another. Finally, in some businesses the marketing unit is organized according to types of customers. This form of internal organization can work well for the firm that has several groups of customers whose needs and problems are quite different. Although marketing units can be structured internally using any one of these approaches, it is common for a firm to use some combination of them. The use of more than one type of organization creates a flexible marketing unit that can develop and implement marketing plans to match customers' needs precisely.

Marketing managers provide purpose, direction, and structure for marketing activities. Until marketing managers implement the marketing plan, exchanges cannot occur. Proper implementation of a marketing plan depends on the coordination of marketing activities, the motivation of marketing personnel, and effective communication within the marketing unit. Because of job specialization and differences in approaches, interests, and timing related to marketing activities, marketing managers must synchronize the activities of the marketing staff within the firm and integrate those activities with the marketing efforts of external organizations such as advertising agencies and retailers. Another part of implementing the marketing plan is to motivate marketing personnel to perform effectively in accomplishing their objectives. Finally, a communication system must be designed to allow the marketing manager to communicate with all units of the firm in order to integrate marketing activities with activities in other areas.

To achieve marketing objectives and to help the organization achieve its overall objectives, a marketing manager must control marketing efforts effectively. The marketing control process consists of establishing performance standards, evaluating actual performance, and reducing the differences between actual and desired performance. There are several requirements for creating and maintaining an effective control process. First, the control process should be designed so that the flow of information is rapid enough to allow the marketing manager to detect differences quickly between actual and planned levels of performance. Second, a variety of control procedures must be developed that accurately monitor different kinds of activities. Third, control procedures should be flexible to accommodate changes. Fourth, the control process must be economical so that its costs are low relative to the costs associated with having no controls. Finally, the control process should be designed so that both managers and subordinates can understand it.

When marketing managers attempt to control marketing activities, they frequently experience several problems. Often, the information required to control marketing activities is unavailable, or is available but costly. Environmental changes can hamper control. Also, the time lag between the performance of marketing activities and the effects of such activities limits a marketing manager's ability to measure the effectiveness of marketing actions.

Since marketing activities often overlap with a firm's other activities, a marketing manager sometimes cannot determine the precise costs of the activities. Finally, marketing control may be hampered because it is extremely difficult to develop precise performance standards related to marketing actions.

# True or False Statements

(T) F   1. The effectiveness of an exchange is determined by the degree to which it helps to achieve a firm's objectives.

T (F)   2. Although an increasing number of businesses are becoming sales oriented, a sizable number of firms remain finance oriented.

T (F)   3. In a marketing-oriented firm, the marketing manager occupies a position above that of the financial, production, and personnel managers.

(T) F   4. A marketing plan is the written blueprint for implementing and controlling the marketing activities of an organization.

(T) F   5. Marketing plans aid the marketing manager in controlling marketing activities because plans include performance standards against which actual performance is measured.

T (F)   6. A marketing plan usually encompasses a period of two to five years.

(T) F   7. Marketing objectives must be consistent with the firm's overall objectives.

(T) F   8. A marketing strategy involves selecting and analyzing a target market and creating and maintaining a marketing mix that will satisfy those people.

T (F)   9. It is not sound marketing planning to aim marketing efforts at several different target markets.

T (F)   10. Marketing encompasses the greatest number of business functions when a firm is sales oriented.

T (F)   11. Organization on the basis of functions generally is considered the best approach for organizing marketing activities because it works well in all businesses.

T (F)   12. Organizing a marketing department by functions works best in a large firm which produces many diverse products.

(T) F   13. Organizing by product groups gives a firm the flexibility to develop special marketing mixes for different products.

T (F)   14. Organizing by type of customers provides a firm with flexibility to develop special marketing programs for specific products.

(T) F   15. A large company that markets products throughout the nation may organize its marketing activities by geographic regions.

(T) F   16. It is common for a firm to use some combination of organization by functions, products, regions, or customer types.

T (F)   17. Marketing planning and organizing provide assurance of a successful marketing strategy.

(T) F   18. In implementing a marketing plan, the marketing manager must coordinate marketing activities with other functions of the firm.

(T)    F    19. Another part of implementing the marketing plan is to motivate marketing personnel to perform effectively in accomplishing their objectives.

T    (F)    20. While proper implementation of a marketing plan depends on communication within the marketing unit, it is not necessary for communication to occur between the marketing manager and high-level executives.

(T)    F    21. Marketing control consists of establishing performance standards, evaluating actual performance by comparing it to established standards, and reducing the differences between desired and actual performance.

T    (F)    22. Performance standards do not apply to a marketer's achievement of budget objectives.

(T)    F    23. To reduce the discrepancies between planned and actual performance, the marketing manager in some cases may change the planned performance standards.

(T)    F    24. Creating and maintaining an effective control process depends heavily on the quantity and quality of information and the speed at which it is received.

T    (F)    25. Marketing controls should focus on the activities of the firm's marketers but should be independent of the actions of personnel in external organizations that provide marketing assistance.

T    (F)    26. The time lag between the performance of marketing activities and the effects of such activities increases marketing management's ability to measure precisely the effectiveness of marketing actions.

T    (F)    27. The information required to control marketing activities is readily available and inexpensive to obtain.

# Multiple-Choice Questions

C    1. Marketing management is a process of planning, organizing, implementing, and controlling marketing activities in order to
   a. increase a firm's sales and profits.
   b. hold down the costs of marketing the firm's product(s).
   c. expedite exchanges efficiently and effectively.
   d. maintain a high level of employee morale.
   e. facilitate highly desirable exchanges.

A

2. According to the text, the role of marketing in a firm is determined mainly by
   a. whether the firm is production, sales, or marketing oriented.
   b. the firm's overall objectives.
   c. the type of customer served and the firm's product offering
      to that customer.
   d. the purpose, direction, and consideration of marketing ac-
      tions.
   e. the relation of marketing to the other activities within the
      firm.

C

3. In a sales-oriented firm the sales manager is on the same level
   as the other functional managers. This type of structure reflects
   the belief that
   a. production is of primary importance.
   b. the fewer the managers, the better.
   c. profits are best generated by personal selling and advertising.
   d. producing high-quality products is the primary objective.
   e. good-quality products require little effort to sell.

D

4. Which of the following statements concerning marketing planning is false?
   a. A marketing plan is the written blueprint for implementing
      and controlling the marketing activities of an organization.
   b. Marketing planning is a circular process.
   c. Some managers do not use formal marketing plans because
      they spend most of their time dealing with daily problems.
   d. Marketing plans usually encompass a period equal to a firm's
      business cycle.
   e. Marketing planning forces the marketing manager to formu-
      late objectives and develop a strategy.

A

5. Marketing planning can be viewed as a process that focuses on
   a. marketing opportunities and resources, objectives, marketing
      strategy, and plans.
   b. marketing organization and purpose.
   c. company purpose and direction.
   d. marketing objectives and organizational objectives.
   e. marketing plans and marketing strategy.

D

6. According to the text, marketing objectives are important to the
   marketing manager because
   a. the marketing manager must be sure that marketing objec-
      tives are consistent with the firm's objectives.
   b. these objectives may focus on one or several dimensions such
      as market share, long-run profits, or short-run profits.
   c. marketing objectives should indicate the future point in time
      by which the objectives are to be accomplished.

d. these objectives provide a foundation for making marketing decisions and implementing and controlling marketing activities.

e. these objectives must be formulated in such a way that the degree of accomplishment can be measured accurately.

_c_    7. To achieve marketing objectives and to contribute to the accomplishment of the organization's overall objectives, the marketing manager should develop

a. a marketing department.

b. organizational strategies.

c. a marketing strategy.

d. the target market toward which activities are aimed.

e. a marketing mix that fits the needs of the target market.

_d_    8. Which of the following statements concerning marketing objectives is *false*?

a. Marketing objectives state what is to be accomplished through marketing activities.

b. Marketing objectives should be stated in clear, simple terms in order to be understood easily.

c. Marketing objectives cannot be established until the firm's overall objectives have been established.

d. Marketing objectives usually focus on implementation of plans.

e. Marketing objectives should be formulated in such a way that the degree of accomplishment can be measured accurately.

_B_    9. A group of persons for whom a firm attempts to create and maintain a marketing mix that fits the needs and preferences of that group is known as a

a. customer group.

b. target market.

c. consumer target.

d. marketplace.

e. primary market.

_e_    10. When a target market is being chosen, which of the following need *not* occur?

a. Managers should try to evaluate possible markets to determine how entry into them would affect the firm's sales, costs, and profits.

b. Marketers should consider whether the firm has the resources to produce a marketing mix that meets the needs of the target market.

c. Marketers must analyze the size and number of competitors who are already selling in the target market.

d. The firm must decide whether to focus its marketing efforts on one or several target markets.

e. Managers should ensure that choosing a particular target market will not adversely affect employee moral.

*e*   11. Which of the following does not commonly serve as a basis for a marketing unit's internal organization within a business?
a. Functions
b. Products
c. Regions
d. Types of customers
e. Types of marketing strategy

*A*   12. An organization that produces a diverse set of products probably would organize its marketing departments according to
a. product groups.
b. functions.
c. regions.
d. types of customers.
e. competitive standards.

*b*   13. When the marketing operations are organized on the basis of products,
a. the product lines are concentrated under a single product manager who is responsible for them.
b. the product manager assumes full responsibility for the marketing of a particular product or product group.
c. the marketing activities can be coordinated to avoid duplication.
d. the product manager's authority in the organizational hierarchy is equal to the financial manager's.
e. benefits would likely be gained by businesses with centralized marketing activities.

*C*   14. A large company that markets products throughout the entire nation may organize its marketing activities by
a. product groups.
b. functions.
c. regions.
d. types of customers.
e. competitive standards.

*C*   15. Which type of organization creates a flexible structure that allows marketers to develop and implement plans to fit customers' needs more precisely?
a. Organization on the basis of regions
b. Organization on the basis of types of customers
c. Organization on several bases
d. Organization on the basis of products
e. Organization on the basis of functions

A   16. To implement a marketing plan properly requires
      a. coordination of marketing activities.
      b. the creation of a flexible marketing unit.
      c. a sales-oriented organization.
      d. first, that a firm produce a good product.
      e. the establishment of strict performance standards.

C   17. The marketing control process requires
      a. that the marketing manager focus on the time dimension and the areas of control.
      b. that the marketing manager focus on developing and maintaining a control process as well as controlling actual problems.
      c. that marketing management establish performance standards, evaluate actual performance, and reduce the difference between actual and desired performance.
      d. that the marketing manager ensure the achievement of individual tasks.
      e. that the marketing manager take steps necessary to improve actual performance.

 18. To be able to ensure the achievement of individual tasks, the marketing manager should
      a. monitor the activities of personnel in external organizations.
      b. monitor the activities of marketers within the firm and reduce the discrepancies between actual and planned performance.
      c. change planned performance standards.
      d. establish general performance standards related to overall objectives.
      e. convert broad performance standards into specific standards.

 19. Which of the following is *not* a requirement for creating and maintaining an effective control process?
      a. The flow of information should be rapid.
      b. A variety of control procedures are necessary to monitor different kinds of activities.
      c. Control procedures should be flexible.
      d. Because of the benefits accrued, the costs of the control process can be high relative to sales.
      e. Both managers and subordinates should understand the control process.

d   20. Which of the following is *not* a good example of possible first steps a marketing manager could take to reduce discrepancies between planned and actual performance standards?
      a. meet with personnel to discuss morale problems
      b. examine competitors' prices
      c. assess product displays in the local sector

d. begin research on a new product line

e. meet with the sales manager to discuss customer reaction to a product

_ß_ 21. What is the *best* reason for attempting to ensure flexibility in marketing control procedures?

a. Marketing personnel are not always motivated to work.

b. The marketing environment is always changing.

c. Managers and workers may need several explanations to be able to understand the procedures.

d. A competitor may suddenly change the price of a product.

e. Plans must sometimes be changed from short range to long range.

# Programmed Completion Exercises

planning, organizing, implementing, controlling

1. Marketing management is a process of _____, _____, _____, and _____ marketing activities in order to facilitate and expedite exchanges effectively and efficiently.

production, sales, marketing

2. The place of marketing in a company is largely determined by whether the firm is _____, _____, or _____ oriented.

framework, implementing, controlling

3. Plans provide a marketing manager with a basic _____ for _____ and _____ the marketing activities of an organization.

formulate objectives

4. Marketing planning forces the marketing manager to _____ _____ and to think systematically about the firm's future marketing activities.

Marketing objectives

5. _____ _____ state what is to be accomplished through marketing activities.

marketing objectives, accomplishment, measured

6. For purposes of control, _____ _____ should be formulated in such a way that the degree of _____ can be _____ accurately.

marketing
manager,
consistent,
organization

7. When creating marketing objectives, the _____ _____ must be sure that the marketing objectives are _____ with the overall objectives of the _____ .

accomplish-
ment,
marketing
strategy

8. To achieve marketing objectives and to contribute to the _____ of the organization's overall objectives, a _____ _____ should be developed.

target market,
sales, costs,
profits

9. When choosing a _____ _____ , a marketing manager tries to evaluate possible markets to determine how entry into the market would affect the firm's _____ , _____ , and _____ .

small, vast

10. A marketing manager may define a target market to include a relatively _____ number of people or the manager may define it to encompass a _____ number of people.

specific
activities,
responsibility,
authority,
activities

11. Organizing involves dividing the work to be done into _____ _____ and delegating _____ and _____ to perform these _____ to persons who occupy various positions in the marketing department or division.

marketing mix,
target

12. Marketing managers must develop a _____ _____ that precisely matches the needs of the people in the _____ market.

products,
product,
product,
product group

13. When the marketing operations are organized on the basis of _____ , the _____ manager assumes full responsibility for the marketing of a particular _____ or _____ _____ .

characteristics,
needs, region

14. The regional approach to organizing is especially effective for a firm that has customers whose _____ and _____ vary greatly from one _____ to another.

types of
customers

15. When marketing activities are organized according to _____ _____ _____ , they can be designed specifically to meet the needs of each customer group.

structured
internally,
combination,
approaches

16. Although marketing units can be _____ _____ using a single base (such as functions, products, regions, or customer types), it is common for a firm to employ a _____ of _____ .

multiple bases,
develop,
implement

17. The use of _____ _____ creates a flexible structure that allows marketers to _____ and _____ marketing plans to fit customers' needs more precisely.

purpose,
direction,
structure

18. Planning and organizing provide _____, _____, and _____ for marketing activities.

communication,
motivation,
coordination

19. Proper implementation of marketing plans depends upon effective _____ among marketing personnel, _____ of persons performing marketing activities, and _____ of these activities.

needs,
motivation

20. To motivate marketing personnel, a marketing manager must ascertain their _____ and then develop and use _____ methods based on these needs.

Communica-
tion, integrate,
activities

21. _____ with managers in other functional areas is required to _____ marketing activities with _____ in other functional areas.

actual, planned,
action, actual,
planned

22. Marketing control is a process by which _____ performance of marketing activities is compared with _____ performance standards and _____ is taken to reduce the disparity between _____ and _____ performance.

planned
performance,
actual
performance

23. To reduce the discrepancy between _____ _____ and _____ _____, a marketing manager can take steps to improve actual performance, to reduce or totally change the performance standards, or to do both.

# Answers to Objective Questions

*True or False*

| | | | |
|---|---|---|---|
| 1. | T | 15. | T |
| 2. | F | 16. | T |
| 3. | F | 17. | F |
| 4. | T | 18. | T |
| 5. | T | 19. | T |
| 6. | F | 20. | F |
| 7. | T | 21. | T |
| 8. | T | 22. | F |
| 9. | F | 23. | T |
| 10. | F | 24. | T |
| 11. | F | 25. | F |
| 12. | F | 26. | F |
| 13. | T | 27. | F |
| 14. | F | | |

*Multiple-Choice*

| | | | |
|---|---|---|---|
| 1. | c | 12. | a |
| 2. | a | 13. | b |
| 3. | c | 14. | c |
| 4. | d | 15. | c |
| 5. | a | 16. | a |
| 6. | d | 17. | c |
| 7. | c | 18. | b |
| 8. | d | 19. | d |
| 9. | b | 20. | d |
| 10. | e | 21. | b |
| 11. | e | | |

# CHAPTER 3

# Marketing Research and Information Systems

## Chapter Summary

Marketing research and the systematic gathering of information increase the probability of success in marketing activities. Marketing intelligence is used by management in problem solving and decision making. Marketing intelligence is a broad term that includes all data gathered as a basis for marketing decisions. Marketing research is that part of marketing intelligence which involves a systematic and orderly gathering of information not supplied through the routine reporting systems. Marketing research is conducted on a special, project basis. A marketing information system (MIS), on the other hand, is that part of marketing intelligence that provides a continuous flow of information from sources both inside and outside the organization. This regular information flow is an ongoing input for the organization's data bank. A data bank or file of information collected through the marketing information system and marketing research projects equip a marketer with many relevant facts important in formulating plans, developing marketing strategies, selecting target markets, creating a marketing mix, and controlling marketing activities. In short, the marketing concept can better be implemented when adequate information about customers is available.

Formal marketing research departments have become increasingly important in overall planning and strategy development in large organizations. This trend reflects not only the increase in the use of research but also the growing importance and acceptance of the role of marketing in overall planning. The real value of marketing research

28

and the systematic gathering of information that supports it is measured by improvements in a marketer's ability to make decisions. Research and information systems provide feedback from customers to the organization. Without this feedback, a marketer cannot understand the dynamics of the marketplace.

Marketing research and information systems are aids to sound management judgment, not a substitute for it. While research provides an objective and practical approach to making decisions, judgment and intuition also are important aspects of decision making. The increase in marketing research activities represents a transition from intuitive to scientific problem solving. Intuition involves personal knowledge and experience. Scientific decision making uses an orderly and logical approach to gathering information. Successful decisions blend both intuition and research.

Planning for marketing research projects has five main steps: (1) defining and locating problems, (2) developing hypotheses, (3) collecting data, (4) interpreting research findings, and (5) reporting research findings. Defining the nature and boundaries of a problem is a necessary first step in launching a research study. Refining a problem from an ambiguous state to an understandable, researchable, and clearly defined statement permits the development of hypotheses. A hypothesis is an assumption about the problem or circumstances under analysis. In order to test a hypothesis, one must gather data. Exploratory, descriptive, and casual investigations are general designs for gathering data. Interpreting research findings is necessary to make the results of hypothesis testing useful. Finally, research must be reported to the appropriate persons so that findings can contribute to decision making.

Marketers must be able to design research procedures that produce reliable and valid data. Reliable research techniques produce identical data in repeated trials. The main concepts used in designing research are sampling and experimentation. The objective of sampling in marketing is to select representative units from the total population. Random, stratified, area, and quota sampling are the major sampling approaches used in developing estimates about population characteristics. Experimentation involves finding out which variable or variables caused an event to occur. Experiments may be conducted in the laboratory or in the field.

There are three basic ways of obtaining data for market research. They are (1) conducting surveys, (2) making observations, and (3) using stored or secondary data. The first two are considered primary-data collection methods; the third, a secondary-data collection method. Surveys are conducted by mail, by telephone, or through personal interviews. The selection of an interviewing approach depends on the nature of the problem, the data needed to test the hypothesis, and the resources available to the researcher. A mail survey is used most often when there is widespread geographic dispersion of the sample and economy is an important consideration. The telephone survey eliminates many of the disadvantages of the mail survey, but it has unique disadvantages too. The traditional survey method used by researchers is the face-to-face interview, primarily because of its flexibility.

The purpose of constructing a questionnaire is to design questions that will elicit information that meets the data requirements of the study. The composition of the questions depends on the nature of and the detail demanded. Several kinds of questions can be designed: multiple-choice questions, dichotomous questions, and open-end questions.

Various observation methods other than surveys can be used to collect primary data. In using the observation method researchers record the overt behavior of respondents, taking note of physical conditions and events. Direct contact is avoided; instead, actions or phenomena are systematically examined and noted. A disadvantage of this method is that analyses of observations of behavior are subject to biased judgments of researchers.

The secondary-data collection method involves the use of records, reports, and information presently available within the marketing information system or from outside sources such as periodicals, government publications, and unpublished data.

# True or False Statements

T  Ⓕ    1. The value of research is measured by improvements in the marketer's ability to implement plans.

Ⓣ  F    2. The feedback mechanism of the marketing information system is necessary to understand consumers and the dynamics of the marketplace.

Ⓣ  F    3. Marketing intelligence is a broad term that includes all data gathered as a basis for marketing decisions.

Ⓣ  F    4. The position within an organization of marketing research director is gaining prominence in higher levels of management.

T  Ⓕ    5. Formal marketing research departments have become less important in the planning and strategy development of large organizations.

T  Ⓕ    6. In general it can be said that marketing research and information systems improve decision making and increase the cost of the product to consumers.

Ⓣ  F    7. Personal knowledge or experience is a source of information on the basis of which managers make decisions.

Ⓣ  F    8. Limited research is valuable when, in terms of the usefulness to decision makers, it would be too expensive to gather complete data.

Ⓣ  F    9. The use of research in planning becomes more desirable as the alternative outcomes to a problem increase and the expected payoff increases.

T  Ⓕ   10. Usually either intuition or research is necessary for successful marketing outcomes, not both.

T  Ⓕ   11. The marketing information system is a discontinuous process within the organization, generating an inconsistent flow of information concerning expenses, sales, and profits.

T  Ⓕ   12. In the MIS, the means of gathering data receive more attention than do the procedures for expediting the flow of information.

T  Ⓕ   13. Marketing research, unlike a marketing information system, does not involve specific investigations into problems related to marketing decisions.

T  Ⓕ   14. Descriptive studies involve the collecting of data that will clarify a research problem.

Ⓣ  F   15. Causal studies assume that an independent variable, $X$, is the cause of a dependent variable, $Y$.

Ⓣ  F   16. Surveys, observation, and secondary-data collection are three basic ways of gathering data used in marketing research.

Ⓣ  F   17. Examples of primary data are surveys and observations.

**T** F 18. A survey is valid if it actually measures what it is supposed to measure and not something else.

T **F** 19. In area sampling, respondents or sample elements are separated into groups or strata according to a common characteristic or attribute.

T **F** 20. If related variables are random, the effect of the experimental variables in the experimentation design can be measured.

T **F** 21. Small organizations normally cannot afford to maintain the data bank required for a marketing information system.

**T** F 22. A variation of the personal interview technique focuses on groups rather than individuals.

T **F** 23. A telephone survey is an example of a good random sample because people have an equal possibility of being selected: virtually all homes have telephones that are listed in the telephone directory.

**T** F 24. Direct contact with respondents is generally avoided by using the observational method of data gathering.

T **F** 25. The "population" for a particular marketing research design refers to that portion of the total target market actually questioned or observed.

**T** F 26. Random sampling requires that all members of a population have an equal chance of appearing in the sample.

**T** F 27. The biggest disadvantage of mail surveys is the strong possibility that the response rate will be low.

T **F** 28. Syndicated data services offer a source of primary data for a particular company.

T **F** 29. The company's own accounting records are probably the most used source of data in the typical marketing division.

T **F** 30. Large businesses rely heavily on marketing research, but there is little likelihood that small businesses will become interested in obtaining marketing research information.

# Multiple-Choice Questions

1. Which of the following statements concerning research and information systems in marketing is *not* true?
   a. They help implement the marketing concept by providing adequate information about consumers.
   b. They increase the chances of success in performing marketing activities.

    c. They are used to plan and develop appropriate strategies.

    d. They provide important input into the development of the marketing mix.

    e. They increase the cost of the product to the consumer.

*C*

2. Marketing research and information systems

    a. represent an information-gathering process for specific situations.

    b. lack a mechanism that would provide feedback from consumers to organizations.

    c. provide valuable insights concerning the desires of consumers.

    d. do not provide inputs into the development of consumer products.

*C*

3. The first thing a marketer must think about when tackling a marketing research project is

    a. gathering data.

    b. developing a hypothesis.

    c. defining and locating the problem.

    d. interpreting the research findings.

*A*

4. The marketing data bank can be described as

    a. a file of data collected through both the MIS and marketing research projects.

    b. an establishment where money is received for the financial aspects of marketing.

    c. a pool of external sources of marketing information.

    d. a subscription to syndicated data services.

*A*

5. Which of the following statements is *not* true?

    a. Causal studies assume that a dependent variable, $X$, is the cause of an independent variable, $Y$.

    b. The purpose of exploratory studies is to refine a tentative hypothesis or to acquire more information about the research problem.

    c. Descriptive studies are concerned with identifying the characteristics of certain phenomena and may require statistical analysis.

*C*

6. Limited research is used in decision making when

    a. cost is no object.

    b. complete data are not necessary and are considered too expensive.

    c. the number of alternative solutions to a problem is very large.

*e*

7. Which of the following is *not* a limitation of field experiments?

    a. Field settings restrict the types of manipulation that can be employed.

    b. Gaining the interest and attention of respondents is difficult.

     c. Carryover effects are present from past experiments and may influence respondents.

     d. Many relevant variables cannot be measured.

     e. Field experiments take place in natural surroundings.

_D_   8. In a laboratory experiment

     a. the development of realism is not a problem.

     b. it is difficult to control independent variables.

     c. the setting is comparable to the real world.

     d. respondents are invited to react to experimental stimuli.

_B_   9. A non-probability sample chosen on the basis of an interviewer's own judgment is called

     a. an intuitive sample.

     b. a quota sample.

     c. a stratified sample.

     d. an area sample.

     e. a random sample.

_e_   10. An example of a primary-data source is

     a. the *Census of Business.*

     b. accounting records.

     c. *Survey of Buying Power.*

     d. unpublished trade association data.

     e. a telephone interview.

_A_   11. The results of a research design are most reliable

     a. when the research techniques produce almost identical data in repeated trials.

     b. if they actually measure what they are supposed to measure and not something else.

     c. when the source of the data is trustworthy.

     d. when measurements provide data that can be used to test a hypothesis.

_D_   12. An example of a sampling design is

     a. cross sampling.

     b. observation sampling.

     c. range sampling.

     d. stratified sampling.

_d_   13. A pitfall of the observational method of research is that

     a. direct contact between the researcher and respondent is not allowed.

     b. only demographic information can be gathered.

     c. it eliminates the need to motivate respondents to state their true feelings.

     d. it tends to be descriptive and may not provide insights into causal relationships.

*e*  14. Which of the following has *not* been a factor in the declining rate of response in personal survey research?
a. Using a survey approach to sell a product
b. Consumers' reluctance to talk to strangers
c. Unethical survey tactics
d. A general trend among the public to clam up on door-to-door solicitors
e. The length and depth of face-to-face interviews.

*d*  15. A characteristic of telephone surveying is that
a. it provides a nonrepresentative sample.
b. it makes it hard to get respondents to cooperate.
c. it is a time-consuming survey method.
d. it permits the interviewer to gain rapport with respondents and to ask them probing questions.

*e*  16. Which of the following statements about personal interviews is *not* true?
a. They offer the interviewer a chance to probe certain questions in depth.
b. They enable the interviewer to develop lines of thought that were not anticipated.
c. They give the interviewer the opportunity to judge socio-economic characteristics.
d. They allow follow-up studies about respondents.
e. They do not lend themselves well to group situations.

*b*  17. One common mistake in constructing questionnaires is
a. developing the questionnaire after defining the specific objectives.
b. asking questions that interest the researcher but do not provide useful information in determining whether to accept or reject a hypothesis.
c. developing questions that are unbiased and objective.

*c*  18. Syndicated data services
a. provide researchers with primary data.
b. are an example of an internal data bank source.
c. provide secondary data.
d. collect specific information for a few clients.

*d*  19. All of the following are steps in the marketing research process *except*
a. developing hypotheses.
b. collecting data.
c. interpreting research findings.
d. surveying the population.
e. defining the problem.

_b_ 20. The sampling design that divides respondents into groups according to geographic divisions is called
   a. random sampling.
   b. area sampling.
   c. group sampling.
   d. stratified sampling.

_b_ 21. In experimentation, that which is observed for changes after manipulation of something else is called the
   a. independent variable.
   b. dependent variable.
   c. hypothesis.
   d. data.

_e_ 22. Which of the following is *not* a primary source of data for marketing research?
   a. A survey
   b. An interview
   c. A questionnaire
   d. An observation
   e. A government census

# Programmed Completion Exercises

defining,
developing,
collecting,
interpreting,
reporting

1. The five basic steps in planning marketing research are (a) _____ problems, (b) _____ hypotheses, (c) _____ data, (d) _____ research findings, and (e) _____ research findings.

Exploratory,
descriptive,
causal

2. _____ studies, _____ studies, and _____ investigations are general designs for gathering data.

surveys,
observation,
secondary

3. The three elementary techniques by which data are usually obtained in marketing research are the primary collection methods of _____ and _____, and _____ data collection.

Personal,
telephone, mail

4. _____ interview, _____, and _____ are three types of survey methods that may be used to obtain information for testing a hypothesis.

Personal

5. _____ survey research is experiencing declining rates of response because the public is clamming up on door-to-door solicitors.

constructing a questionnaire, accept, reject

6. One of the most common mistakes in _____ _____ _____ is asking questions that are interesting to the researcher but do not provide information that can be used in deciding whether to _____ or _____ a hypothesis.

Dichotomous

7. _____-type questions are frequently called "yes or no" questions because there are only two possible responses.

observational

8. The _____ method of data gathering is an approach in which direct contact is avoided; instead, action is systematically examined and noted.

descriptive, causal relationships

9. Two disadvantages of the observational method are that it tends to be _____ and may not provide insights into _____ _____, and reliability is subject to the biased judgments of researchers.

reliable, valid

10. Well-founded marketing data must be developed by using _____ data provided by an accurate estimate of the population and a _____ measurement that gauges what it is supposed to measure.

independent, dependent

11. Experimentation involves the manipulation of _____ variables to measure changes in the _____ variable.

intuitive, scientific

12. The increase in marketing research activities represents a transition from _____ to _____ problem solving.

specific situations

13. The marketing information system is a continuous process within the organization, whereas marketing research is an information gathering process for _____ _____.

intuitive

14. The _____ manager makes decisions based on personal knowledge and experience, whereas the research approach to decision making is an orderly and logical approach.

marketing
information
system

15. The _____ _____ _____ establishes a framework for the managing and structuring of regularly gathered information.

realism

16. Laboratory experiments lack _____ and total comparability to the real world, but they simulate a real-world situation and offer the opportunity to control variables.

open-end,
dichotomous,
multiple-choice

17. Several kinds of questions can be designed for use on questionnaires including _____ , _____ , and _____ questions.

independent
variable,
dependent
variable,

18. In causal relationship studies, it is assumed that a particular _____ _____ , X, is the cause of variation in the _____ _____ , Y.

Marketing
intelligence

19. _____ _____ is a broad term that includes all data gathered as a basis for making marketing decisions.

## Answers to Objective Questions

*True or False*

| | | | |
|---|---|---|---|
| 1. | F | 16. | T |
| 2. | T | 17. | T |
| 3. | T | 18. | T |
| 4. | T | 19. | F |
| 5. | F | 20. | F |
| 6. | F | 21. | F |
| 7. | T | 22. | T |
| 8. | T | 23. | F |
| 9. | T | 24. | T |
| 10. | F | 25. | F |
| 11. | F | 26. | T |
| 12. | F | 27. | T |
| 13. | F | 28. | F |
| 14. | F | 29. | F |
| 15. | T | 30. | F |

*Multiple-Choice*

| | | | |
|---|---|---|---|
| 1. | e | 12. | d |
| 2. | c | 13. | d |
| 3. | c | 14. | e |
| 4. | a | 15. | d |
| 5. | a | 16. | e |
| 6. | c | 17. | b |
| 7. | e | 18. | c |
| 8. | d | 19. | d |
| 9. | b | 20. | b |
| 10. | e | 21. | b |
| 11. | a | 22. | e |

# CHAPTER 4

# Analyzing Buyer Behavior

## Chapter Summary

Buyer behavior is important to marketers for three reasons. First, the ways that buyers behave toward a firm's marketing strategy or strategies have great impact on the firm's success. Second, a major component of the marketing concept is that a firm should create a marketing mix that satisfies consumers. Third, by gaining a better understanding of the factors that influence consumer behavior, marketers are in a better position to predict how consumers will respond to their marketing strategies.

To analyze the behavior of consumers effectively, marketers should view buyers as decision makers. Consumers make purchasing decisions in order to create and maintain an assortment of products that provide current and future satisfaction. A buyer's decision-making process may range from routine to extensive. Routine decision making is customarily used to purchase lower-priced, frequently bought products. Consumers employ extensive decision making, on the other hand, when purchasing a product for the first time and when buying items that are expensive and purchased infrequently.

To understand consumer behavior, marketers should analyze both the psychological factors and the social forces that influence buyer behavior. Psychological factors include perception, motives, learning, attitudes, and personality. Social factors include roles, family influences, reference groups, social classes, and culture and subcultures.

Perception is a process by which an individual selects, organizes, and interprets information inputs to create a meaningful picture of the world. A person receives many information inputs but selects only a small portion of them to reach awareness at a specific time. Once an individual receives information inputs, he or she organizes them. Once organization of information inputs occurs, interpretation occurs. When making an interpretation, people usually interpret in terms of what is familiar to them.

Motives are internal energizing forces that direct a person's behavior toward goals. A buyer's actions are influenced by a set of motives that vary in strength. Many different types of motives influence buyer behavior. Motives are analyzed through motivation research. Motivation research is performed through either interviews or projective techniques.

Learning is a change in an individual's behavior that arises from prior behavior in similar situations. Learning refers to the effects of direct and indirect experiences on future behavior. Marketers may try to influence the direct experiences of consumers even before they purchase products by sending out free product samples. Consumers' indirect experiences are influenced by associates, salespersons, and advertisements.

Attitudes consist of knowledge and positive or negative feelings about an object. Attitudes are learned and, therefore, can be changed. Consumers' attitudes toward an organization and its products strongly influence the success or failure of that organization's marketing strategy.

Personality is an internal structure in which experience and behavior are related in an orderly way. Some marketers believe that personality influences the types and brands of products that consumers purchase. Marketers sometimes aim advertising campaigns at general types of personalities.

Roles are one type of social influence that affect consumer behavior. All of us occupy positions within groups, organizations, and institutions. Associated with each position is a set of actions and activities that are supposed to be performed by the person in that position. This set of actions and activities is called a role. Marketers need to be aware of how roles affect buying behavior. They need to know not only who does the actual buying, but also who influences the purchasing decisions because of their roles.

A group is a reference group when an individual identifies with the group so much that he or she takes on many of the values, attitudes, or behaviors of the group members. The success of using reference-group influence in advertising depends on advertising's effectiveness in communicating the message, the type of product, and the individual's susceptibility to reference-group influence.

A social class is an open aggregate of people with similar social ranking. Social class influences an individual's buying decisions in terms of the type, quality, and quantity of goods purchased and the types of stores patronized.

Culture is everything in our surroundings that is made by human beings. Cultural influences have broad effects on buying behavior because they touch so many aspects of our daily lives. On the basis of geographic differences or human characteristics such as age or ethnic background, a culture can be divided into parts called sub-cultures. Subcultural differences may result in considerable variations in what, how, and when people buy.

# True or False Statements

T   (F)     1. Consumer behavior is highly predictable.

(T)   F     2. Low-priced, frequently bought items may be called habitual purchases.

T   (F)     3. Psychological factors operate independently of external forces.

(T)   F     4. A person becomes aware of only a small number of the information inputs he or she receives.

(T)   F     5. If an event is anticipated, inputs regarding that event are more likely to reach one's awareness.

T   (F)     6. If the intensity of an input changes significantly, it is not likely to reach awareness.

(T)   F     7. Motives can move an individual toward positive accomplishment of a goal; therefore, they can serve to reduce tension.

(T)   F     8. An individual is influenced by a set of motives rather than just one motive.

T   (F)     9. Personality is the internal energizing force that directs a person toward goals.

(T)   (F)     10. Motives that influence where a person purchases products on a regular basis are called purchase motives.

(T)   (F)     11. Consumers learn about products directly by experiencing them and indirectly through information from salespersons, advertisements, friends, and relatives.

(T)   (F)     12. Direct questioning of people about their motives is an effective method for marketers to determine consumers' motives.

T   (F)     13. Projective techniques are tests in which subjects are asked to project their motives through a depth interview.

T   (F)     14. Learning refers to the effects of direct and indirect experiences, such as hunger and fatigue, on future behavior.

T   (F)     15. Attitudes are hereditary and, therefore, cannot be changed.

(T)   F     16. Personality is an internal structure in which experience and behavior are related in an orderly way.

(T)   F     17. Researchers have not been able to prove conclusively that a person's personality strongly affects buying behavior.

(T)   F     18. A role is a set of actions and activities that a person in a particular position is supposed to perform.

(T)   F     19. The degree to which a reference group influences a purchase decision depends on an individual's susceptibility to reference-group influence and the strength of involvement with the group.

(T)   F     20. The decision to buy cigarettes as well as which brand to buy is influenced by one's reference group.

T  (F)    21. A social class is a closed aggregate of individuals with similar social ranking.

(T)  F    22. One's social class influences the type, quality, and quantity of products one consumes.

T  (F)    23. Culture consists only of tangible man-made items in our society, such as furniture, buildings, and clothes.

(T)  F    24. Subcultures are divisions of a culture based on geographic region or human characteristics.

T  (F)    25. Consumer dissatisfaction exists because all marketers have adopted the marketing concept.

# Multiple-Choice Questions

__b__    1. Marketers are concerned with consumer behavior because
   a. consumers are predictable.
   b. the way consumers behave toward an organization's marketing strategies has a great impact on the success of the marketing program.
   c. consumer behavior is influenced by many factors.
   d. marketers are able to control consumer behavior.
   e. a consumer must make purchasing decisions.

__e__    2. Which of the following statements concerning purchasing decisions is *most* correct?
   a. Brand loyalty would be expected to play a much greater role in the selection of expensive items because the cost of making a wrong decision is greater.
   b. As the price of an item increases, the amount of time spent in making a purchasing decision increases proportionally.
   c. The amount of satisfaction a product gives a consumer when it is purchased determines whether or not the selection process will be routine or extensive.
   d. A housewife would be expected to make more routine purchases than a working wife.
   e. A consumer may use extensive decision making when a product that was purchased routinely in the past no longer satisfies.

    3. Which of the following products would probably require extensive decision making before the purchase?
   a. Products purchased frequently
   b. Products to be purchased in the future

c. Products that are purchased routinely

d. Expensive products

e. Products purchased as a result of social influences

*A*　4. Which of the following statements concerning perception is *least* correct?

a. All the inputs of information to which an individual is exposed are used in forming a perception of the world.

b. Perception is a process by which an individual selects, organizes, and interprets information inputs into a meaningful picture of the world.

c. A person selects only a small number of inputs to reach awareness.

d. A person is likely to allow an input to reach consciousness if the information helps to satisfy current needs.

e. If the intensity of an input changes significantly, it is more likely to reach awareness.

*e*　5. Perception is

a. the major factor within the individual that influences both general behavior and consumer behavior.

b. the selection of a small number of inputs and the disregard of many other inputs.

c. the organization of inputs that a person receives.

d. the interpretation of inputs that allows an individual to avoid mental confusion.

e. a process in which an individual selects, organizes, and interprets inputs into a meaningful picture of the world.

*e*　6. Which of the following statements is most correct concerning the organization of inputs that reach awareness?

a. Generally, inputs are organized by individuals to produce meaning, and this organization process is usually a slow one.

b. Organization of information inputs is not always needed to produce meaning.

c. Inputs that reach awareness are organized and interpreted in pretty much the same way by all consumers.

d. Because a person interprets information in terms of what is familiar, only one interpretation of the organized inputs is usually possible.

e. Inputs that reach awareness are organized to produce meaning, and this meaning is interpreted in light of what is familiar to an individual.

*b*　7. When buyers perceive information inputs that are inconsistent with their beliefs, they

a. are likely to use this information.

b. are likely to forget the information quickly.

c. will pass the information on to others.

d. are likely to remember the information.

e. should consider whether they perceived the information as intended by the seller.

 8. The best definition of a motive is

  a. behavior that results in tension reduction.

  b. an internal behavioral factor that operates within people and determines their behavior as consumers.

  c. a determinant of consumer behavior.

  d. an internal force that directs one's behavior toward goals.

  e. an internal structure in which experience and behavior are related.

 9. Which of the following statements concerning motives is true?

  a. Motives can reduce or increase tension within a person.

  b. A buyer's actions at any given time usually are affected by one dominant motive.

  c. The strength of motives tends to remain constant from one period of time to another.

  d. An individual's motives drive him or her toward goals, and tension tends to increase as the person accomplishes goals.

  e. Product characteristics such as durability or styling are usually not related to motives during the purchasing decision process.

 10. In regard to motives, which one of the following statements is *most* accurate?

  a. At any given time a consumer's behavior is usually affected by just one motive.

  b. Conflict among motives will result in tension building, which is eliminated by a purchasing decision.

  c. Motives that influence where one purchases products on a regular basis are called patronage motives.

  d. A group interview is more effective than a depth interview because greater interaction is possible in group discussion.

  e. Projective techniques are tests whereby groups of individuals are asked to talk freely in the hope that they will reveal subconscious motivation.

 11. Studies dealing with internal forces that direct one's behavior toward goals are called

  a. motivation research.

  b. attitude research.

  c. personality research.

  d. attribution theory.

  e. reflective introspection.

*b*    12. The interview technique that tries to generate discussion among people regarding one or more topics is known as the
   a. projective interview.
   b. group interview.
   c. depth interview.
   d. conversation technique.
   e. sentence completion test.

*A*    13. Learning
   a. refers to the effects of direct and indirect experience on future behavior.
   b. is a change in an individual's behavior that arises from physiological conditions such as hunger, fatigue, or growth.
   c. is knowledge and positive or negative feelings about an object.
   d. is seldom influenced by attitudes and motives.
   e. has no bearing on consumers' behavior.

*C*    14. Which of the following is an example of direct experience of a product by a consumer?
   a. A consumer receives a letter that explains the features of the product.
   b. A salesperson gives a consumer a "sales pitch" about a particular product.
   c. A consumer test drives an automobile.
   d. A consumer hears a friend tell about using a product and how he or she was satisfied with the product.
   e. A consumer reads an advertisement for a particular product.

*D*    15. Attitudes
   a. are learned and, therefore, cannot be changed.
   b. possessed by a person at a particular time are all of equal strength.
   c. of consumers toward a particular firm have no influence on the firm's marketing strategy.
   d. are acquired through experience and interaction with other people.
   e. have little influence on consumer behavior.

*b*    16. Which one of the following statements regarding personality is true?
   a. Personalities are possessed only by outgoing people.
   b. Personality is an internal structure in which experience and behavior are related.
   c. Studies have shown that buying behavior reliably reflects personality characteristics.
   d. All types of personalities are represented, when possible, in advertising campaigns.
   e. Personality is a structure in each individual that operates independently of other people.

*b* 17. Social influences can be grouped into four major areas:
   a. roles and family influences, psychographics, reference groups, and social class.
   b. roles and family influences, reference groups, social class, and culture and subcultures.
   c. roles and family influences, reference groups, psychographics, and social class.
   d. roles and family influences, reference groups, social class, and personality structures.
   e. roles and family influences, reference groups, social class, and dissonant groups.

*A* 18. If an individual purchases a certain product, he or she may be fulfilling another person's expectations for his or her behavior. This best illustrates the influence of
   a. roles.
   b. product attractiveness.
   c. motives.
   d. personality influence.
   e. personal autonomy.

*e* 19. Roles
   a. are associated with positions that only leaders occupy.
   b. are unchanging.
   c. influence only general behavior and have little influence on a person's behavior as a consumer.
   d. are numerous, but each individual has only one role.
   e. consist of a set of actions and activities that are supposed to be performed by a person in a particular position.

*d* 20. Which one of the following would not be considered a reference group?
   a. A consumer's family
   b. The American Medical Association
   c. A group from which a consumer derives information
   d. An organization that has little influence on an individual
   e. A church group

*A* 21. A marketer uses reference-group influence in advertisements
   a. to promote the message that people in a specific group buy the product and are highly satisfied by it.
   b. to show general satisfaction with the product regardless of reference-group size or the number of people who identify with it.
   c. because reference-group influence is more effective than all other influences in advertisements.
   d. because most people have only one reference group that influences them significantly.
   e. to determine which product satisfies a particular reference group.

_c_    22. Products for which both the purchasing decision and the brand
           decision are influenced strongly by reference groups are
           a. magazines.
           b. clothing.
           c. cigarettes.
           d. television sets.
           e. furniture.

_c_    23. Factors such as income level, occupation, religion, and education
           level are used to
           a. influence consumer behavior.
           b. measure personality traits.
           c. group people into various social classes.
           d. group people into various reference groups.
           e. determine the personality characteristics of a person.

_b_    24. Culture is defined as
           a. the characteristics of various social classes.
           b. everything in our surroundings that is man-made.
           c. a set of actions and activities that an individual is expected to
              perform.
           d. an open aggregate of people with similar social ranking.
           e. a group with which an individual identifies.

_c_    25. Consumer dissatisfaction still exists for several reasons: (1) mar-
           keters cannot accurately determine what is highly satisfying to
           consumers, (2) marketers may not be capable of providing what
           satisfies consumers, and (3)
           a. consumers' actions strongly influence the success or failure
              of a marketing program.
           b. the consumer movement is becoming widespread.
           c. some marketers have not adopted the marketing concept.
           d. consumer behavior is unimportant to marketers.
           e. consumers are not viewed as decision makers.


# Programmed Completion Exercises


marketing mix    1. A major component of the marketing concept is the belief that

                    a firm should create a _____ _____ that satisfies

                    consumers.

                 2. Even though some social critics give marketers credit for being

                    able to manipulate consumers, marketers depend upon infor-

behavioral sciences

mation from the _____ _____ to understand consumer behavior.

routine, frequently, extensive, expensive, infrequently

3. In making decisions, a buyer generally uses one of two different types of decision-making processes: (a) _____ decision making for low-priced, _____ bought items; and (b) _____ decision making for _____, _____ bought items.

perception, motives, learning, attitudes, personality

4. The primary internal elements that affect consumer behavior are (a) _____, (b) _____, (c) _____, (d) _____, and (e) _____.

Perception

5. _____ is a process by which an individual selects, organizes, and interprets information inputs.

aware, inputs

6. A person becomes _____ of only a small portion of the information _____ that are received at any given time.

anticipated event, satisfying, current, intensity

7. An input is more likely to reach awareness if it is related to an _____ _____, if the information is useful in _____ one's _____ needs, and if the input changes significantly in _____.

motives, motive

8. A buyer's actions at any given time are affected by a set of _____, not just one _____.

reduce, increase

9. Motives can _____ or _____ tension, depending upon whether they move one toward or away from goals.

interviews, projective techniques

10. Motivation research is performed through either _____ or _____ _____.

Learning, Free samples, directly, indirectly

11. _____ refers to the effects of direct and indirect experiences on future behavior. _____ _____ are used by a marketer to get potential consumers to _____ experience the product. Consumers' learning also is affected _____ by experiencing products through information from salespeople, advertisements, friends, and relatives.

acquires
attitudes

12. Through experience and interaction with other people, an individual _____ _____ .

Consumers'
attitudes,
strongly
influence

13. _____ _____ toward a firm and its products _____ _____ the success or failure of the organization's marketing program.

long, expensive,
difficult

14. Changing people's attitudes is generally a _____ , _____ , and _____ task.

social
influences,
roles, family
influences,
reference
groups, social
class, culture,
subcultures

15. Consumers' buying decisions are affected partially by the people around them. These people and the forces they exert upon a buyer are called _____ _____ , and may be grouped into four major areas: (a) _____ and _____ _____ , (b) _____ _____ , (c) _____ _____ , and (d) _____ and _____ .

general
behavior,
consumers,
roles, who,
buying,
purchasing
decision

16. Numerous expectations are placed on people's behavior both by themselves and by many persons around them. People's roles influence not only their _____ _____ but also, to some extent, their behavior as _____ . Marketers need to be aware of how _____ affect buying behavior. They need to know not only _____ does the _____ but also who influences the _____ _____ because of their roles.

role

17. Each person occupies positions within groups, organizations, and institutions. The set of actions that a person is expected to perform within a position is called a _____ .

roles

18. Since a person occupies numerous positions, he or she has many _____ .

buying behavior

19. Marketers need to be aware of how roles affect _____ _____ .

buy, brand

20. Reference-group influence may affect the decision to _____ and the choice of a _____, depending upon the type of product purchased.

involvement

21. The degree to which a reference group influences a purchasing decision depends upon the strength of the individual's _____ with the group.

reference group, reference-group, advertisements

22. A group is a _____ _____ when an individual identifies with the group so much that he or she takes on many of the values, attitudes, or behaviors of group members. A marketer sometimes uses _____-_____ influence in _____ to promote the message that people in a specific group buy the product and are highly satisfied by it.

information, comparison

23. A reference group acts as a source of _____ and as a point of _____ for an individual.

Culture, Cultural, buying behavior, subcultural differences

24. _____ is everything in our surroundings that is man-made. _____ influences have broad effects on _____ _____ because they touch so many aspects of our daily lives. When trying to create a satisfying marketing mix, marketers must recognize that even though their operations may be confined to the United States, to one state, or to only one city, _____ _____ may result in considerable variations in what, how, and when people buy.

social class

25. A _____ _____ is an open aggregate of people with similar social ranking.

susceptibility

26. When a marketer uses reference-group influence in advertising, the success of the advertising depends on how effective the advertisement is, the type of products, and an individual's _____ to reference-group influence.

common patterns of behavior

27. Individuals within social classes to some degree develop and take on _____ _____ _____ _____.

criteria

28. The _____ used to group people into classes varies from one society to another.

beer, drugs,
cigarettes, cars

29. A product for which both the purchasing decision and the brand decision are influenced strongly by reference groups is _____ (one example).

determines

30. Marketers need to be aware of the impact of social class upon a person's behavior as a consumer. An individual's social class to some extent _____ the type, quality, and quantity of products consumed.

purchased,
used

31. Since culture, to some degree, determines the ways that products are _____ and _____, it, in turn, affects the development, distribution, pricing, and promotion of products.

marketing
mixes

32. International marketers find that people in other cultures have different attitudes, values, and needs, which, in turn, call for different methods of doing business as well as different types of _____ _____.

subcultures

33. On the basis of geographic differences or human characteristics such as age or ethnic background, a culture can be divided into parts called _____.

# Answers to Objective Questions

| *True or False* | | *Multiple-Choice* | |
|---|---|---|---|
| 1. F | 14. F | 1. b | 14. c |
| 2. T | 15. F | 2. e | 15. d |
| 3. F | 16. T | 3. d | 16. b |
| 4. T | 17. T | 4. a | 17. b |
| 5. T | 18. T | 5. e | 18. a |
| 6. F | 19. T | 6. e | 19. e |
| 7. T | 20. T | 7. b | 20. d |
| 8. T | 21. F | 8. d | 21. a |
| 9. F | 22. T | 9. a | 22. c |
| 10. F | 23. F | 10. c | 23. c |
| 11. T | 24. T | 11. a | 24. b |
| 12. F | 25. F | 12. b | 25. c |
| 13. F | | 13. a | |

CHAPTER 5

# Selecting and Evaluating Target Markets

## Chapter Summary

To provide customer satisfaction, a marketer identifies the group of customers on whom the firm wishes to focus its marketing activities. This group is the firm's target market. The marketing manager then attempts to develop and maintain a marketing mix (product, price, distribution, and promotion) that satisfies these customers' needs.

A market is an aggregate of people who, as individuals or as organizations, have needs for products in a product class and who have the ability, willingness, and authority to purchase such products. There are three major types of markets: consumer, industrial, and reseller. Consumer markets are ones in which purchasers intend to consume or to benefit from the purchased products. Industrial markets consist of individuals, groups, or organizations that buy products to be directly used to produce other products or to be used in the daily operation of the organization. Industrial markets can be divided into three categories: producer markets, government markets, and institutional markets. Reseller markets consist of intermediaries who buy finished products and resell them for the purpose of making a profit.

The two general ways that marketers approach target markets are the total market approach and the market segmentation approach. When a firm designs a single marketing mix and directs it at an entire market for a particular product, the firm is using a total market approach. This method can only be effective when a large proportion of individuals in the total market have similar product needs and the organization is capable of developing and maintaining a single marketing mix that satisfies these people's needs. A variation of this approach is the product differentiation strategy, with which a firm aims one type of product at the total market and attempts to differentiate the product in customers' minds as being superior and preferable to competing brands.

Sometimes a firm cannot satisfy the total market with a single marketing mix because the individuals within the market have diverse needs. Such a market is called a heterogeneous market. In such situations, a marketer must use a market segmentation approach to divide the total market into market segments, or groups of individuals who have relatively similar product needs. A marketer then can design a marketing mix (or mixes) that fit more precisely the needs of individuals in the selected segment (or segments).

There are two major types of market segmentation strategies: (1) the concentration strategy and (2) the multisegment strategy. When a firm focuses its marketing efforts on a single market segment through one marketing mix, it is using a concentration strategy. The firm using this strategy can often generate large sales through penetration of a single segment. The drawback of this strategy is that if demand in that segment falls, total sales will decline. A firm using the multisegment strategy designs a particular marketing mix for each of two or more selected segments.

For segmentation to be effective, five conditions must exist: (1) consumers' needs must be heterogeneous; (2) the segments must be identifiable and divisible; (3) the estimated sales potential, cost, and profits for each segment must be measurable; (4) at least one segment must have enough profit potential to support a special marketing mix; and (5) the firm must be able to reach the chosen segment with a particular marketing mix.

A segmentation variable is the basis for dividing the total market into segments. The four general categories of segmentation variables are socioeconomic, geographic, psychographic, and product-related. One or several variables can be used in dividing a market.

*Market sales potential* refers to the amount of a product that would be purchased by specific customers within a specified time period at a specific intensity of industry marketing activity. *Company sales potential* is the amount of a product that an organization could sell during a specified time period. When attempting to measure company sales potential, a marketer may use either the breakdown approach or the buildup approach.

For developing a forecast of actual company sales for a specific time period, marketers have several methods at their disposal: (1)

executive judgment, which is based on the intuition of executives; (2) surveys of customers, sales personnel, or experts; (3) time series analysis, which relies on historical data; (4) correlation methods, used to develop a mathematical relationship between past sales and one or more selected variables; and (5) market tests, which measure actual consumer purchases and consumer responses to promotion, price, and distribution efforts.

# True or False Statements

T  (F)  1. An individual who has the desire, the buying power, and the willingness to purchase certain products may certainly do so.

(T)  F  2. The consumer market is composed of persons who do not buy products to resell at a profit.

(T)  F  3. A person cannot be categorized neatly into only a single market but is part of numerous consumer markets.

(T)  F  4. More exchanges occur in industrial markets than in consumer markets.

T  (F)  5. The federal government spends over two-thirds of the total amount spent by the government sector.

(T)  F  6. Institutional markets may require special types of marketing activities.

T  (F)  7. The segmentation approach is most appropriately used in a homogeneous market.

(T)  F  8. A company sometimes defines the total market as its target market.

T  (F)  9. When employing a product differentiation strategy, the marketer designs the product to be significantly different physically from competing brands.

(T)  F  10. Companies in the gasoline industry sometimes use a product differentiation strategy.

(T)  F  11. Using a concentration strategy allows a firm to carefully analyze the needs of a specific group of customers.

T  (F)  12. Multisegment strategy is one in which the organization directs its marketing efforts at two or more segments by developing one marketing mix to be used in all selected segments.

(T)  F  13. For market segmentation to be effective, a firm must be able to reach a chosen segment with a particular marketing mix.

(T)  F  14. Socioeconomic dimensions of markets can be measured readily through observations or surveys.

T  (F)  15. *Target market* refers to the number of potential customers within a unit of land area.

T  (F)  16. Psychographic segmentation variables are being used more often because they are relatively easy to measure.

(T)  F  17. A market can be divided in terms of the benefits that customers want from a particular product.

(T)  F  18. The major disadvantage of using multivariable segmentation is that as more segments are produced, the sales potential of many of the segments declines.

(T)   F     19. The major advantage in using more than one segmentation variable is the precision that additional information may provide.

T   (F)     20. The analysis of sales potential should be limited to one specific level of marketing activity.

(T)   F     21. A sales forecast must be specific in terms of time.

T   (F)     22. The customer survey is the most feasible sales forecasting method for a soft-drink company.

(T)   F     23. The customer survey method is generally easier to use with industrial customers than with customers in consumer markets.

(T)   F     24. Time series analysis seeks a pattern in a firm's sales volume based on historical data.

T   (F)     25. Correlation methods are the most useful methods for forecasting the sales of a new product.

# Multiple-Choice Questions

*b*     1. Which is not a requirement for a market?
   a. Ability to purchase
   b. Measurable relationship between supply and demand
   c. Need for a product
   d. Authority to buy
   e. Willingness to purchase

*d*     2. A professor who buys a typewriter to prepare a textbook for publication is in what type of market?
   a. Consumer
   b. Government
   c. Nonbusiness
   d. Industrial
   e. Reseller

*c*     3. Reseller markets consist mainly of
   a. consumers.
   b. retailers.
   c. wholesalers and retailers.
   d. manufacturers.
   e. industrial users.

*e*     4. A total market approach can be effective if
   a. many individuals have similar needs and are satisfied by several marketing mixes.
   b. the individuals have diverse product needs but are satisfied by a single marketing mix.

   c.  used only in the consumer market.
   d.  many individuals have diverse product needs that can be satisfied by a single marketing mix.
   e.  many individuals have similar product needs that can be satisfied by a single marketing mix.

_c_   5. The marketing mix consists of
   a.  price, product, promotion, and package.
   b.  promotion, package, distribution, and product.
   c.  price, promotion, distribution, and product.
   d.  price, distribution, advertising, and product.
   e.  product, package, selling, and distribution.

_d_   6. A strategy that relies heavily on promotional activity to differentiate a product from competing brands is
   a.  concentration strategy.
   b.  multisegment strategy.
   c.  total market strategy.
   d.  product differentiation strategy.
   e.  segmentation strategy.

_b_  •7. Markets made up of individuals with diverse product needs are called
   a.  homogeneous markets.
   b.  heterogeneous markets.
   c.  differentiated markets.
   d.  segmented markets.
   e.  market segments.

_c_   8. This is a diagram of what marketing strategy?
   a.  Undifferentiated
   b.  Multisegment
   c.  Concentration
   d.  Product differentiation
   e.  Total market

_c_   9. One major difference between a total market approach and a multisegment approach is
   a.  the number of product modifications.
   b.  the number of marketing mixes required.

c.  the relative size of the target market.
d.  the number of prices used.
e.  the homogeneity of the target group.

_C_  10. Firms in the auto industry generally use which marketing strategy?
a.  Product differentiation
b.  Total market
c.  Multisegment
d.  Concentration
e.  Mass marketing

_A_  11. Which is not a condition necessary for effective segmentation?
a.  Consumers' needs must be homogeneous.
b.  The segments must be divisible.
c.  The estimated sales potential of the segments must be measurable.
d.  At least one segment must provide enough profit to support a special marketing mix.
e.  The segments must be accessible.

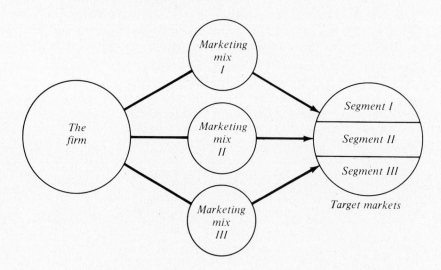

_d_  12. This type of segmentation
a.  is effective when customers' needs are homogeneous.
b.  is used when a firm directs its efforts at the market with a particular product.
c.  is used when a firm attempts to differentiate a particular product in customers' minds.
d.  ordinarily entails higher marketing costs than a concentration strategy.
e.  is used by all producers of staple food items.

_b_  13. The segmentation variable that is measured most easily pertains to
  a. product benefits.
  b. socioeconomic characteristics of buyers.
  c. buyer behavior.
  d. buyer motives.
  e. personality.

_c_  14. The number of potential customers within a unit of land area is referred to as the
  a. target market.
  b. market objective.
  c. market density.
  d. market segment.
  e. total market.

_d_  15. Personality characteristics, motives, and lifestyles are
  a. product-related customer characteristics.
  b. variables for segmenting institutional markets.
  c. socioeconomic characteristics.
  d. psychographic dimensions for segmenting markets.
  e. behavioral segmentation variables.

_e_  16. If a market were divided into heavy users and light users of a particular product, then this market would have been segmented by
  a. psychological dimensions.
  b. geographical variables.
  c. types of organizations.
  d. product uses.
  e. product-related customer characteristics.

_d_  17. A major disadvantage of multivariable segmentation is that
  a. one or more variables are used to divide a market.
  b. a marketing mix is developed that more precisely satisfies customers in a given segment.
  c. the firm cannot concentrate on any one segmentation variable.
  d. the larger the number of variables, the greater the number of segments created, which reduces the sales potential in many of the segments.
  e. the cost is greater than single-variable segmentation.

_b_  18. The amount of a product that would be purchased by specific customer groups within a specified time period at a specific level of industry-wide marketing activity is referred to as
  a. company sales potential.
  b. market sales potential.
  c. consumer buying potential.

d. sales forecast.

e. market ability.

*A*   19. The amount of a product that an organization could sell during a specified time period is referred to as

a. company sales potential.

b. market sales potential.

c. sales forecast.

d. profitability margin.

e. sales breakdown schedule.

*b*   20. The company sales forecast

a. is unaffected by the industry's activities.

b. should be based on the assumption that the company will operate at a certain level of marketing effort.

c. is the amount of a product that could be sold.

d. can be determined accurately only through mathematical models.

e. considers what sales levels are possible at various intensities of company marketing activities.

*C*   21. Through a customer survey, the forecaster gains information regarding consumers'

a. past purchases.

b. actual purchases.

c. intended purchases.

d. buying power.

e. minimum purchases.

*e*   22. A major justification for a firm to survey its own sales personnel is that they are

a. least biased.

b. least likely to be overly pessimistic.

c. able to devote more time to the study.

d. the best at setting reasonable quotas.

e. closer to customers.

*d*   23. The sales forecasting method that relies specifically on historical data is

a. market tests.

b. executive judgment.

c. expert surveys.

d. time series analysis.

e. forecasts of sales personnel.

*d*   24. A disadvantage of using expert surveys is that the experts

a. seldom have the needed experience.

b. often lack necessary information.

c. are not expedient.

d. may not be motivated.

e. are too expensive.

_b_    25. Through a market test a forecaster gains information regarding consumers'
    a. past purchases.
    b. actual purchases.
    c. intended purchases.
    d. estimated purchases.
    e. minimal purchases.

_b_    26. A market-test method can be effective for estimating the sales of an existing product in new geographic areas because
    a. it correlates new sales with those in existing markets.
    b. it is not dependent on historical data.
    c. it can measure consumers' intended purchases accurately.
    d. it is the least expensive method available.
    e. the product demand will stabilize quickly.

# Programmed Completion Exercises

ability, willingness, authority to buy

1. For an aggregate of people to be a market, the people must have needs for the product, as well as the _____, _____, and _____ _____ _____.

consumer, industrial, reseller

2. The three major types of markets are _____, _____, and _____ markets.

Consumer, Industrial

3. _____ markets are those in which the purchaser intends to reap the utility of the product. _____ markets are those in which the product can be used to create another product.

Reseller

4. _____ markets consist of middlemen, such as wholesalers and retailers, who buy finished goods and resell them at a profit.

total market, market segmentation

5. The two approaches to finding target markets are the _____ _____ approach and the _____ _____ approach.

total market

6. A _____ _____ approach is effective if many individuals have similar product needs that can be satisfied by a single marketing mix.

total market,
customers'
minds

7. Product differentiation is a strategy by which a firm aims one type of product at the _____ _____ and attempts to differentiate its product from competitors' products in _____ _____ mainly through promotion.

segmentation
variable

8. A _____ _____ is the basis on which a marketer divides a total market into segments.

concentration

9. A disadvantage of the _____ strategy is that by developing strong brand recognition in one market segment a firm may be prevented from successfully entering another segment.

multisegment
strategy

10. A _____ _____ is employed when a firm directs its marketing efforts at two or more segments by developing a marketing mix for each segment.

heterogeneous

11. Market segmentation is used when consumers' needs are _____ .

family life cycle

12. Characteristics such as marital status and the presence and age of children are combined into the single dimension of the _____ _____ _____ .

climate

13. Producers of air conditioners often use _____ as a segmentation variable.

market density

14. The number of potential customers per unit of land is referred to as _____ _____ .

personality
dimensions

15. Competitiveness, ambitiousness, and aggressiveness are _____ _____ .

geography, type
of organization,
customer size,
product use

16. The variables used to segment industrial markets are _____ , _____ _____ _____ , _____ _____ , and _____ _____ .

producer,
government,
institutional

17. The industrial category of markets includes _____ , _____ , and _____ markets.

Single-variable
segmentation

18. _____ _____ is the simplest form of segmentation and is the easiest to perform.

Market sales potential, Company sales potential

19. _____ _____ _____ refers to the amount of a product that would be purchased by specific customer groups within a specified period of time at a specific intensity of industry marketing activity. _____ _____ _____ is the amount of a product that an organization could sell during a specified time period.

breakdown, buildup

20. The _____ approach and the _____ approach are used to measure company sales potential.

executive judgment, time series analysis, correlation, market tests

21. The most commonly used forecasting techniques are (a) surveys, (b) _____ _____, (c) _____ _____ _____, (d) _____, and (e) _____ _____.

expedient, inexpensive, stable, experience

22. The advantages of the sales forecast method based on executive judgment are that it is _____ and _____. This method works reasonably well when product demand is _____ and when the forecaster has extensive _____.

relatively small

23. The customer survey can be useful to a firm that has a _____ _____ number of customers.

actual, intended

24. Through a market test, a forecaster gains information regarding consumers' _____ purchases rather than _____ purchases.

actual purchases, promotion, price, distribution

25. A market test measures _____ _____ and can be used to measure consumers' responses to _____, _____, and _____ efforts.

# Answers to Objective Questions

| *True or False* | | |
|---|---|
| 1. F | 14. T |
| 2. T | 15. F |
| 3. T | 16. F |
| 4. T | 17. T |
| 5. F | 18. T |
| 6. T | 19. T |
| 7. F | 20. F |
| 8. T | 21. T |
| 9. F | 22. F |
| 10. T | 23. T |
| 11. T | 24. T |
| 12. F | 25. F |
| 13. T | |

| *Multiple-Choice* | | |
|---|---|
| 1. b | 14. c |
| 2. d | 15. d |
| 3. c | 16. e |
| 4. e | 17. d |
| 5. c | 18. b |
| 6. d | 19. a |
| 7. b | 20. b |
| 8. c | 21. c |
| 9. c | 22. e |
| 10. c | 23. d |
| 11. a | 24. d |
| 12. d | 25. b |
| 13. b | 26. b |

# CHAPTER 6

# Product Concepts

## Chapter Summary

Products are among a firm's most important and most visible contacts with buyers. If products do not meet the desires and wants of buyers, failure will result. The product's role in satisfying customers cannot be overstressed. The total product is more than a physical product and/or service that satisfies customers' needs. It includes everything that one receives in an exchange; it is a complexity of tangible and intangible attributes including functional, social, and psychological utilities or benefits. A product can be an idea, a service, a good, or any combination of these three; it includes packaging, manufacturer's and retailer's prestige, accessories, installation, instruction about use, and the assurance that service facilities will be available to meet customers' needs after the purchase. Products not only have functional value; they also act as vehicles through which people express their values and enhance their self-images. Since a product can play a variety of roles in consumers' lives, it is important for marketers to understand what a product means to consumers and to know what consumers' expectations are about products.

The classification of products is based on the intention of the buyer. Products purchased for satisfaction of personal and family needs are consumer products. Those bought for use in a firm's operations or to produce other products are industrial products. The classification of products as industrial or consumer products is important in selecting target markets. Consumer products, moreover, are traditionally broken down into three categories, based primarily on the characteristics of buyers' purchasing behavior. Convenience products are relatively inexpensive and frequently purchased items for which buyers want to exert only minimal efforts to obtain. Shopping products are items for which buyers are willing to put forth considerable effort in planning and making the purchase. Specialty products possess one or more unique characteristics and are products that buyers are willing to expend considerable purchasing efforts to obtain.

Industrial products can be broken down into categories based on their characteristics and intended uses. Industrial products include raw materials, major equipment, accessory equipment, component parts, process materials, supplies, and industrial services.

Products are like living organisms; they are born, they live, and they die. The product life cycle has four major stages. During the introduction stage, the first stage, sales are just taking off and profits are negative. Potential buyers must be made aware of the product's features, uses, and advantages. During the growth stage, sales rise rapidly; profits reach a peak and then start to decline. In the maturity stage, the sales curve peaks and starts to fall as profits continue to decline. This stage is characterized by a high degree of competition. During the decline stage sales fall rapidly, and the marketer may cut promotional efforts, eliminate marginal distributors, and, finally, make plans for phasing out the product. Most enterprises have a product mix, and various products in the mix can be at different life cycle stages. Since a product's life span is too short from the firm's viewpoint, marketers must deal with the dual problems of prolonging existing products and introducing new ones to meet organizational sales goals.

A brand identifies a seller's product and differentiates it from competitors' products. A brand name is that part of a brand that can be spoken—letters, words, numbers. The element of a brand that cannot be spoken, such as a symbol or design, is called a brand mark. A trademark is a legal designation indicating that the owner has exclusive use of a brand or part of a brand and that others are prohibited by law from using it. Buyers benefit from branding because it identifies a manufacturer or company whose products buyers may or may not like. Sellers benefit from branding because it facilitates repeat purchases. In addition, branding facilitates promotional efforts because each branded product indirectly promotes all of the firms' products that are branded similarly. Manufacturer brands are initiated by producers and enable producers to be identified with their products at the point of purchase. Private distributor brands are initiated and owned by resellers.

The choice of a brand is a critical decision because the brand affects customers' attitudes toward a product and, therefore, their purchase decisions. The brand name should be easy to say, spell, and recall and, if possible, should allude to the product's uses, benefits, or special characteristics in a positive way. To protect the firm's exclusive rights to a brand, the company should be certain that the selected brand name does not infringe on brands already registered with the U.S. Patent Office. Also, a firm must guard against allowing a brand name to become a generic term which is used to refer to a general product category, because generic terms cannot be protected as exclusive brand names.

In attempting to establish branding policies, the first decision to be made is whether the firm should brand its products at all. When an organization's product is very similar to competitors' products, it may be difficult to brand. Assuming that a firm does choose to brand its products, marketers may choose one or more of the following branding policies: individual branding, overall family branding, line family branding, or brand-extension branding. Individual branding is a policy in which every product is named something different. In overall family branding, all of a firm's products are branded with the same name or at least part of the name. Brand-extension branding occurs when a firm uses one of its existing brand names as part of a brand for an improved or new product that is usually in the same product category as the existing brand.

Packaging involves development of a container and a graphic design for a product. Like a brand name, a package influences customers' attitudes toward a product. The impressions that buyers obtain about a product at the point of purchase or through use may be greatly influenced by the package characteristics. A package can perform several functions, among them protection, economy, convenience, and promotion. Marketers, however, must consider many factors when developing packages. One major consideration is cost. Marketers should try to determine how much customers are willing to pay for packages that are more protective, convenient, safe, or attractive. Another consideration is whether to package the product singularly or in multiple units. When developing packages within an already existing organization, marketers should consider how much continuity among package designs is desirable. A package can thus be a major component of a marketing strategy. An effective package may help to give a firm more promotional impact than it could possibly afford with conventional advertising efforts.

A label is another product feature. It is that part of a product that carries written information about the product and serves both promotional and informational purposes. The label is one of the most visible features of the product to consumers; it is therefore an important element in the marketing mix.

Other product-related features are the physical characteristics of the product and supportive services. Physical characteristics include colors, textures, and sizes. A marketer is also concerned with developing product warranties and establishing a system to provide replacement parts and repair services. Finally, a firm sometimes must provide credit services to customers.

# True or False Statements

(T)  F    1. The product is an important variable in the marketing mix.

(T)  F    2. A product is a complexity of tangible and intangible attributes including functional, social, and psychological utilities or benefits.

(T)  F    3. When people purchase a product, they are also buying the benefits and satisfaction that they believe the product will provide.

T  (F)    4. Products bought for use in a firm's operations to produce other products are classified as consumer products.

(T)  F    5. The classification of consumer products is based primarily on the characteristics of buyers' purchasing behavior.

T  (F)    6. A consumer product can be classified as a convenience, shopping, or specialty good, but cannot fit into more than one category.

(T)  F    7. Classifying a product as to whether it is an industrial or a consumer product is important in determining marketing strategies.

(T)  F    8. Electrical appliances are typical shopping products.

(T)  F    9. Specialty products require consumers to expend considerable searching efforts.

(T)  F    10. Supplies are consumed indirectly in the production of other products.

T  (F)    11. The product mix refers to a related group of products in the product line.

(T)  F    12. A specific product in a product line should satisfy a definite target market.

T  (F)    13. Lathes, cranes, and stamping machines are examples of industrial products classified as accessory equipment.

(T)  F    14. A brand is a name, term, symbol, design, or combination of these that identifies a seller's products and differentiates them from competitors' products.

T  (F)    15. Manufacturer brands give retailers higher gross profit margins.

T  (F)    16. The primary function of packaging is to promote a product.

(T)  F    17. Profits are negative in the introductory stage of the product life cyle.

(T)  F    18. Marketers should avoid overpackaging or buying more packaging protection than is required to prevent product damage.

(T)  F    19. Because there are so many similar products on the grocery shelf, a creative label can act as a "silent" salesperson to attract attention to a particular product.

(T)  F    20. When packaging a product, a manufacturer must consider both the target market and government laws and regulations.

T    (F)    21. Branding benefits mainly the sellers of a product.

T    (F)    22. Private distributor brands identify the product's manufacturer.

(T)    F    23. A product's name may be a major factor in making it a winner or a loser.

T    (F)    24. A marketer should strive to have a brand name become a generic term.

T    (F)    25. In overall family branding each product is named something different.

T    (F)    26. An idea can be a consumer good but not an industrial good.

(T)    F    27. Product packaging—such as unique closure, better box, or more durable container size—may give a firm a competitive advantage in the market.

(T)    F    28. A product may fail during its introductory stage because it does not provide benefits that consumers want.

# Multiple-Choice Questions

_b_    1. An organization's products
  a. are not part of the marketing mix.
  b. represent visible contacts with consumers.
  c. are not information sources.
  d. are purchased for functional reasons only.

_d_    2. Packaging design directly involves all of the following *except*
  a. labeling.
  b. environmental impact.
  c. cost considerations.
  d. production.
  e. decisions about colors.

_e_    3. The definition of a product *excludes*
  a. functional utilities.
  b. side effects.
  c. social utilities.
  d. psychological utilities.
  e. production techniques.

_b_    4. Consumer product classifications are based primarily on
  a. how consumers use the product.
  b. the characteristics of buyers' purchasing behavior.
  c. where the product is purchased.
  d. how consumers view the product.
  e. the cost of the product.

_c_    5. In purchases of industrial products
   a. organizational goals are often secondary.
   b. psychological considerations outweigh functional considerations.
   c. functional considerations outweigh psychological considerations.
   d. government buyers constitute the largest market.

_c_    6. The total group of products that a seller makes available to consumers is termed the
   a. product line.
   b. marketing mix.
   c. product mix.
   d. product items.
   e. market line.

_d_    7. Which of the following is *not* an example of an industrial product?
   a. Screws used to mount engine blocks on cars
   b. Steel used for manufacturing drill bits
   c. Gasoline for a salesperson's car
   d. A pencil used to write a weekly grocery list
   e. A chair used for a weekly meeting room in a business

_b_    8. All of the following are classes of industrial products *except*
   a. raw materials.
   b. semi-finished supplies.
   c. accessory equipment.
   d. supplies.
   e. process materials.

_c_    9. A product line refers to
   a. the composite of products that an organization makes available to consumers.
   b. a specific version of a product that can be designated as unique among an organization's products.
   c. a group of closely related products that are considered a unit.
   d. product information provided to a customer by a salesperson.
   e. the width of the product mix.

_d_    10. Which of the following characterizes the maturity stage of the product life cycle?
   a. Sales fall rapidly, and new technology as well as social trends may cause profits to fall also.
   b. Sales are zero, and profits are negative.
   c. Sales rise rapidly, and profits reach a peak.
   d. The sales curve peaks and starts to decline as profits continue to decline.
   e. Minimal competition exists among sellers.

_e_    11. Which stage in the product life cycle is characterized by negative profits, zero sales, and an emphasis on communicating product benefits to buyers?
   a. Maturity stage
   b. Planning stage
   c. Decline stage
   d. Growth stage
   e. Introduction stage

_e_    12. Which of the following is a typical marketing strategy when managing a product in the growth phase?
   a. Maintaining a constant price
   b. Concentrating on advertising and dealer-oriented promotion
   c. Encouraging strong brand loyalty and thus competing with aggressive product emulators
   d. Eliminating marginal distributors
   e. Making potential buyers aware of the product's features, uses, and advantages

_b_    13. Which of the following is *least* likely to be the goal in a retailer's decision to use a private distributor brand?
   a. To purchase products of a specified quality at the lowest cost
   b. To promote a manufacturer
   c. To develop an efficient promotion scheme
   d. To generate higher gross profit margins
   e. To improve a store image

_c_    14. Which of the following has resulted from the competition between manufacturer and private distributor brands?
   a. Manufacturer brands are becoming more popular.
   b. Competition between manufacturer and private brands is leveling off.
   c. Manufacturers are developing multiple brands and distribution systems.
   d. Consumers are buying fewer private distributor brands.
   e. The market shares for manufacturer and private brands are about equal.

_d_    15. The classification of industrial products is useful in
   a. production.
   b. purchasing activities.
   c. understanding consumers' buying motives.
   d. developing a marketing mix.

_d_    16. Brands aid buyers in all of the following *except*
   a. identifying specific products the buyer likes or doesn't like.
   b. assisting buyers in evaluating the quality of products.
   c. providing the buyer with psychological rewards.
   d. making product selection a random process.

_C_ 17. Selection of a branding policy is influenced by all of the following *except*
  a. the number of products and product lines produced by the firm.
  b. target market characteristics.
  c. package size.
  d. the extent of the firm's resources.
  e. the number and types of competing products available.

_d_ 18. Which of the following statements about labeling is false?
  a. Labels can be used to promote other products of the manufacturer.
  b. Labels are "silent salespersons."
  c. Labels can be used to encourage proper use of products.
  d. Labels are primarily promotional devices and provide little useful information.
  e. None of the above is false.

_A_ 19. When developing products, marketers must consider all of the following *except*
  a. production specifications.
  b. product textures.
  c. types of warranties.
  d. establishing a system to provide replacement parts.
  e. credit services.

# Programmed Completion Exercises

protection,
economy,
convenience,
promotion

1. Packaging as a marketing activity is concerned with _____, _____, _____, and _____.

label,
information

2. The _____ is that part of a product which carries _____ about the product or the seller; it may be part of a package, or it may be attached to the product.

introduction,
growth,
maturity,
decline

3. The four stages of a product's life cycle are _____, _____, _____, and _____.

life cycle

4. As a product moves through the product _____ _____ strategies must be evaluated continually, especially

those relating to competition, promotion, distribution, and market information.

product

5. The life expectancy of a _____ is based on buyers' wants, the availability of competing products, and other considerations.

decline, phase

6. In the _____ stage of the product life cycle, the marketer may cut promotional efforts, eliminate marginal distributors, and, finally, make plans to _____ the product out of the market.

industrial, consumer

7. The functional aspects of an _____ product are usually considered more significant than the psychological rewards that sometimes are associated with _____ products.

raw materials, major equipment, accessory equipment, component parts, process materials, supplies, industrial services

8. On the basis of their characteristics and intended uses, industrial products can be classified into several categories, including _____ _____, _____ _____, _____ _____, _____ _____, _____ _____, _____, and _____ _____.

good, service, idea

9. A product can be a _____, a _____, or an _____.

product line

10. A _____ _____ includes a group of closely related products that are considered a unit because of technical, marketing, or end-use considerations.

product mix

11. The _____ _____ is the composite of products that an organization makes available to consumers.

product, tangible, intangible

12. A _____ is a complexity of _____ and _____ characteristics or attributes, including functional, social, and psychological utilities or benefits.

consumer, industrial

13. A product can be classified in one of two general categories, as a _____ product or as an _____ product, on the basis of its intended use.

Convenience

14. _____ products are relatively inexpensive, frequently purchased items for which buyers exert only minimal effort to obtain.

shopping

15. Consumers purchase _____ products after going to several stores to compare price, quality, and service.

specialty

16. A _____ product has some unique attraction for which consumers are willing to make a special search effort; in general, economy is not the major consideration.

depth, width

17. The _____ of a product mix is measured by the number different products offered to buyers in each product line, whereas the _____ of the product mix measures the number of product lines in the company.

name, term, symbol, design

18. A brand is a _____, _____, _____, or _____, or a combination of these, that identifies a seller's products.

trademark, brand, prohibited

19. A _____ is a legal designation indicating that the owner has exclusive use of a _____ and that others are _____ by law from using it.

Manufacturer

20. _____ brands are initiated by the producer and enable the producer to be identified with the product at the point of purchase.

private distributor

21. Retailers and wholesalers use _____ _____ brands in order to achieve more efficient promotion, higher gross margins, and improved store images.

Resellers, manufacturers

22. _____ and _____ are competing to determine who will control brand names.

individual branding, overall family branding, line family branding, brand-extension branding

23. Assuming a firm chooses to brand its products, marketers may use one or more branding policies including _____ _____, _____ _____ _____, _____ _____ _____, and _____-_____ _____.

Multiple, increase

24. _____ packaging is likely to _____ demand because it increases the amount of the product available at the point of consumption.

Warranties,
repair services,
credit services

25. _____ , _____ _____ , and _____ _____ are examples of supportive product-related services.

## Answers to Objective Questions

*True or False*

| | | | |
|---|---|---|---|
| 1. | T | 15. | F |
| 2. | T | 16. | F |
| 3. | T | 17. | T |
| 4. | F | 18. | T |
| 5. | T | 19. | T |
| 6. | F | 20. | T |
| 7. | T | 21. | F |
| 8. | T | 22. | F |
| 9. | T | 23. | T |
| 10. | T | 24. | F |
| 11. | F | 25. | F |
| 12. | T | 26. | F |
| 13. | F | 27. | T |
| 14. | T | 28. | T |

*Multiple-Choice*

| | | | |
|---|---|---|---|
| 1. | b | 11. | e |
| 2. | d | 12. | c |
| 3. | e | 13. | b |
| 4. | b | 14. | c |
| 5. | c | 15. | d |
| 6. | c | 16. | d |
| 7. | d | 17. | c |
| 8. | b | 18. | d |
| 9. | c | 19. | a |
| 10. | d | | |

# CHAPTER 7

# Developing and Managing Products

## Chapter Summary

Developing a marketing mix that succeeds in the marketplace is an important task for marketing management. Marketers must blend product, price, distribution, and promotion into a final marketing mix that provides benefits which match buyers' wants and needs. Too often companies have to cope with product failures because they have not thought carefully enough about what buyers' reasons are for purchasing particular products. Such mistakes can be avoided by developing a consumer-oriented marketing strategy that communicates and then delivers desired benefits.

A marketing manager must determine an organizational approach to developing and managing products. Three organizational approaches that have been used successfully to manage products are the product manager system, the market manager system, and an approach that combines the two. The product manager system is sometimes used when a company has multiple products flowing into a common market; the products are sold in one location or to the same dealers and may be designed to appeal to different target markets. The market manager system is sometimes used when different markets desire a single product line. When products and markets crisscross, then these two approaches may be combined. A product manager holds a staff position in a multiproduct company in which the large number of products makes it difficult for market managers to make decisions that enhance the profitability of one product or a group of products on a continuing basis. Product managers are responsible for a product, a product line, or several distinct products that are considered to be an interrelated group. A brand manager is a type of product manager who is responsible for a single brand. When the number of a company's products increases, the firm may separate its products according to the markets it seeks, assigning a single market manager to the products directed at the same market. While the market manager seeks modifications in existing products or product additions to meet the needs of a target market, the product manager has the basic responsibility to coordinate all product decisions that relate to all target markets served.

A venture team is an organizational innovation to create entirely new products that may be aimed at unfamiliar markets. The venture team, unlike the product manager or market manager, is responsible for all aspects of a product's development process and has authority to execute plans for product development. Members of the team come from different functional areas of the organization. When the commercial potential of a new product has been demonstrated, members of the venture team may return to their functional areas, or they may join an existing or new division to manage the product.

To provide products that satisfy people in a firm's target market(s) and to achieve the organization's objectives, a marketer must be able to improve the product mix. Three alternatives that may be used to improve a product mix are developing a new product, modifying an existing product, and deleting a product.

Developing new products is frequently expensive and risky. It goes through six phases. The first phase is idea generation, which is a more or less systematic approach for gathering new product ideas. New ideas may come from internal sources or from sources outside the firm. Next, ideas are screened. Those that do not match organizational objectives are rejected, and those with the greatest potential are selected for further development. The third phase is a business analysis that provides a tentative sketch of a product's compatibility in the marketplace, including its probable profitability. The next phase is product development. The primary purpose of the development phase is to ascertain whether it is technically feasible to produce the product and whether the product can be produced at costs low enough to result in a reasonable price. If a product idea survives to the development point, it then is ready to be transformed into a prototype that should reveal tangible and intangible attributes associated with the product in consumers' minds. The fifth phase of new-product development is test marketing, a limited introduction of a product in areas chosen to represent the intended market in order to determine probable buyers' reactions. The last phase is commercialization, during which plans for full-scale manufacturing and marketing must be refined and settled, and budgets for the projects must be prepared. And, finally, the product is introduced into the market.

Product modification refers to changing one or more of a product's characteristics and often is used in the maturity stage of the product life cycle to give a brand a competitive advantage. Existing products can be changed in three major ways: quality modifications, functional modifications, and style modifications. Quality modifications are changes that relate to a product's dependability and durability and usually are executed by alterations in the materials or production process employed. Changes that affect a product's versatility, effectiveness, convenience, or safety are called functional modifications and usually require redesigning one or more parts of the product. Style modifications are directed at changing the sensory appeal of a product by altering its taste, texture, sound, smell, or visual characteristics.

A product, however, cannot satisfy target-market customers and contribute to achieving an organization's overall goals indefinitely. To maintain an effective product mix, a firm has to get rid of some products. This is called product deletion. Although some organizations drop weak products only after they have become severe financial burdens, a better approach involves some form of systematic review in which each product is evaluated periodically to determine its impact on the overall effectiveness of the firm's product mix.

When a marketer introduces a product, attempts are made to position it so that it projects an image of possessing the characteristics most desired by target-market members at whom the product is aimed. A product's position refers to the customers' concept of the product's attributes relative to their concepts of competitive brands. If a product has been planned properly, its attributes and its brand image will give it the distinct appeal needed. When some preferred attributes are not being offered, then room exists for a new product or for repositioning of an existing product.

Most new products start off slowly and seldom generate enough sales to produce profits immediately. As buyers learn about the product, marketers should be alert for product weaknesses and make corrections quickly to prevent the early death or crippling of demand. As the sales curve moves upward and the breakeven point is reached, the growth stage begins. During the growth stage product models might be expanded to appeal to more specialized markets. After development costs have been recovered, it may be possible to lower prices. During the growth period gaps in the distribution network should be filled. Promotional efforts should continue to develop brand loyalty during the growth stage, but as sales increase promotional costs may decline.

In the maturity stage of the product life cycle marketers may need to change the product's quality or make other modifications. Pricing strategies become more mixed and marketers usually place strong emphasis on encouraging dealers to support the product. During the maturity stage large expenditures on advertising may be necessary to maintain the product's market share.

As a product's sales curve turns downward, profits usually decline, and the product enters the decline stage of the life cycle. At this stage an important decision is to determine when to eliminate the product. Usually, a declining product has lost its distinctiveness, and marketers do little to change its style, design, or other attributes. The fact that a product returns a profit may be more important to marketers than maintaining a certain market share through repricing. During a product's decline, those outlets with the core sales are maintained, and unprofitable outlets are weeded out. Promotion becomes less important during this stage.

# True or False Statements

T   F    1. Venture teams are usually groups used to develop new products.

T   F    2. Product planning tends to reduce the probability of product failure.

T   F    3. Products often fail because companies have not adequately considered consumers' reasons for buying.

T   F    4. A market manager has the responsibility to coordinate all product decisions concerning all target markets served.

T   F    5. Most new products are commercially successful.

T   F    6. A brand manager is a type of market manager.

T   F    7. A properly planned and managed product mix should not require alterations to maintain its effectiveness.

T   F    8. Idea generation is the first stage in developing and introducing new products.

T   F    9. One purpose of screening ideas is to assess the firm's overall ability to produce and market a new product.

T   F    10. The primary purpose of the development phase is to provide a tentative sketch of a product's compatibility in the marketplace, including its probable profitability.

T   F    11. Test marketing is a widespread introduction of a product to determine if it will sell.

T   F    12. The product adoption model implies that promotion should be used to create widespread awareness of a new product and its benefits.

T   F    13. As products are commercialized, they are usually introduced on a national basis very quickly.

T   F    14. Gradual product introduction allows competitors to enter the same target market quickly with similar products.

T   F    15. For product modification to be successful, existing customers must be able to perceive that a modification has been made.

T   F    16. Quality modifications are changes that affect a product's versatility, effectiveness, convenience, or safety.

T   F    17. Style modifications are directed at changing the sensory appeal of a product.

T   F    18. A weak product may generate unfavorable images that rub off onto some of the firm's other products.

T   F    19. Weak products should be deleted only after they have become severe financial burdens.

T   F    20. Product positioning refers to the shelf space location given to a product by a reseller.

(T)  F   21. Segmentation means that a firm is aiming a given brand at only a portion of the total market.

T  (F)   22. Head-to-head positioning is critical when a firm is introducing a brand into a market in which it already has one or more brands.

(T)  F   23. As sales for a product increase, the momentum must usually be supported by adjustments in the marketing strategy.

T  (F)   24. Price always falls during the maturity stage.

(T)  F   25. The goal during the growth stage of a product's life cycle is to establish the product's position and encourage brand loyalty.

(T)  F   26. Salespersons usually object if a product is dropped when a loyal core market exists.

T  (F)   27. During a product's decline marketers usually place strong emphasis on encouraging dealers to support the product.

(T)  F   28. During the maturity stage of the product life cycle pricing strategies become more mixed.

# Multiple-Choice Questions

_c_   1. An alternative to the functional organization that sometimes is used when a company has multiple products flowing into a common market is called
   a. the traditional system.
   b. the market manager system.
   c. the product manager system.
   d. the market-oriented system.
   e. the consumer-oriented system.

_d_   2. Changes in consumers' wants and needs can best be met by
   a. advertising extensively.
   b. lowering prices.
   c. adopting the product manager system.
   d. altering the marketing mix.

_d_   3. Which of the following indicates the way in which a venture team is *unlike* a product manager or market manager?
   a. A venture team is limited to planning and coordination.
   b. A venture team never manages a product following its development.
   c. A venture team seeks to modify existing products.
   d. A venture team is responsible for all aspects of a product's development, including research, engineering, finance, and marketing.
   e. A venture team is not highly flexible.

_C_     4. Which of the following is *not* an intrafirm device for developing new product ideas?
   a. Rewards
   b. Brainstorming
   c. Management consultants
   d. Incentives

_b_     5. One purpose of idea screening is to
   a. brainstorm for new ideas.
   b. provide an early projection of economic payoffs.
   c. secure consultants to provide ideas.
   d. select products to be produced.
   e. determine how a product will affect sales, costs, and profits.

_C_     6. One purpose of the business analysis stage of new product development is to
   a. provide an early projection of economic payoffs.
   b. ascertain whether it is technically feasible to produce the product.
   c. determine if similar marketing channels, outlets, and promotional resources can be used.
   d. test market the product.
   e. commercialize the product.

_b_     7. In which stage of product development is a product transformed into a working model?
   a. Screening
   b. Development
   c. Testing
   d. Business analysis
   e. Commercialization

_C_     8. Test marketing
   a. helps guarantee a product's success.
   b. is the unlimited introduction of a product into a geographic area.
   c. is a sample launching of the entire marketing mix for a product.
   d. should be conducted for all products.

_a_     9. Commercialization does *not* involve
   a. jamming.
   b. full-scale distribution.
   c. final budget preparation.
   d. scheduling and coordination.
   e. making the marketing program final.

_d_     10. What percentage of products that are test marketed are then placed into commercialization?
   a. 65 percent
   b. 50 percent

c. 40 percent

d. 30 percent

e. 15 percent

_e_    11. The product adoption process consists of all of the following stages *except*

a. awareness.

b. interest.

c. evaluation.

d. adoption.

e. rejection.

_c_    12. During which stage of the product life cycle does the competitive situation usually stabilize.

a. Introductory stage

b. Growth stage

c. Maturity stage

d. Decline stage

e. Development stage

_b_    13. Gradual product introduction is often used because it

a. prevents competitors from monitoring new product introduction.

b. reduces the risk associated with introducing a new product.

c. is less expensive than rapid product introduction.

d. prevents competitors from entering the market with similar products.

e. maximizes the effectiveness of the product mix.

_a_    14. Style modifications are directed at changing a product's

a. sensory appeal.

b. convenience or safety.

c. durability.

d. price.

e. quality.

_b_    15. A run-out approach to deleting a product

a. lets the product decline without changing the marketing strategy.

b. exploits any strengths left in the product.

c. involves the sudden termination of an unprofitable product.

d. lets weak products be dropped only after they have become severe financial burdens.

_c_    16. Product positioning refers to

a. distributing products in a good location.

b. exaggerating product attributes.

c. creating and maintaining the product concept in customers' minds.

d. a product's shelf location.

e. a product's hierarchy in the distribution channels.

  C 17. Product managers are essentially
      a. salespeople.
      b. generators of creative ideas.
      c. planners and coordinators.
      d. financial managers.
      e. communications experts.

  c 18. The majority of products are in which stage of the product life
      cycle?
      a. Introductory stage
      b. Growth stage
      c. Maturity stage
      d. Decline stage
      e. Extinction stage

  b 19. Marketers should establish a market position and encourage
      brand loyalty during which life cycle stage?
      a. Introductory stage
      b. Growth stage
      c. Maturity stage
      d. Decline stage

  C 20. Large advertising expenditures may be necessary to maintain the
      market share during which life cycle stage?
      a. Introductory stage
      b. Growth stage
      c. Maturity stage
      d. Decline stage

# Programmed Completion Exercises

commercializa- 1. The _____ phase is equivalent to the early introductory
tion, marketing
    period of the product life cycle, and it involves plans for full-

    scale _____ of the product.

Awareness, 2. _____, _____, _____, _____, and
interest,
evaluation, trial, _____ are the stages of the adoption process generally
adoption
    recognized as those that buyers go through in accepting a prod-

    uct.

product 3. In multiproduct companies the _____ manager, who

    holds a staff position, coordinates product efforts and becomes

    the strategy center for the product in all markets.

venture team,
new products,
unfamiliar

4. A _____ _____ is an organizational structure established to create _____ _____ that may be aimed at _____ markets.

test marketing

5. A competitor may try to jam the _____ _____ program by increasing advertising, lowering prices, and developing special retailer incentives.

ideas

6. New product _____ may be obtained from sources outside the firm such as advertising agencies, management consulting firms, and private research organizations.

new product
ideas

7. Screening _____ _____ _____ involves a general assessment of the organization's resources and attempts, through forecasting techniques, to make an early projection of economic payoffs.

develop, alter,
maintain,
product mix

8. To provide products that satisfy the firm's target market(s) and to achieve the organization's objectives, a marketer must be able to _____, _____, and _____ an effective _____ _____.

growth

9. During the _____ period of the product life cycle the tendency is to move from an exclusive or selective exposure to a more extensive distribution network of dealers.

idea generation,
screening,
business
analysis,
product
development,
test marketing,
commercialization

10. The six phases of new-product development are _____ _____, _____, _____ _____, _____ _____, _____ _____, and _____.

J S b a P a T C

technically
feasible, low,
price

11. The primary purpose of the product development phase is to ascertain whether it is _____ _____ to produce the product at costs _____ enough to result in a reasonable _____.

modifiable,
perceive,
modification,
consistent,
desires

12. Product modification can be effective under certain conditions: the product must be _____, existing customers must be able to _____ that a _____ has been made, and the modification should make the product more _____ with customers' _____.

consumes, time,
resources, new
products,
unfavorable
images

13. A weak product not only costs the firm financially but also _____ too much of a marketer's _____, reduces the time and _____ available for developing _____ _____, and may generate _____ _____ among customers.

position, head-
on, avoid
competition

14. A firm can _____ a product in order to compete _____ with another brand, or a product can be positioned to _____ _____.

modification,
rejuvenation

15. A marketing strategy for a mature product may involve product _____ or _____ through packaging, new models, or style changes.

phased out, run
out, dropped
immediately

16. A product can be deleted in several ways; it can be _____ _____, _____ _____, or _____ _____.

growth,
distribution
network

17. During the _____ stage, gaps in the _____ _____ should be filled in.

interface

18. Managers who make product decisions must have an _____ with departments and individuals who influence the product's destiny.

# Answers to Objective Questions

| *True or False* | | | |
|---|---|---|---|
| 1. T | 15. T |
| 2. T | 16. F |
| 3. T | 17. T |
| 4. F | 18. T |
| 5. F | 19. F |
| 6. F | 20. F |
| 7. F | 21. T |
| 8. T | 22. F |
| 9. T | 23. T |
| 10. F | 24. F |
| 11. F | 25. T |
| 12. T | 26. T |
| 13. F | 27. F |
| 14. T | 28. T |

| *Multiple-Choice* | |
|---|---|
| 1. c | 11. e |
| 2. d | 12. c |
| 3. d | 13. b |
| 4. c | 14. a |
| 5. b | 15. b |
| 6. c | 16. c |
| 7. b | 17. c |
| 8. c | 18. c |
| 9. a | 19. b |
| 10. d | 20. c |

# CHAPTER 8

# Pricing Decisions

## Chapter Summary

Price is the value placed on what is exchanged. Something of value—usually purchasing power—is exchanged for satisfaction or utility. It is a mistake to believe that price is always money paid or some other financial consideration. The oldest form of exchange is barter, the trading of products. Buyers' concern for and interest in price is related to their expectations about the satisfaction or utility associated with a product. Since buyers have limited resources, they must allocate their purchasing power and decide whether the utility gained in an exchange is worth the purchasing power sacrificed. Price is one of the easiest variables in the marketing mix to adjust. It can be changed quickly to respond to changes in demand or the actions of competitors. Because price times quantity equals revenue, price is important in determining profits. The economic role of price is to allocate products according to market opportunities, which depend on increases or decreases in demand.

The eight steps involved in pricing are: (1) selecting the pricing objectives, (2) identifying the target market's evaluation of price and its ability to purchase, (3) determining demand, (4) ascertaining the relationships among demand, cost, and profit, (5) analyzing competitors' prices, (6) selecting a pricing policy, (7) selecting a pricing method, and (8) selecting a price. The first step in pricing is the consideration of pricing objectives, that is, overall goals that indicate the role of price in an organization's long-range plans. Survival is the broadest and most fundamental pricing objective. Since price is a flexible variable, it can be adjusted to help achieve a sales volume that is consistent with the organization's expenses. Sometimes the management of a business claims that its pricing objective is to maximize profits for the firm's owners; such an objective rarely works, however, since its achievement is difficult to measure. Pricing for a targeted return on investment is another kind of pricing objective. Many firms establish pricing objectives to maintain or increase market share. A cash flow and recovery objective is used to recover cash as quickly as possible. In some instances, an organization may be in a favorable position and therefore sets an objective of maintaining the status quo, that is, deciding not to take on further risk. There is no one best objective; objectives should be consistent with organizational goals.

The next step in setting prices is identifying the target market's evaluation of price and its ability to purchase. Price plays a major role in customers' overall evaluations of a marketing mix. Therefore, identifying the values that specific types of buyers expect from exchanges is important. Customers' ability to buy also has direct consequences for marketers setting a price. The ability to purchase involves resources such as money, credit, wealth, and other products that could be traded in exchange.

Marketers also need to examine the price elasticity of demand to determine consumer responsiveness to changes in price. If demand is price elastic, a change in price causes an opposite change in total revenue. An inelastic demand results in a parallel change in total revenue.

Having determined the role that demand plays in setting price, marketers next must examine the relationships among demand, costs, and profits. There are two approaches to understanding demand, cost, and profit relationships: breakeven analysis and marginal analysis.

To set prices effectively, an organization must be aware of the prices charged by competitors. After competitors' prices are determined, a company can use price to increase sales.

The next step in setting prices is selecting a pricing policy. A pricing policy is a guiding philosophy or course of action designed to influence and determine pricing decisions. One common pricing policy is pioneer pricing, of which there are two kinds: price skimming and penetration pricing. Price skimming permits an organization to charge the highest possible price that buyers who most desire the product will pay. A penetration price is a lower price designed to penetrate the market so as to increase unit sales. Another pricing policy is psychological pricing, which is designed to encourage purchases that are based on emotional, rather than rational, responses. It is used most often at the retail level and has limited use in pricing industrial products. Professional pricing is another pricing policy and is used by persons who provide highly skilled services. Professional pricing encompasses ethical pricing and gentlemen's pricing. Finally, price often is coordinated with promotion. Promotional pricing includes price leaders and special-event pricing.

After selecting a pricing policy, a marketer must choose a pricing method. Pricing methods provide techniques for assigning a price to a specific product. In using cost-oriented pricing methods a firm determines price by adding a dollar amount or a certain percentage onto the product's cost. Two cost-oriented pricing methods are cost-plus pricing and markup pricing. Demand-oriented pricing methods use the level of demand for a product as the basis for price setting. If demand for the product is strong a high price will be chosen; if demand is weak, a low price will be used. Finally, competition-oriented pricing considers cost and revenue secondary to prices of competitors.

Pricing policies and methods of determining prices should provide the direction and structure for selecting a final price. The target market, demand, costs, price elasticity, government regulations, and competition are all important variables to consider before selecting the final price.

Quoting and adjusting prices for industrial markets is based on differences in costs that result from serving different markets. Two commonly used industrial pricing policies are price discounting and geographic pricing. Price discounts can be classified as trade, quantity, and cash discounts. Geographic pricing involves reductions for transportation costs or other costs associated with the physical distance between buyer and seller.

# True or False Statements

T  (F)  1. The price of a product usually has a minor effect upon purchase decisions made by consumers.

(T)  F  2. It is a mistake to believe that the price is always money or some other financial consideration.

(T)  F  3. Pricing decisions involve the relationship of the variables of quantity times the variables of price.

(T)  F  4. Interest payments and tolls are examples of prices.

T  (F)  5. Status quo pricing objectives can increase a firm's risk by creating a climate of severe price competition in an industry.

(T)  F  6. An inverse relationship exists between the price of most products and the quantity demanded.

T  (F)  7. Demand for a product should be the major consideration in setting a price for a product.

T  (F)  8. It is easy for a marketer to use an economic model to isolate the effect of price changes on the quantity demanded.

(T)  F  9. The manipulation of price is one of the most visible and convenient decision variables available to marketers.

T  (F)  10. If demand is elastic, a change in price results in a smaller change in total revenue.

(T)  F  11. Ideas, services, rights, tangible items—anything of value—can be assessed in terms of price.

(T)  F  12. A buyer's concern for and interest in price is related to expected satisfaction or utility associated with a product.

(T)  F  13. To stay in business, a company has to set prices that cover all its costs in supplying products to meet demand.

(T)  F  14. Pricing objectives influence decisions in most functional areas and must be consistent with an organization's overall goals.

T  (F)  15. The point at which marginal costs are equal to marginal revenues is called the breakeven point.

(T)  F  16. Professional pricing is based on the belief that professionals who provide services have an ethical responsibility not to overcharge customers.

T  (F)  17. The purpose of price discrimination is to decrease marginal cost by gaining additional revenue from buyers who may be reluctant to purchase the product even at low prices.

(T)  F  18. Superficial discounting is considered unethical, and legislation outlaws it in some states.

(T)  F  19. Cost-plus pricing is a pricing method in which a specified dollar amount or percentage of the seller's cost is added to the seller's cost to set the price.

Ⓣ  F    20. Financial price is the basis of most market exchanges.

Ⓣ  F    21. The purpose of a systematic pricing approach is to set a price based on all considerations that could influence the attainment of an organization's pricing objectives.

T  Ⓕ   22. Demand-oriented pricing involves using a low price if demand for a product is strong and a high price if product demand is weak.

Ⓣ  F    23. Quantity discounts may be cumulative or noncumulative.

Ⓣ  F    24. A reduction of list price given to a middleman by a producer is called a trade discount.

T  Ⓕ   25. A price quoted as F.O.B. factory means that the manufacturer pays for shipping the product from the factory.

T  Ⓕ   26. The economic approach to pricing means that the optimum price is the one at which marginal cost equals average cost.

T  Ⓕ   27. A pricing policy is a systematic procedure for calculating prices on a regular basis.

Ⓣ  F    28. A fundamental pricing objective is to survive.

Ⓣ  F    29. Penetration pricing may allow a marketer to gain a larger market share.

T  Ⓕ   30. Odd-even pricing, customary pricing, symbolic pricing, and price-lining are types of promotional pricing.

Ⓣ  F    31. Price leaders are products that management prices below cost in the hope of attracting new customers.

Ⓣ  F    32. Knowing competitors' prices may help a marketer increase his or her own sales.

## Multiple-Choice Questions

_c_    1. Which pricing objective is oriented to the quick recovery of cash and is favored for products with a short life cycle?
   a. Return on investment pricing
   b. Profit pricing
   c. Cash flow pricing
   d. Market share pricing
   e. Status quo pricing

_b_    2. According to the text, price is best described as
   a. purchasing power.
   b. the value placed on what is exchanged.
   c. utility associated with a product.
   d. how much something costs in monetary terms.
   e. money paid or some other financial consideration.

_d_      3. For which of the following reasons is price *not* important?
        a. Price can be changed quickly to respond to changes in demand.
        b. Price has a psychological impact on customers and can be used symbolically to emphasize a product's quality.
        c. Price is important in determining profits.
        d. Price can be used as a tool to lower production costs.
        e. Price allocates products that must be matched to market opportunities.

_c_      4. The demand schedule illustrates the effect of
        a. a change in price caused by an equal change in total revenue.
        b. different pricing policies.
        c. one variable, price, on the quantity demanded.
        d. dependent variables such as the environment.

_a_      5. Which of the following helps to identify the target market's evaluation of price?
        a. Understanding customers' need, willingness, authority, and ability to buy
        b. Discovering the top price customers will pay for a product
        c. Stretching demand for a product
        d. Evaluating competitors' prices
        e. Discovering the lowest price customers will pay for a product

_a_      6. Pricing objectives are overall goals that describe the role of price and
        a. aid an organization in its long-range plans.
        b. have a minimal effect on other functional areas of a business.
        c. help determine the maximum allocation of buyers' purchasing power.
        d. should not have any effect on the functional areas of a business.

_b_      7. Which of the following is viewed as the broadest and most fundamental pricing objective?
        a. Market share
        b. Survival
        c. Sales growth and expansion
        d. A return on investment
        e. Cash flow and recovery

_c_      8. Which of the following statements is true?
        a. Price is an unimportant ingredient in the marketing program.
        b. Price is the most difficult variable to adjust in the marketing mix.
        c. Price can be adjusted quickly to change the quantity demanded and revenue received.
        d. Since cost times quantity equals profit, the slope of the demand schedule will be fixed at any point.

_a_    9. Elasticity of demand describes
   a. the change in quantity demanded due to changes in price.
   b. the change in total revenues resulting from a change in de-
      mand.
   c. the change in price resulting from a change in demand.
   d. an inverse change in total revenue resulting from a change in
      price.
   e. a parallel change in total revenue resulting from a change in
      price.

_e_   10. The breakeven point is the point where
   a. marginal revenues are equal to marginal costs.
   b. a reasonable profit has been earned.
   c. all variable costs have been recovered.
   d. marginal revenues are equal to total revenues.
   e. the costs of producing the product equal the revenue earned
      from selling the product.

_b_   11. A pricing policy is
   a. designed to encourage purchases that are based on emotional
      reactions.
   b. a guiding philosophy that determines how price will be used
      as a variable in the marketing mix.
   c. a method for calculating the base price of a product.
   d. a mechanical procedure for setting prices on a regular basis.
   e. the same thing as a pricing objective.

_a_   12. A psychological price is designed to encourage purchases based
      on emotional, rather than rational, responses. One approach to
      psychological pricing is
   a. customary pricing.
   b. loss leader pricing.
   c. gentlemen's pricing.
   d. unit pricing.
   e. cash discounting.

_d_   13. A penetration price
   a. is a price established primarily by tradition.
   b. is a price that is set artificially high to provide a prestige
      image.
   c. is used by persons who have great skill in a particular field.
   d. can allow a marketer to gain a larger market share and dis-
      courage competitors from entering the market.
   e. usually requires the firm to employ a price leader.

_a_   14. The advantage of using marginal analysis as opposed to break-
      even analysis is that marginal analysis
   a. combines the increasing costs of production with the price
      elasticity of the demand schedule as a way of obtaining op-
      timum profits.

b. equates the cost of producing a product with the revenues earned from selling the product.

c. is a precise pricing method.

d. is of great help in pricing new products before costs and revenues are established.

___a___ 15. What effect does quantity discounting have on the marketing function?

a. Large purchases reduce selling costs and may shift some of the storage, finance, and risk-taking expenses onto buyers.

b. Since discounts are usually small, they provide no incentive for middlemen to furnish transportation, storage, final processing, and other service functions.

c. Discounts usually decrease the total number of marketing functions that are necessary in getting the product to buyers.

d. Price discounting has no effect on the marketing function.

___c___ 16. The eight steps in setting prices

a. do not necessarily require an integration and coordination of objectives, theory, and practice.

b. should begin with the organization, not buyers.

c. explain how an organization should set and evaluate prices.

d. disregard the current environmental situation.

___d___ 17. In using a cost-oriented pricing method, a firm determines price

a. by using marginal analysis.

b. based on the level of demand for a product.

c. based on a consideration of competitors' prices.

d. by adding a dollar amount or a percentage to the cost of the product.

e. by determining the breakeven point.

___e___ 18. A commonly employed pricing method among retailers is

a. skimming.

b. demand-oriented pricing.

c. competition-oriented pricing.

d. penetration pricing.

e. markup pricing.

___c___ 19. An example of a professional pricing policy is

a. symbolic pricing.

b. customary pricing.

c. gentlemen's pricing.

d. base-point pricing.

___c___ 20. A marketer sometimes uses a demand-oriented pricing method, called price differentiation, when the firm

a. wants to use one price to market several different products.

b. wants to encourage purchases based on emotional, rather than rational, responses.

c. wants to use more than one price to market a specific product.

           d. offers cash discounts.

           e. wants to penetrate a specific target market.

*c* 21. Which of the following statements is *not* true?

           a. Market share, or sales in relation to competition, is a meaningful bench mark of success for a company.

           b. An organization's sales may increase while its actual market share decreases.

           c. Market share is important but cannot be considered a pricing objective.

           d. Market share can increase even though sales are decreasing for the total industry.

*a* 22. Which of the following statements is *not* true?

           a. Profits are the residual amount after expenses are paid and are included in costs to determine the breakeven point.

           b. The breakeven point is the point at which variable costs and fixed costs equal total revenue.

           c. At the breakeven point, no losses have been incurred, nor have any profits accumulated.

           d. Breakeven analysis assumes the quantity demanded to be fixed.

*a* 23. On a graph, the average revenue for a product would be the same as the

           a. demand curve.

           b. marginal revenue curve.

           c. supply curve.

           d. marginal cost curve.

*b* 24. The advantage of knowing competitors' prices is that

           a. it eliminates a marketer's need to develop cost objectives.

           b. it may enable a marketer to set prices slightly lower and thus increase sales.

           c. it ensures profits for a marketer who charges the same price.

           d. it ensures an accurate estimate of sales.

*d* 25. If, in introducing a new product in a product line, a marketer's objective is to gain maximum unit sales volume, then the pricing policy should be

           a. market skimming.

           b. psychological pricing.

           c. customary pricing.

           d. penetration pricing.

*b* 26. A trade discount is

           a. a deduction from the list price that reflects the economies of purchasing in large quantities.

           b. a reduction of list price given to a middleman by a producer for performing certain functions.

      c. a price reduction to the buyer given for prompt payment or cash payment.

      d. is considered unethical and has been outlawed in some states.

_C_   27. Price discrimination

      a. is always discriminatory.

      b. is discriminatory only when customers are not in competition with each other.

      c. is legal when price differentials can be justified on the basis of cost savings.

      d. is specifically prohibited by the Clayton Act.

# Programmed Completion Exercises

survival, profits, return on investment, market share, cash, status quo

1. Pricing objectives may be based on _____, maximizing _____, attaining a _____ _____, maintaining or increasing _____ _____, recovering _____, or maintaining _____ _____.

objectives, target markets, demand, competitors' prices, policy, method

2. Prior to selecting a final price, marketers should select pricing _____, identify _____ _____, determine _____, ascertain demand, cost, and profit relationships, analyze _____ _____, select a pricing _____, and select a pricing _____.

value, exchanged

3. To a buyer, price is the _____ placed on what is _____.

marketing mix, demand, competitors

4. Price is one of the easiest variables in the _____ _____ to adjust; it can be changed quickly to respond to the dynamics of _____ or the actions of _____.

Pricing objectives, organizational

5. _____ _____ will influence decisions in most functional areas, such as finance, accounting, and production; thus, it must be consistent with overall _____ goals.

marginal cost, marginal revenue

6. Economic analysis shows that maximum profit is achieved at the point where _____ _____ equals _____ _____.

elastic, inelastic

7. If demand is _____, a change in price causes an opposite change in total revenue; and _____ demand results in a parallel change in total revenue.

method, policy

8. A pricing _____ is a mechanical procedure for setting prices on a regular basis; a pricing _____ is a guiding philosophy designed to influence and determine price decisions.

pioneer

9. Market skimming and penetration pricing are _____ pricing policies.

price leaders, special-event pricing

10. Promotional pricing policies include _____ _____ and _____-_____ _____.

discriminatory

11. Differentiation in price becomes _____ when one reseller is able to obtain products at a lower price than similar customers are able to.

breakeven analysis, marginal analysis

12. There are two ways of understanding demand, cost, and profit relationships: _____ _____ and _____ _____.

financial price

13. In our society, the _____ _____ quantifies value and is the basis of most market exchanges.

penetration, market share

14. A marketer uses a _____ price when introducing a product in order to gain a larger _____ _____.

cost-plus, markup

15. Two common cost-oriented pricing methods are _____ and _____ pricing.

buyers

16. As with all elements in the marketing mix, price setting should start with _____ and work back through the marketing system.

Price elasticity

17. _____ _____ of demand is the relative responsiveness of the slope of the demand curve to the percentage change in quantity demanded caused by a percentage change in price.

high, strong, low, weak

18. Demand-oriented pricing results in using a _____ price if demand for the product is _____ and a _____ price if product demand is _____.

cost-oriented, demand-oriented, competition-oriented

19. Three types of pricing methods are _____ pricing, _____ pricing, and _____ pricing.

odd-even, customary, symbolic, price lining

20. Psychological pricing includes _____ pricing, _____ pricing, _____ pricing, and _____.

Ethical pricing, gentlemen's pricing

21. _____ _____ and _____ _____ are two types of professional pricing.

industrial customers

22. Quoting and adjusting prices to _____ _____ reflect cost differences in serving different markets.

cash, trade, quantity, cumulative, noncumulative

23. The types of price discounting policies are _____ discounts, _____ discounts, and _____ discounts, the latter of which may be _____ or _____.

differentials, cost, competition

24. Price _____ are legal if they can be justified as _____ savings that meet _____ in good faith or if they do not damage competition.

# Answers to Objective Questions

*True or False*

| | | | |
|---|---|---|---|
| 1. | F | 17. | F |
| 2. | T | 18. | T |
| 3. | T | 19. | T |
| 4. | T | 20. | T |
| 5. | F | 21. | T |
| 6. | T | 22. | F |
| 7. | F | 23. | T |
| 8. | F | 24. | T |
| 9. | T | 25. | F |
| 10. | F | 26. | F |
| 11. | T | 27. | F |
| 12. | T | 28. | T |
| 13. | T | 29. | T |
| 14. | T | 30. | F |
| 15. | F | 31. | T |
| 16. | T | 32. | T |

*Multiple-Choice*

| | | | |
|---|---|---|---|
| 1. | c | 15. | a |
| 2. | b | 16. | c |
| 3. | d | 17. | d |
| 4. | c | 18. | e |
| 5. | a | 19. | c |
| 6. | a | 20. | c |
| 7. | b | 21. | c |
| 8. | c | 22. | a |
| 9. | a | 23. | a |
| 10. | e | 24. | b |
| 11. | b | 25. | d |
| 12. | a | 26. | b |
| 13. | d | 27. | c |
| 14. | a | | |

# CHAPTER 9

# Marketing Channels

## Chapter Summary

Distribution is concerned with making products available; marketing channels and physical distribution are the two major considerations in distribution decisions. Various intermediaries and facilitators assist in moving products to customers. Physical distribution is concerned with transportation, storage, warehousing, inventory control, and any other decisions relating to the physical movement of products.

Marketing channels consist of an interrelated group of marketing institutions, including such intermediaries as retailers and wholesalers, that perform marketing activities necessary to direct products to customers. The marketing channel also can be described as a structure of intraorganizational units and extraorganizational agents and merchants through which exchange activities are facilitated. Channel members hold different role responsibilities within the distribution system's overall structure.

Channel structure describes the arrangement and order of links and units in the distribution system. The channel implies a linkage of units to carry product flows to the marketplace. The different levels in a channel represent the institutions that have managerial responsibility in the distribution process. Channels for consumer or industrial products may be direct or indirect. A channel structure consisting of a producer, wholesaler, retailer, and consumer represents one of the most traditional channels to consumers. Retailers usually do not exist in the industrial channel, since industrial purchasers use products in the production of other products. Agents, brokers, and dealers often are used in the industrial channel for products that are standardized and when information gathering and selling functions are important.

The channel system builds up a collection of utilities or product benefits by performing activities that facilitate exchanges. The development of assortments involves the accumulation of products to serve market needs. Allocating and rationing products to match demand in various locations should be managed by marketing intermediaries, by the producer, or by buyers. The number and types of middlemen used in the channel are determined by assortments desired by buyers and the opportunity for efficiency in channel arrangements.

The channel intermediaries perform sorting activities to aid the distribution of goods to other channel members. The sorting activities include sorting out, accumulating, allocating, and assorting. Through these activities, the channel network makes mass distribution possible and still satisfies the different tastes and preferences of consumers.

The total channel system may include facilitating agencies such as transportation companies, insurance companies, advertising agencies, and financial institutions that may perform marketing functions necessary to effectively develop and facilitate exchanges. Channel functions may be passed on to buyers, or the producer may perform the functions rather than passing them on to other channel members.

Bringing together the various links or stages of the channel under the management of one organization can be accomplished by both vertical and horizontal integration. The integration may stabilize supply, reduce costs, and increase channel control.

A channel system should be designed to provide the desired intensity of market coverage; thus it should be able to offer the right products when and where customers demand them. Intensive distribution aims to make the product ready and available to all potential dealers. Selective distribution attempts to use the most qualified middlemen to expose the product properly. In exclusive distribution, a limited number of outlets are used to distribute products.

The channel operates as a system that results in role differentiation and a division of labor. The role associated with each channel position defines how channel members interact. The ability of one channel member to facilitate or hinder the goal attainment of other channel members defines the power relationship. Channel cooperation is required if each party expects to gain something from other members. Role deviance or malfunction is a major source of channel conflict, since role expectations are the means of integration and coordination.

Each channel member occupies a position involving role relationships with other channel members. Leadership is a power relationship, and manufacturers, wholesalers, agents, or retailers can assume leadership positions and guide the channel. Cooperation among the channel members, as well as the leadership role, is influenced by power bases such as authority, coercive techniques, rewards, referents, and experts.

# True or False Statements

T   (F)     1. Fewer opportunities for middlemen exist when large distances intervene between buyers and producers.

(T)   F     2. Middlemen deal with the general need for distribution.

T   (F)     3. Channel functions cannot be passed on to buyers or performed by producers.

T   (F)     4. Middlemen play a minor role in marketing channel systems.

(T)   F     5. Although the activities performed by channel members and facilitating agencies are largely facilitating, it is difficult for consumers to see the benefits associated with distribution costs.

T   (F)     6. The channel is a system of unrelated functions that expedite the distribution of goods.

(T)   F     7. Producers may be willing to supply products, and consumers may be demanding them, yet no transactions can take place unless a relationship between buyers and sellers is facilitated.

T   (F)     8. Agents and brokers are the chief types of merchants.

T   (F)     9. Agents take title to merchandise and resell it.

T   (F)     10. Facilitating agencies generally play a major role in controlling channel decisions with regard to getting the product to the consumer.

(T)   F     11. Any sequence of interrelated intermediaries from producers to final users or consumers is called a marketing channel.

T   (F)     12. Channel leadership is primarily involved with whether or not the product is new to the marketplace.

T   (F)     13. A common misunderstanding is that an increase of links or middlemen in the channel means that costs are lowered automatically.

(T)   F     14. Bringing together the various links of a channel can be accomplished by vertical integration.

(T)   F     15. Horizontal integration is accomplished by combining the leadership of several institutions.

(T)   F     16. Different intermediaries, including transportation companies and warehouses, can assume the physical risks in marketing channel flows.

T   (F)     17. Combining various links in the marketing channel always increases efficiency.

(T)   F     18. As the channel moves from intensive to exclusive distribution, it gives up exposure in return for some other advantage—including, but not limited to, greater dealer control over the channel.

T (F) 19. Channel power involves the ability of all members in a channel to facilitate or hinder the attainment of their respective goals.

(T) F 20. Referents can assume the role of channel leader when channel members feel the need to please referents.

T (F) 21. Wholesaler channel leaders include stores such as Sears, Penney's, and K-Mart.

(T) F 22. Retailers can be agents.

T (F) 23. Merchants expedite exchanges for a commission or fee.

# Multiple-Choice Questions

_e_ 1. Middlemen, especially large-scale retailers, can create conflict by demanding
   a. large discounts.
   b. special promotional allowances.
   c. special shipping arrangements.
   d. protection against price changes.
   e. all of the above.

_c_ 2. Of the following, which is the most important dimension of a marketing channel?
   a. The number of retailers involved
   b. The total amount of goods distributed
   c. The number of activities performed at a particular stage
   d. The economic environment

_b_ 3. What type of integration brings the processes and functions of two or more stages of the channel together under one management?
   a. Conventional
   b. Vertical
   c. Traditional
   d. Horizontal

_a_ 4. When horizontal integration occurs, reduced costs result because
   a. the combined units operate more efficiently than independent institutions.
   b. the market is made more heterogeneous.
   c. a number of institutions are combined under a common management.
   d. the functions of an intermediary are performed at some other channel level.
   e. government regulations prevent independent institutions.

_c_    5. Changes in which of the following would have the most profound effect on the structure of a marketing channel?
   a. Industrial technology
   b. Marketing technology
   c. Consumer purchase patterns
   d. Wholesaling
   e. Integrative technology

_e_    6. Channel leadership is based on control over many factors. According to the text, which of the following is *not* one of them?
   a. Products
   b. Markets
   c. Technology
   d. Institutions
   e. Consumer behavior

_d_    7. Retailers can be all of the following except
   a. merchants.
   b. agents.
   c. marketing channel members.
   d. wholesalers.
   e. channel leaders.

_b_    8. A wholesaler can be either an agent or a merchant. Of the following terms, which describes a wholesaler who receives a commission or fee for expediting exchanges?
   a. Merchant
   b. Agent
   c. Facilitating agency
   d. Negotiation merchant

_a_    9. Which of the following terms can be used to describe the marketing channel?
   a. Channel of distribution
   b. Communication channel
   c. Promotional channel
   d. Trade flow

_d_    10. Which sorting activity refers to an inventory of homogeneous products?
   a. Allocation
   b. Combining
   c. Assorting
   d. Accumulation
   e. Sorting out

_d_    11. According to the text, what is the overall goal of each channel member?
   a. To build up a collection of products
   b. To determine the most appropriate method of product distribution at the consumer level

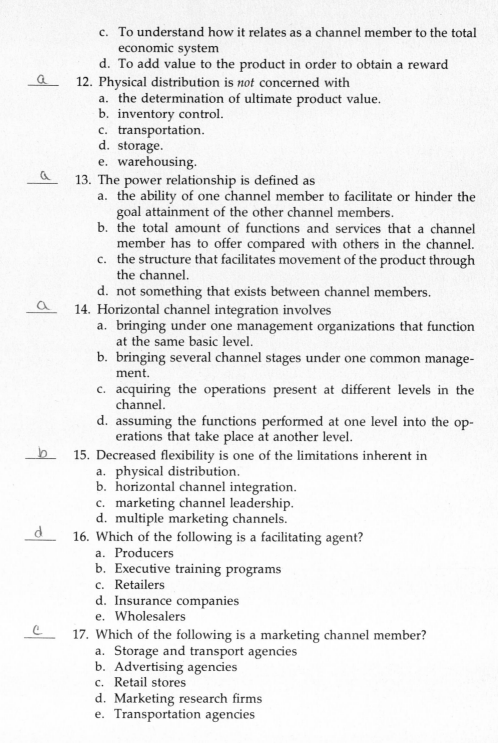

    c. To understand how it relates as a channel member to the total economic system

    d. To add value to the product in order to obtain a reward

*a*   12. Physical distribution is *not* concerned with
    a. the determination of ultimate product value.
    b. inventory control.
    c. transportation.
    d. storage.
    e. warehousing.

*a*   13. The power relationship is defined as
    a. the ability of one channel member to facilitate or hinder the goal attainment of the other channel members.
    b. the total amount of functions and services that a channel member has to offer compared with others in the channel.
    c. the structure that facilitates movement of the product through the channel.
    d. not something that exists between channel members.

*a*   14. Horizontal channel integration involves
    a. bringing under one management organizations that function at the same basic level.
    b. bringing several channel stages under one common management.
    c. acquiring the operations present at different levels in the channel.
    d. assuming the functions performed at one level into the operations that take place at another level.

*b*   15. Decreased flexibility is one of the limitations inherent in
    a. physical distribution.
    b. horizontal channel integration.
    c. marketing channel leadership.
    d. multiple marketing channels.

*d*   16. Which of the following is a facilitating agent?
    a. Producers
    b. Executive training programs
    c. Retailers
    d. Insurance companies
    e. Wholesalers

*c*   17. Which of the following is a marketing channel member?
    a. Storage and transport agencies
    b. Advertising agencies
    c. Retail stores
    d. Marketing research firms
    e. Transportation agencies

_b_    18. Channel leaders are responsible for
  a. physical possession.
  b. coordination of channel members.
  c. market risk.
  d. market possession.
  e. channel integration.

_d_    19. Which of the following is *not* a power base involved in channel leadership?
  a. Authority
  b. Reference groups that channel members try to please
  c. Coercion
  d. Desire to influence overall channel performance
  e. Expertise about products, markets, or technology

_d_    20. Selective distribution is the form of distribution utilized with
  a. specialty products.
  b. infrequently purchased products.
  c. highly available products.
  d. products which require controlled sales and special services.

_c_    21. Guitars are generally marketed by means of
  a. physical distribution.
  b. intensive distribution.
  c. selective distribution.
  d. exclusive distribution.

_b_    22. Which of the following occurs when one of the members of a marketing channel fails to fulfill its expected role?
  a. Channel cooperation
  b. Channel conflict
  c. Channel leadership
  d. Channel integration
  e. Channel distribution

_c_    23. Which of the following statements is true?
  a. Selective distribution is commonly needed for convenience goods.
  b. Intensive distribution refers to the desire to sell through a few responsible and suitable outlets in a given area.
  c. Consumers are likely to devote more time and effort when shopping for products available through selective distribution.
  d. Only products that are marketed through exclusive distribution will require special services or information.

# Programmed Completion Exercises

authority,
reference,
coercion,
expertise

1. Power bases involved in channel leadership include _____, _____, _____, and _____.

authority,
coercive,
reward, expert

2. Power in a distribution channel can be developed on _____, _____, _____, referent, or _____ bases.

agents,
merchants

3. The marketing channel includes marketing intermediaries that can be either _____ or _____.

channel

4. The _____ implies a linkage of units to carry product flows to the marketplace.

assortment

5. An _____ is a collection of products that complement each other or possess some common want-satisfying attributes.

middlemen

6. The number and character of _____ in the channel are determined by assortments desired by buyers and the opportunity for efficiency in channel arrangements.

Facilitating
agencies

7. _____ _____ perform special tasks for channel members but do not get involved in directing or controlling channel decisions.

leader

8. The channel _____ may establish distribution policies and coordinate the development of the marketing mix.

coordinating,
flexibility

9. The limitations of integration include difficulties in _____, a decrease in _____, and an increase in planning and research.

retailers,
wholesalers

10. Marketing channels are an interrelated group of marketing institutions including intermediaries such as _____, _____, and facilitating agencies that perform marketing activities necessary to direct products to customers.

producers,
wholesalers,
retailers,
consumers

11. The most traditional channel for consumer products consists of _____, _____, _____, and _____.

assortments

12. Basic functions of channels include developing product types and accumulating, allocating, and providing _____ for buyers.

Agents, brokers, dealers

13. _____, _____, and _____ often are used in the industrial channel for products that are standardized and when information gathering and selling functions are important.

utilities, product benefits

14. The channel system builds up a collection of _____ or _____ _____ by performing activities that facilitate exchanges.

facilitating agencies

15. Channel members are assisted by _____ _____ such as transportation companies, insurance companies, advertising agencies, and financial institutions that may perform marketing functions necessary to develop efficiency and facilitate exchanges.

Horizontal, vertical

16. _____ or _____ integration strategies may be used to stabilize supply, reduce costs, and increase channel control.

conflict

17. Role deviance or malfunction is a major source of channel _____ .

integration, coordination

18. Role expectations are the means of _____ and _____ to enhance channel effectiveness and efficiency.

Producers, wholesalers, retailers

19. _____, _____, or _____ can assume leadership and guide the channel.

# Answers to Objective Questions

| *True or False* | | | *Multiple-Choice* | | |
|---|---|---|---|---|---|
| 1. F | 13. F | | 1. e | 13. a | |
| 2. T | 14. T | | 2. c | 14. a | |
| 3. F | 15. T | | 3. b | 15. b | |
| 4. F | 16. T | | 4. a | 16. d | |
| 5. T | 17. F | | 5. c | 17. c | |
| 6. F | 18. T | | 6. e | 18. b | |
| 7. T | 19. F | | 7. d | 19. d | |
| 8. F | 20. T | | 8. b | 20. d | |
| 9. F | 21. F | | 9. a | 21. c | |
| 10. F | 22. T | | 10. d | 22. b | |
| 11. T | 23. F | | 11. d | 23. c | |
| 12. F | | | 12. a | | |

CHAPTER 10

# Wholesaling

## Chapter Summary

Wholesaling involves all exchange activities among organizations and individuals except for transactions with ultimate consumers. Wholesaling activities and wholesaling establishments are concerned primarily with selling products directly to industrial, reseller, and institutional users, and additionally to other wholesalers. The importance of wholesaling is represented by the existence of over 580,000 wholesaling establishments in the United States and by the fact that they have a higher sales volume than retail establishments. This is because all wholesalers' transactions are measured, including multiple transactions of products as they move through the marketing channel.

Wholesaling activities must be performed during distribution for all goods, whether or not a wholesaling institution is involved. Wholesalers offer management advice, and they can assist retail customers with various aspects of their operations, including stocking techniques, displaying, point-of-sale promotions, training of sales and service personnel, and marketing research. In addition, wholesalers often handle credit for producers and retailers. The use of wholesalers is a distinct advantage to producers because this distribution link provides accumulation and allocation roles for a number of products, thus saving producers money and permitting them to concentrate on producing, assembling, and developing quality products to match consumers' wants. By buying in large quantities and delivering to customers in small lots, a wholesaler may perform physical distribution activities such as transportation, materials handling, inventory planning, communication, and warehousing more efficiently and may provide more service than a producer or retailer can achieve with its own physical distribution system.

Wholesalers are classified by the activities they perform and by the nature of their operations. Merchant wholesalers take title and assume risk and generally are involved in buying and reselling products to industrial or retail customers. The two broad categories of merchant wholesalers are full-service and limited-service wholesalers. Full-service wholesalers provide as much service as customers desire. Types of full-service wholesalers include general merchandise wholesalers who carry a very wide product mix, limited-line wholesalers who carry only a few product lines, and specialty-line wholesalers who specialize in stocking a narrowly defined line of products such as shellfish. Limited-service merchant wholesalers are distinguished by offering a limited number of services. Typical types of limited-service wholesalers are cash-and-carry wholesalers, truck merchants, rack jobbers (service merchandisers), drop shippers, and mail-order wholesalers.

Agents and brokers negotiate purchases and expedite sales, but they do not take title to products. They are called functional middlemen because they perform a limited number of marketing activities for a commission. Agents and brokers usually perform fewer marketing functions than merchant wholesalers; they are used when merchant wholesaling services may not be needed or when the establishment of retail or manufacturer wholesaling operations is too expensive. Manufacturers' agents, selling agents, commission merchants, and brokers (food and real estate) are typical kinds of functional middlemen.

Manufacturers' sales branches and offices are wholesaling operations that are part of the vertically integrated distribution channel of the producer. The distinguishing characteristic of the sales branch or office is that it is owned and controlled by the manufacturer.

Facilitating organizations perform highly specialized wholesaling functions. Sometimes these organizations make it unnecessary for manufacturers or retailers to use a wholesaling establishment. Common types of facilitating organizations are public and field warehouses, finance and transportation companies, and trade shows and trade marts.

Changing trends in wholesaling indicate the adaptability of this marketing activity to the buying patterns of consumers. Two kinds of shifts have been taking place in wholesaling activities. First, merchant wholesalers have increased, while manufacturers' sales branches have declined. Second, the share of trade for manufacturers' sales offices has increased, while agents' and brokers' shares have declined. Furthermore, there has been an increasing trend to bypass traditional wholesaling establishments when alternative channels provide advantages for retailers or manufacturers. In general, there is a trend toward simplified marketing channels, fewer distribution points, and a corresponding opportunity for greater centralization and control of distribution. The kinds of wholesaling establishments that will emerge in the future will depend on the changing mix of activities performed by producers and retailers. The future of independent wholesalers, agents, and brokers is a function of their ability to delineate markets and provide services that these markets desire.

# True or False Statements

T  (F)  1. Future wholesaling patterns will adapt to the buying patterns of retailers, since the latter are viewed as the focus of all channel activities.

(T)  F  2. Wholesaling includes all marketing transactions in which purchases are intended for resale or are used in making other products.

T  (F)  3. Eliminating wholesalers would eliminate the need for the functions they provide because direct channels are more efficient.

T  (F)  4. Wholesaling involves exchange activities among organizations that deal directly only with ultimate consumers.

(T)  F  5. One major advantage of using wholesalers is that this distribution link provides accumulation and allocation roles for a number of products, thus saving producers money and permitting them to concentrate on producing, assembling, and developing quality products.

T  (F)  6. One way of recognizing a wholesaler is through the collection of retail sales tax on sales made to retailers.

T  (F)  7. Wholesaling exists to provide services and functions; these activities are, for the most part, unrelated to basic marketing functions.

(T)  F  8. Wholesaling activities must be performed during distribution for all goods, whether or not a wholesaling institution is involved.

(T)  F  9. Wholesalers provide research that monitors changing attitudes toward products or that pinpoints typical buyers, and this helps retailers understand consumers.

T  (F)  10. Financing inventories and collecting, handling, and billing accounts is one area of service rarely handled by wholesalers.

(T)  F  11. In general, wholesalers serve producers that already possess established products.

T  (F)  12. Wholesaling is concerned only with those marketing transactions that are related to the actual handling and moving of physical goods.

T  (F)  13. Wholesalers provide form utility, which allows manufacturers to avoid risks associated with holding large inventories.

(T)  F  14. Buying, selling, storing, transporting, financing, risk taking, and gathering market information are the basic activities of wholesalers.

T  (F)  15. Wholesalers have to be generalists in understanding market conditions and in performing their selling functions.

Ⓣ F    16. Any classification of wholesalers is meaningful only at a point in time because the activities performed by wholesalers adjust continuously to changes in the marketing environment.

T Ⓕ    17. Wholesalers are classified according to their position in the marketing channel.

T Ⓕ    18. Merchant wholesalers do not take title to products.

T Ⓕ    19. Agents and brokers take title to products and are compensated by commissions for negotiating transactions between manufacturers and retailers.

Ⓣ F    20. The broad categories of merchant wholesalers are full-service wholesalers and limited-service wholesalers.

Ⓣ F    21. General merchandise wholesalers are full-service merchant wholesalers who carry a very wide product mix.

Ⓣ F    22. Drop shippers take title to products and negotiate sales but do not physically handle products.

T Ⓕ    23. A rack jobber provides transportation, delivering products directly to customers for inspection and selection.

Ⓣ F    24. Manufacturers' sales branches are part of the vertically integrated distribution channel of the producer.

T Ⓕ    25. Public and field warehouses, finance and transportation companies, and trade shows and marts are all agencies that are classified as limited-service merchant wholesalers.

T Ⓕ    26. In general, there is a trend toward more complex marketing channels, more distribution points, and a greater decentralization of distribution.

# Multiple-Choice Questions

_a_    1. Wholesalers
     a. perform marketing activities necessary to expediting exchanges.
     b. usually can be eliminated with no loss in efficiency.
     c. are engaged primarily in selling products to ultimate consumers.
     d. cause higher prices to consumers in the performance of their functions.

_c_    2. Which service is *not* usually offered by a wholesaler?
     a. Management assistance and marketing research
     b. Handling credit and financing
     c. Selling activities

d. Physical distribution activities

e. Collecting retail sales tax from ultimate consumers

_b_   3. Wholesaling functions are performed
   a. when products are produced.
   b. during marketing transactions in which purchases are intended for resale or are used in making other products.
   c. when ultimate consumers buy products.
   d. when ultimate consumers allocate products.

_d_   4. The general trend in the structural pattern of wholesaling is toward
   a. more distribution points.
   b. more complex marketing channels.
   c. greater dependency on traditional wholesale establishments.
   d. more centralization and control of distribution.

_a_   5. A reaction to the integrated wholesaling activities of large corporate chain retailers has been
   a. the evolution of voluntary chain wholesalers.
   b. the increase of manufacturers' sales branches and the decrease in merchant wholesalers.
   c. an increase in agents' and brokers' share of trade because of their efficiency.
   d. the decreasing efficiency of manufacturers' sales offices due to their reliance on traditional selling methods.

_c_   6. Which of the following is *not* a major category of facilitating organizations?
   a. Finance companies
   b. Transportation companies
   c. Food brokers
   d. Field warehouses

_a_   7. Which of the following statements is true?
   a. Accumulation, allocation, and assortment are all roles performed by wholesalers.
   b. The distinguishing characteristic of rack jobbers is that these middlemen do not physically handle products but they do take title to products and negotiate sales.
   c. Products offered by the manufacturer's agent must, of necessity, be competing and noncomplementary.

_d_   8. Limited-service wholesalers are characterized by
   a. providing as much service as desired by customers.
   b. being specialists in most of the wholesaling functions.
   c. being restricted to boundaries of competition set forth by the government.
   d. providing only some marketing services and specializing in a few functions.

_c_    9. By buying in large quantities and delivering to customers in smaller lots, a wholesaler may perform all of the following activities *except*
   a. transportation.
   b. materials handling.
   c. selling the retailer's product.
   d. inventory planning.
   e. warehousing.

_d_    10. The classification of wholesalers is based on
   a. the state of the economy.
   b. the categories set forth by the government.
   c. only a particular time.
   d. the activities they perform.

_c_    11. The product distribution network operated by wholesalers
   a. increases the total number of negotiations and selling transactions among manufacturers and consumers
   b. increases the costs associated with exchanges through intermediaries.
   c. promotes both specialized mass production and the satisfaction of differentiated needs of consumers.

_e_    12. Wholesaling usually does not include the marketing activities performed by
   a. manufacturers' sales branches.
   b. agents.
   c. commission merchants.
   d. resellers.
   e. retailers.

_c_    13. Which of the following are *not* considered to be a limited-service merchant wholesaler?
   a. Rack jobbers
   b. Mail-order wholesalers
   c. Specialty-line wholesalers
   d. Drop shippers
   e. Truck wholesalers

_c_    14. Agents and brokers
   a. take title and assume risk and generally are involved in buying and reselling products to industrial or retail customers.
   b. take title to products and negotiate sales but do not physically handle products.
   c. negotiate purchases and expedite sales but do not take title to the product.
   d. are part of the vertically integrated distribution channel of the producer.
   e. are highly specialized wholesalers who act as facilitating agencies for a producer.

_e_    15. Which of the following conditions favors circumvention of traditional wholesalers?
    a. Customers are widely dispersed, and there is a large number of them.
    b. The product is a nonperishable item.
    c. The cost of installation and repair is low.
    d. The manufacturer is small and has only moderate financial strength.
    e. None of the above.

_a_    16. An increase in merchant wholesalers accompanied by a decrease in manufacturers' sales branches indicates that
    a. merchant wholesalers have provided more efficient stocking operations than manufacturers could provide for themselves.
    b. traditional wholesaling establishments are becoming obsolete.
    c. manufacturers' sales offices have less effective selling methods than independents.
    d. there is inefficiency in the market channel.

_a_    17. A distinct advantage of wholesalers is their ability to
    a. provide time and place utility.
    b. deal directly with ultimate consumers.
    c. increase the number of sales contacts.
    d. offer trade discounts to retailers.

# Programmed Completion Exercises

Full-service,
limited-service

1. _____ wholesalers provide most services that can be performed by wholesalers, and _____ wholesalers provide only some marketing services and specialize in a few functions.

centralization

2. In general, there is a trend toward simplified marketing channels, fewer distribution points, and a corresponding opportunity for greater _____ and control of distribution.

ultimate
consumers

3. Wholesaling is defined as all exchange activities among organizations and individuals except for transactions to _____ _____ .

distribution,
wholesaling

4. Wholesaling activities must be performed during _____ for all goods, whether or not a _____ institution is involved.

public, field,
finance,
transportation,
trade
exhibitions

5. Facilitating organizations that perform wholesaling functions include _____ and _____ warehouses, _____ and _____ companies, and _____ _____.

general
merchandise,
limited-line,
specialty-line

6. Three types of full-service merchant wholesalers are _____ _____ wholesalers, _____ wholesalers, and _____ wholesalers.

Facilitating
agencies

7. _____ _____ are organizations that sometimes make it unnecessary for manufacturers or retailers to use wholesaling establishments.

increased,
decreased

8. One major trend of wholesaling is that merchant wholesalers have _____ while manufacturers' sales branches have _____.

activities

9. The kinds of wholesale establishments that develop in the future will depend on the changing mix of _____ that retailers and producers perform.

industrial,
reseller,
institutional,
wholesalers

10. Wholesale establishments are engaged primarily in selling products directly to _____, _____, and _____ users, and additionally to other _____.

multiple
transactions

11. Wholesaling establishments in the United States have a higher sales volume than retail establishments. This results from _____ _____ as products move through the distribution channel.

Sales offices,
vertically
integrated

12. _____ _____ provide service normally associated with agents and are part of the _____ _____ distribution channel of the producer.

large, small,
transportation,
materials
handling,
inventory
planning,
communication,
warehousing

13. By buying in _____ quantities and delivering to customers in _____ lots, a wholesaler may perform physical distribution activities such as _____, _____ _____, _____ _____, _____, and _____.

wholesalers,
accumulation,
allocation

14. The use of _____ is a distinct advantage to producers because this distribution link provides _____ and _____ roles for a number of products.

Merchant, title

15. _____ wholesalers take _____ and assume risk and generally are involved in buying and reselling products to industrial or retail customers.

agents, several,
product line

16. Manufacturers' _____ represent _____ sellers and sell products to customers as a _____ _____.

Cash-and-carry,
drop shippers,
truck, mail-
order, rack
jobbers

17. _____ wholesalers, _____ _____, _____ merchants, _____ wholesalers, and _____ _____ are typical limited-function wholesalers.

functional
middlemen

18. Agents and brokers are called _____ _____, and their distinguishing characteristic is that they do not take title to products.

mass,
differentiated
tastes

19. The distribution network makes possible specialized _____ production on the one hand, and the satisfaction of _____ _____ of consumers on the other.

full-service,
limited-service

20. Two broad categories of merchant wholesalers are _____ wholesalers and _____ wholesalers.

branches,
offices

21. Manufacturers' sales _____ and _____ perform wholesaling activities that are part of a vertically integrated distribution channel.

wholesaler

22. Although the _____ can be considered an establishment, the activities can be performed by any marketing channel member.

# Answers to Objective Questions

*True or False*

| 1. F | 14. T |
|------|-------|
| 2. T | 15. F |
| 3. F | 16. T |
| 4. F | 17. F |
| 5. T | 18. F |
| 6. F | 19. F |
| 7. F | 20. T |
| 8. T | 21. T |
| 9. T | 22. T |
| 10. F | 23. F |
| 11. T | 24. T |
| 12. F | 25. F |
| 13. F | 26. F |

*Multiple-Choice*

| 1. a | 10. d |
|------|-------|
| 2. e | 11. c |
| 3. b | 12. e |
| 4. d | 13. c |
| 5. a | 14. c |
| 6. c | 15. e |
| 7. a | 16. a |
| 8. d | 17. a |
| 9. c | |

# CHAPTER 11

# Retailing

## Chapter Summary

Retailing offers great opportunity for individuals interested in serving consumers at the ground level. Retailers are important links in the marketing channel because they are both sellers and buyers. Retailers create place, time, and possession utilities by providing assortments of products that match consumers' wants. Retailers often recognize that services are different from goods because of the intangible nature of services, the inseparableness of the retailer and the product, and the perishability of services. Retailing focuses on the activities required to finalize exchanges with ultimate consumers. While the retailer stands closest in the marketing channel to the consumer, most products are still developed by the initiative of producers. Retailers will develop product assortments, a variety of products from several competing lines, to satisfy the consumer. The product assortment must be evaluated in terms of status, purpose, and completeness.

Because a consumer may not have a specific reason for going to a retail store, retailing requires the development of a stimulating and interesting shopping environment. The store's image deals with the customers' self-image. All ill-defined image may alienate all potential customers and ruin any chance the store has to succeed. The atmosphere is designed to have emotional effects that will strengthen the consumers' probability to buy.

The width and depth of the product mix and line create different types of stores. The department store has a wide product mix, though the depth of the product line may vary. The mass merchandisers tend to offer fewer customer services and focus more on lower prices, high turnover, and large sales volumes. Examples of mass merchandisers are discount houses, warehouse and catalog showrooms, supermarkets, and superstores. The specialty stores carry a narrow product mix with deep product lines. Nonstore retailing takes place without consumers visiting a store. It may involve personal contact with the consumer (in-home retailing), direct personal contact by telephone, or several varieties of nonpersonal selling such as automatic vending or mail-order or catalog retailing.

Franchising is an arrangement in which a supplier grants a dealer the right to sell products in exchange for some type of consideration (such as a percentage of sales). The supplier may franchise a number of stores to sell a particular brand of product, it may franchise wholesalers to sell to retailers, or it may simply supply brand names, techniques, and other services.

The shopping center has replaced the central business district as a place for shopping, cultural, or recreational opportunities. The neighborhood shopping center usually consists of convenience and specialty stores and serves the small area around it. The community shopping center may include some department stores and more specialty stores, and its sphere of influence is much larger. The regional shopping center has the largest department stores, the widest product mix, and the deepest product lines; their target market will usually be 150,000 customers or more.

The *wheel of retailing* hypothesis refers to the idea that new types of retailers enter the market as low-status, low-margin, low-price operators. They acquire more elaborate establishments and facilities, with increased investments and higher operating costs. They then mature into high-cost, high-price merchants, susceptible to newer types, who go through the same pattern.

A marketing strategy for a retailer involves (1) segmenting the market by type of product, (2) identifying competition, (3) assessing resources as compared to competition, (4) defining the specific market target, and (5) developing a retailing mix. The retailing mix includes location, hours, facilities, organizational structure and strength, merchandise planning and control, pricing, buying, promotion, service, and expense management.

There are new trends and developments in retailing to be aware of. Retail buying may be carried out by means of in-home computer systems. Specialty stores seem to be moving ahead, since there is a widening range of consumer interests and activities. Also, the increase of mass merchandisers seems to be continuing. The growth of nonstore retailing seems destined to continue. Lastly, the retailer must be very conscious of special problems that the energy bind may cause.

# True or False Statements

Ⓣ   F   1. The wheel of retailing hypothesis holds that new types of retailers enter the market as low-status, low-margin, and low-priced operators.

Ⓣ   F   2. In community shopping centers there is more emphasis on shopping and specialty products that are not available in neighborhood shopping centers.

T   Ⓕ   3. Today, many specialty retailers appear to be following the wheel of retailing by offering more service, better locations, quality inventory, and therefore higher prices.

T   Ⓕ   4. Atmospherics are important to the appearance of a store, but there is no evidence to support the belief that this can affect sales.

T   Ⓕ   5. Understanding the nature and the development of marketing methods is the guiding philosophy of retailing.

T   Ⓕ   6. Retailers are not middlemen because they sell to ultimate consumers.

Ⓣ   F   7. Retailing involves primarily the development of a satisfying assortment of products for some market segment.

Ⓣ   F   8. In some cases, retailers create form, place, time, and possession utilities.

Ⓣ   F   9. Retailers are customers for the marketing efforts of suppliers, wholesalers, and manufacturers.

Ⓣ   F   10. Satisfaction of a market segment is an attribute strived for by retailers in their product assortments.

T   Ⓕ   11. Franchising has been characterized by efficient and well-planned management.

T   Ⓕ   12. Shopping centers are planned, coordinated, and promoted to appeal to homogeneous groups of customers.

Ⓣ   F   13. Mass merchandisers tend to offer fewer services to customers than department stores and to emphasize lower margins as a way of achieving higher turnover.

Ⓣ   F   14. Discount houses can be described as self-service, general merchandise stores that carry a wide assortment of products comparable to department stores.

T   Ⓕ   15. Retailing is the final part of the marketing process and is oriented toward accomplishing exchanges for the purposes of industrial and business use.

Ⓣ   F   16. Mail-order catalogs represent a form of nonstore retailing.

Ⓣ   F   17. The effective and efficient functioning of the marketing channel depends on the ability of retailers to provide a satisfying assortment of product utilities.

T   Ⓕ    18. Retailers typically take a "back seat" approach in reflecting consumer demands back to manufacturers.

T   Ⓕ    19. A business that develops a vague image, bordering between a discount store and department store, can then draw from both clienteles.

T   Ⓕ    20. Retailers are inflexible in controlling the product mix, the product line depth, the store location, and the level of service.

Ⓣ   F    21. It is reasonable to say that there is a relationship between shoppers' perceptions of a store's "personality" and shoppers' self-perceptions.

T   Ⓕ    22. It is impossible for a retailer to create dual atmospheres in one store to appeal to multiple segments.

Ⓣ   F    23. It is correct to assume that if the target customers do not think a store is going to satisfy their needs, they will not shop there and therefore will have no exposure to the products there.

T   Ⓕ    24. Mass merchandisers are typically organized into separate departments to facilitate such store functions as marketing services and accounting.

T   Ⓕ    25. Labeling a store according to the consumer's image of the product assortment limits the store to one type of merchandise.

T   Ⓕ    26. According to the text, the two types of retailing that do not conform to the wheel of retailing are mail-order selling and door-to-door selling.

T   Ⓕ    27. The superstore prototype is usually the same size as a discount house or supermarket.

T   Ⓕ    28. A major weakness of the wheel of retailing theory is that it predicts what and when new innovations will develop rather than describing new retail stores.

Ⓣ   F    29. The wheel of retailing theory states that increasing the level of services and thus the costs makes established retail institutions vulnerable to the entry of new institutions.

T   Ⓕ    30. The retailing mix consists of products, prices, promotion, and distribution.

## Multiple-Choice Questions

_c_    1. The guiding philosophy of retailing can best be stated as
a. convincing target customers that they have the best store to shop in.
b. foreseeing changes and estimating their impact on the existing retail structure as well as on one's own channel.

    c. developing product assortments and distribution methods that satisfy consumers' wants.

    d. offering products at a profitable price and convincing target customers that they have the best selection of merchandise.

2. The most visible middlemen to ultimate consumers are
    a. agents.
    b. brokers.
    c. distributors.
    d. retailers.

3. Which of the following statements is false?
    a. Most personal income is spent in retail stores.
    b. Retailers constitute the majority of middlemen.
    c. There are more retailers than any other institutions in the marketing channel.
    d. Services offered at the retail level are an imperishable commodity.

4. What do retailers do that distinguishes their role in the marketing channel?
    a. Provide assortments of products that match consumers' wants
    b. Develop and design products to match consumers' wants
    c. Offer an attractive building to shop in
    d. Perform marketing functions that wholesalers refuse to perform

5. The effectiveness and efficiency of the retailer is dependent upon
    a. the development of a marketing strategy to increase traffic in a store.
    b. convincing the target segment that the products will satisfy their wants.
    c. the ability of consumers to search out the retailer.
    d. the ability of retailers to provide the right combination of products.

6. Which of the following is an example of a nonstore retailer?
    a. A telephone directory
    b. A vending machine
    c. A specialty retailer
    d. A beautician

7. What term is used to describe the conscious designing of store space to create emotional effects that enhance the probability of purchase?
    a. Merchandising
    b. Trading-up
    c. Marketing
    d. Atmospherics

_e_    8. Which of the following is *not* a consumer service typically offered by department stores?
   a. Delivery
   b. Personal assistance
   c. A pleasant atmosphere
   d. Credit
   e. Central checkout counters

_c_    9. Which of the following statements describes a customer's view of a specialty store?
   a. The customer wants to compare both products and store product mixes.
   b. The customer will buy any brand at the most accessible store.
   c. The customer prefers both a particular product and a particular store.
   d. The customer likes the wide product mix found there.

_e_    10. What caused the franchising industry to acquire a bad image?
   a. Franchising wholesalers
   b. Highly controlled marketing strategies
   c. Rigid adherence to the marketing concept
   d. Limited expansion
   e. Inefficient management

_b_    11. Which of the following statements is false?
   a. When a retailer allows expenses and prices to increase, vulnerability to competition from new institutions also increases.
   b. There is today a sharp delineation between discount houses and department stores.
   c. The wheel of retailing hypothesis works reasonably well in industrialized, expanding economies.
   d. A retailer should develop a retailing mix.

_a_    12. Which of the following statements characterizes a superstore?
   a. It has three times the sales and four times as many products as department stores.
   b. It is a combination specialty store and supermarket.
   c. It carries few nonfood products.
   d. It is a low-cost, high-volume, limited-service operation.
   e. It is the original mass merchandising concept.

_d_    13. According to the text, which of the following is a step in developing a marketing strategy for retailing?
   a. Developing the store's image
   b. Franchising the store
   c. Pinpointing the wheel of retailing
   d. Segmenting the market for the type of product
   e. Developing a promotional mix

_d_ 14. Today's shopping centers are replacing the central business district not only as a place for shopping, but also for what other opportunities?
   a. Physical and spiritual
   b. Business and nonbusiness
   c. Banking and finance
   d. Cultural and recreational
   e. Athletic and educational

_d_ 15. One trend in retailing is
   a. decreased fragmentation and segmentation of the consumer market.
   b. a public that is more tolerant of retail practices.
   c. a less-informed public.
   d. the growth of specialty stores.

_b_ 16. Specialty stores differ from department stores in that specialty stores usually have a very narrow
   a. product line.
   b. product mix.
   c. product type.
   d. product perspective.
   e. product angle.

_a_ 17. Superstores have been designed to sell products efficiently by means of
   a. their size and operating methods.
   b. their legal advantages.
   c. a direct approach to consumers.
   d. their services to consumers.

_c_ 18. Status in the product assortment identifies the relative importance of each product by
   a. purpose.
   b. purchase.
   c. rank.
   d. selection.

_d_ 19. A welcome change for consumers dissatisfied with the impersonality of retailers can be found in the close, personal contact at
   a. superstores.
   b. department stores.
   c. supermarkets.
   d. specialty stores.
   e. fast-food franchises.

# Programmed Completion Exercises

in-home selling, mail-order selling, automatic vending

1. Three types of nonstore retailing are _____ _____, _____ _____, and _____ _____.

personal, nonpersonal

2. Nonstore retailing includes _____ sales such as in-home and telephone retailing and _____ sales such as mail-order, vending, and catalog retailing.

franchise

3. The _____ system is an arrangement in which a supplier grants to dealers the right to sell products in exchange for some type of consideration.

link

4. Retailers are an important _____ in the marketing channel.

Superstores

5. _____ have three times the sales and four times as many products as supermarkets.

wheel of retailing

6. The _____ _____ _____ concept states that as the level of services increases, established retail institutions become vulnerable to the entry of newer institutions, which also go through the same cycle.

central management, control

7. The expansion of the franchise system to many industries illustrates the advantages of _____ _____ and _____ of coordinated marketing efforts for franchise members.

low-margin, low-service

8. The wheel of retailing is a hypothesis that suggests that retail innovations start in _____, _____ outlets and that gradually, as competition increases, the expenses of these new outlets increase because of trading-up.

benefits

9. Consumers are more concerned with _____ obtained in shopping than with the type of retailer they patronize.

location, hours, facilities, organizational structure, strength, merchandise planning, control, pricing, buying, promotion, service, expense management

10. The retailing mix may contain such variables as _____, _____, _____, _____ _____ and _____, _____ _____ and _____, _____, _____, _____, _____, and _____ _____ .

retailers

11. The most visible middlemen are _____ in that the majority of their contacts are with ultimate consumers.

place, time, possession

12. Retailers create _____, _____, and _____ utilities by providing assortments of products that match consumers' wants.

product mix, product line depth

13. One of the main functions of retailers is to provide a _____ _____ and a _____ _____ _____ that give consumers opportunities to compare, shop, and make purchasing decisions.

Purpose, status, completeness

14. _____, _____, and _____ are three attributes of the product assortment that are provided by retailers.

Atmospherics

15. _____ is the term used to describe the purposeful designing of store space to create emotional conditions that enhance the probability of purchasing.

marketing efforts, internal management

16. Department stores have a wide product mix and are organized into different departments to facilitate _____ _____ and _____ _____ .

narrow, deep

17. Specialty retailers are stores carrying a _____ product mix and _____ product lines.

department store

18. A good example of a shopping store, where the consumer compares the prices, quality, and services of one store with its competitors is the _____ _____ .

warehouse
showroom

19. The introduction of sophisticated mass merchandising to the highly fragmented furniture industry stimulated the birth of the _____ _____ .

neighborhood,
community,
regional

20. Types of planned shopping centers include _____, _____, and _____ shopping centers.

Mass
merchandisers

21. _____ _____ appeal to large heterogeneous target markets, and both the image of efficiency and economy distinguish the atmosphere of the store.

volume of sales,
expenses, cost
of goods sold

22. By increasing _____ _____ _____, decreasing _____, or decreasing the _____ _____ _____ _____, retailers can reduce the selling price.

consumers,
manufacturers

23. Retailers are in a strategic position to gain feedback from _____ and to channel these communications back to _____ or resellers.

## Answers to Objective Questions

*True or False*

| 1. T | 16. T |
|---|---|
| 2. T | 17. T |
| 3. F | 18. F |
| 4. F | 19. F |
| 5. F | 20. F |
| 6. F | 21. T |
| 7. T | 22. F |
| 8. T | 23. T |
| 9. T | 24. F |
| 10. T | 25. F |
| 11. F | 26. F |
| 12. F | 27. F |
| 13. T | 28. F |
| 14. T | 29. T |
| 15. F | 30. F |

*Multiple Choice*

| 1. c | 11. b |
|---|---|
| 2. d | 12. d |
| 3. d | 13. d |
| 4. a | 14. d |
| 5. d | 15. d |
| 6. b | 16. b |
| 7. d | 17. a |
| 8. e | 18. c |
| 9. c | 19. d |
| 10. e | |

# CHAPTER 12

# Physical Distribution

## Chapter Summary

The concept of physical distribution deals with the integration of activities that help to store, transport, handle, and process orders for products and that are necessary to provide a level of service satisfactory to customers. Physical distribution creates time and place utility, thus maximizing the value of products. The major decisions related to physical distribution as discussed in this chapter include inventory planning and control, transportation, warehousing, materials handling, and communications.

Physical distribution is the integrated set of activities that deal with the movement of products within firms and through marketing channels. Planning an effective means of physical distribution can be a significant decision point in developing an overall marketing strategy. Physical distribution activities should be coordinated with decisions relating to the marketing channel. The physical distribution system may often, in fact, be adjusted to meet the unique needs of a channel member.

Inventory planning and control aid in the development and maintenance of adequate assortments of products for the target markets. The inventory control decision that is most important in terms of customers and costs is the average number of units carried in inventory. A systematic approach must be taken to determine efficient reorder points to prevent shortages and to avoid having too much capital tied up in inventory. There is often a trade-off between inventory carrying costs and the probability of stockouts. The economic order quantity (EOQ) is the order size that minimizes the total cost of ordering and carrying inventory. Inventory decisions have a strong impact on physical distribution costs and on the level of customer service provided.

Transportation is an essential physical distribution activity. Cost, capability, reliability, and availability are the considerations in choosing a transportation mode. Transportation helps a firm to create time and place utility for its products. Various transportation decisions are required during the production, storage, and delivery stages of operation. The transportation mode selected affects all elements of the physical distribution system. The marketing strategy itself can sometimes be based on a unique transportation system. Because individual transportation companies often specialize in one mode of transportation, various modes sometimes must be coordinated and integrated. The task of coordination and integration can be handled by the firm or by some special transportation agency. Since costs for small shipments are sharply higher than costs for full loads in railroad cars and trucks, consolidated shipments with firms sharing costs and services are increasing.

Warehousing is another important physical distribution activity; it refers to the design and operation of facilities to store and move goods. The essential functions of a warehouse include receiving, identifying, and sorting goods and dispatching them to storage. The warehouser also holds, recalls, selects or picks goods from storage, marshals the shipment, and dispatches the shipment. Trends in public warehousing indicate a shift from providing space for the storage of goods to offering services for the distribution of goods. Private warehouses are established or purchased usually when a firm believes its warehouse needs are so stable that it can make a long-term commitment to fixed facilities. For many firms the best approach may be a combination of private and public warehousing.

Physical handling of products is important in efficient warehouse operations as well as in transportation from points of production to points of consumption. Materials-handling procedures and techniques should increase the usable capacity of a warehouse, reduce the number of times a good is handled, and improve service to customers as well as their satisfaction with a product. Containerization has revolutionized physical distribution by broadening the capabilities of our transportation system, enabling shippers to transport a wider range of cargoes with speed, reliability, and stable costs.

A communication system for physical distribution should link producers, intermediaries, and customers. Computers, memory systems, display equipment, and other communication technology facilitate the flow of information among channel members. The utilization of advanced computer hardware with appropriate software has greatly increased productivity in communications. Low-cost minicomputers and decentralized computer systems within firms have increased the use of computers in physical distribution.

Changes in customers or technology may have profound effects on the overall structure of physical distribution in the marketing strategy. Physical distribution should meet the requirements of an organization's marketing strategy. Marketers should be substantially responsible for the design and control of the physical distribution system. They must relate costs to customer satisfaction. The physical distribution system must be able to adjust to changing environmental circumstances and continue to give customers what they want. In short, decreasing costs while increasing service should be the main objective in physical distribution.

# True or False Statements

(T)  F     1. When sales volumes are fairly stable, the ownership and control of a private warehouse may provide several gains, including financial ones such as property appreciation and tax shelters realized through depreciation of the facility.

(T)  F     2. While the characteristics of the product itself often determine how it will be handled, the handling process may change those characteristics or qualities.

(T)  F     3. Materials-handling procedures and techniques can reduce the number of times a good is handled, and improve service to customers as well as their satisfaction with the product.

(T)  F     4. Transportation systems must take into account both cost factors and customer requirements.

(T)  F     5. The protective functions of packaging are an important consideration in physical distribution.

(T)  F     6. The development of an efficient physical handling system is dependent on the decisions about packaging materials and methods.

(T)  F     7. Containerization has revolutionized physical distribution by broadening the capabilities of the materials-handling system, enabling shippers to handle a wider range of cargoes with speed, reliability, and stable costs.

(T)  F     8. The availability of low-cost minicomputers and decentralized computer systems within firms has increased the use of computers in physical distribution.

T  (F)     9. Changes in customers or technology may not necessarily have profound effects on the overall structure of physical distribution in the marketing strategy.

(T)  F     10. Speed of delivery, reliability, and availability of service are marketing considerations that help develop the total product in customers' eyes.

(T)  F     11. A physical distribution system must be able to adjust to changing environmental circumstances while continuing to give customers what they want.

(T)  F     12. Changes in transportation, warehousing, materials handling, and inventory may increase or decrease services such as speed of delivery.

T  (F)     13. A physical distribution system should be the last component of the marketing mix to be designed.

T  F  14. Physical distribution is an integrated set of activities that deal with managing the movement of products within firms and through the marketing channels.

T  F  15. Physical distribution creates time and place utility by the performance of activities that store, transport, handle, and process orders for products.

T  F  16. Whatever the role of physical distribution in the marketing strategy, distribution decisions must be made by someone in order for the physical movement of goods to occur.

T  F  17. Inventory planning and control require a systematic approach to determining efficient reorder points, which will help eliminate stockouts and avoid having too much capital tied up in inventory.

T  F  18. The problem of making trade-offs between the costs of carrying larger average inventories and the costs of frequent orders can be solved by finding an optimal marginal order quantity (MOQ).

T  F  19. Transportation decisions should be integrated with other marketing strategy decisions.

T  F  20. The selection of a transportation mode is usually based on cost, transit time, reliability, capability, accessibility, and security.

T  F  21. Warehousing involves only the design and operation of facilities to store goods.

T  F  22. Materials handling, or the physical handling of products, is an important element of the inventory planning and control system.

T  F  23. Often, one channel member will arrange the movement of goods for all channel members involved in exchanges.

T  F  24. The physical distribution system should be adjusted to meet the unique needs of each channel member.

T  F  25. An inventory control decision that is most significant in terms of customers and costs has to do with the average number of units maintained in inventory.

# Multiple-Choice Questions

b  1. According to the text, activities that help to store, transport, handle, and process orders for products facilitate
   a. a sale.
   b. an exchange.
   c. the process of physical distribution.
   d. the flow of goods within the firm.
   e. the movement of goods among marketing channels.

C    2. Which of the following statements about physical distribution is
        true?
        a. Physical distribution usually deals with the physical move-
           ment of goods and raw materials between storage and pro-
           duction facilities within a firm.
        b. Physical distribution deals with the holding of inventory until
           it is needed.
        c. Physical distribution deals with the physical movement and
           inventory holding within and among intermediaries.
        d. Physical distribution concerns the sorting, grading, sampling,
           and physical movement of goods within and among inter-
           mediaries.
        e. Physical distribution deals only with the physical movement
           of goods from producer to the ultimate consumer.

d    3. Inventory planning and control are essential to
        a. production planning and control.
        b. reducing inventory carrying and ordering costs.
        c. inventory pricing.
        d. a sound physical distribution system.
        e. inventory financing.

A    4. The total time that a carrier has possession of goods is known as
        a. transit time.
        b. holding time.
        c. lead time.
        d. carrying time.
        e. possession time.

d    5. To buyers, speed of delivery, service, and dependability
        a. are less important than the cost of the product.
        b. are more important than the quality of the product.
        c. are unimportant when compared to price.
        d. are as important as cost to the consumer in evaluating the
           product.
        e. have no significance whatsoever.

e    6. Ace Tea, Rosedale Distribution, and Hilltop Stores are a group
        of interrelated organizations that direct the flow of various food
        products to customers. This group can best be described as
        a. a sales channel.
        b. a distribution channel.
        c. a marketing force.
        d. an intermediary.
        e. a marketing channel.

b    7. Which of the following are responsible for delays in delivery,
        thereby causing a loss of sales and customers?
        a. Wide assortments of bulky goods
        b. Stockouts

c.  Late deliveries
d.  Inadequate transportation facilities
e.  Distant business locations

_b_   8. According to the text, which of the following is a major consideration in a firm's decision to develop its own transportation system?
a.  A need to make deliveries at the proper place
b.  A need to make deliveries at the right time
c.  A need to make deliveries at minimum cost
d.  The availability of funds
e.  The geographical distribution of customers

_b_   9. Which of the following is *not* a criterion in selecting a transportation mode?
a.  Reliability
b.  Variety
c.  Security
d.  Accessibility
e.  Capacity

_a_  10. Assuming similar benefits and services, which of the following remains an important consideration in selecting a transportation mode?
a.  Cost
b.  Security
c.  Speed
d.  Dependability
e.  Capability

_a_  11. The ability of a carrier to move goods over a specific route or network is known as its
a.  accessibility.
b.  dependability.
c.  reliability.
d.  capability.
e.  capacity.

_a_  12. The design and operation of facilities to store and move goods is an important
a.  physical distribution activity.
b.  selling activity.
c.  facilitating function.
d.  inventory planning and control activity.
e.  transportation activity.

_b_  13. According to the text, changes in which of the following may have profound effects on the overall structure of physical distribution in the marketing strategy?
a.  Transportation
b.  Customers

c. Communications
d. Physical handling system
e. Materials handling practices

*c*    14. Which of the following is *not* one of the functions performed by a warehouse?
a. Identifying goods
b. Sorting goods
c. Bearing the loss of damage to goods while in storage
d. Recalling, selecting, or picking goods from storage
e. Dispatching the shipment

*c*    15. There is often a trade-off between inventory carrying costs and
a. stockouts.
b. inventory holding costs.
c. the probability of stockouts.
d. the chance of losing sales.

*d*    16. Economic order quantity (EOQ)
a. reduces the inventory carried in stock.
b. minimizes the cost per unit of inventory.
c. guarantees a sufficient inventory level at all times.
d. minimizes the total cost of ordering and carrying inventory.
e. minimizes only total carrying costs.

*c*    17. When goods are lost or delivered in a damaged condition by the carrier, the firm
a. incurs costs.
b. sues the carrier.
c. does not incur costs.
d. buys new goods.
e. has to reduce sales proportionately.

*c*    18. According to the text, which of the following represents a considerable cost in physical distribution?
a. Maintaining rail facilities
b. Renting materials-handling equipment
c. Maintaining or renting warehouse facilities
d. Expanding warehouse facilities
e. Maintaining transportation facilities

*d*    19. Which of the following has, as one of its primary functions, accepting merchandise delivered from outside transportation or an attached factory, and taking responsibility for it?
a. A public warehouse
b. A wholesaler
c. A channel member
d. A warehouse
e. A field warehousing company

<u>d</u>   20. The text indicates that transit time affects a marketer's ability to
   a. select a suitable marketing mix.
   b. increase sales volume.
   c. utilize a carrier to capacity.
   d. provide service.
   e. transport the largest quantity of goods to the market.

<u>c</u>   21. The integration of all those activities that help to store, transport, handle, and process orders and that are necessary to provide a level of service satisfactory to customers is known as
   a. production strategy.
   b. sales strategy.
   c. physical distribution.
   d. inventory planning and control.
   e. physical movement of goods.

<u>a</u>   22. Planning an effective means of physical distribution can be a significant decision point in developing
   a. a marketing strategy.
   b. a product strategy.
   c. a promotion strategy.
   d. a sales strategy.
   e. a transportation system owned by the firm.

<u>c</u>   23. A systematic approach must be taken to determine efficient reorder points in order to
   a. ensure higher levels of inventories.
   b. decrease shortages.
   c. eliminate stockouts or avoid having too much capital tied up in inventory.
   d. ensure regular and uniform supply.
   e. minimize inventory ordering costs.

<u>b</u>   24. The overall safety stock
   a. must be greater than the average inventory.
   b. depends on the general level of demand.
   c. depends on the level of supply.
   d. is determined by the inventory cost.
   e. is determined by the costs of stockouts.

# Programmed Completion Exercises

exchange, store, process orders

1. An _____ usually is facilitated through the performance of activities that help to _____, transport, handle, and _____ _____ for products.

integration,
provide, satisfy

2. The concept of physical distribution deals with _____ of all those activities that are necessary to _____ a level of service that will _____ customers.

time, place,
value

3. Physical distribution creates _____ and _____ utility, which maximizes the _____ of products by delivering them when and where they are wanted.

Physical
distribution,
managing,
through

4. _____ _____ is an integrated set of activities that deal with _____ the movement of products within firms and _____ marketing channels.

Planning,
physical
distribution,
developing

5. _____ an effective means of _____ _____ can be a significant decision point in _____ an overall marketing strategy.

important
variable, costs,
customer
satisfaction

6. Physical distribution can be seen as an _____ _____ in a marketing strategy, in that it can decrease _____ and increase _____ _____ .

speed, delivery,
services,
dependability

7. To buyers, _____ of _____, _____ and _____ are often as important as cost.

marketing
channel,
interrelated,
direct

8. The _____ _____ is a group of _____ organizations that _____ products to customers.

physical
distribution,
adjusted,
unique

9. The _____ _____ system is often _____ to meet the _____ needs of a channel member.

Inventory
planning,
control,
development,
maintenance

10. _____ _____ and _____ are physical distribution activities that aid in the _____ and _____ of adequate assortments of products for the target markets.

costs,
inventory,
controlled

11. The _____ involved in obtaining and maintaining _____ must be _____ so that desired profits can be obtained.

planned,
products sold,

12. An inventory system should, first of all, be _____ so that the number of _____ _____ and the number of

products, stock

_____ in _____ can be determined at certain checkpoints.

decision, customers, costs, average

13. An inventory control _____ that is most significant in terms of _____ and _____ is the _____ number of units maintained in inventory.

systematic, efficient, shortages, avoid

14. A _____ approach must be taken to determine _____ reorder points to eliminate _____ or _____ having too much capital tied up in inventory.

size, independent, reordered

15. The _____ of the inventory needed to prevent stockouts is _____ of the size that should be _____ for efficient order processing.

safety stock

16. The overall _____ _____ depends on the general level of demand.

reorders, larger, processing

17. Individual _____ depend on the trade-off between the cost of carrying _____ average inventory and the cost of _____ small orders.

communication system, coordinated effort, physical distribution

18. Inventory management requires a well-tuned _____ _____ and a _____ _____ to make sure that the inventory control system supports the overall objectives of marketing and _____ _____ .

advantage, physical handling, transfers

19. Transportation technology involves taking _____ of each transportation mode's strengths by adopting _____ _____ procedures to permit the most effective _____ among different types of carriers.

transportation modes, marketers, risk

20. Since all _____ _____ have security problems, _____ must determine the relative _____ associated with each appropriate transportation mode in making a selection.

consolidating, container, destination, containerization

21. The practice of _____ many items into one _____ , sealed at the point of origin and opened at the _____ is generally referred to as _____ .

Warehousing, design, operation, activity

22. _____ refers to the _____ and _____ of facilities to store and move goods and is another physical distribution _____.

public warehousing, storage, goods, services

23. Most current trends in _____ _____ indicate a shift from providing space for the _____ of _____ to offering _____ for the distribution of goods.

Materials handling, warehouse, production, consumption

24. _____ _____ is important in efficient _____ operations as well as in transportation from points of _____ to points of _____.

usable capacity, number, times, product

25. Materials-handling procedures should increase the _____ _____ of a warehouse, reduce the _____ of _____ a good is handled, and improve service to customers as well as their satisfaction with the _____.

communication, flow, information, channel

26. Computers, memory systems, display equipment, and other _____ technology facilitate the _____ of _____ among _____ members.

# Answers to Objective Questions

*True or False*

| 1. T | 14. T |
|------|-------|
| 2. T | 15. T |
| 3. T | 16. T |
| 4. T | 17. T |
| 5. T | 18. F |
| 6. T | 19. T |
| 7. T | 20. T |
| 8. T | 21. F |
| 9. F | 22. F |
| 10. T | 23. T |
| 11. T | 24. T |
| 12. T | 25. T |
| 13. F | |

*Multiple-Choice*

| 1. b | 13. b |
|------|-------|
| 2. c | 14. c |
| 3. d | 15. c |
| 4. a | 16. d |
| 5. d | 17. c |
| 6. e | 18. c |
| 7. b | 19. d |
| 8. b | 20. d |
| 9. b | 21. c |
| 10. a | 22. a |
| 11. a | 23. c |
| 12. a | 24. b |

# CHAPTER 13

# Promotion: An Overview

## Chapter Summary

The role of promotion is to communicate with individuals, groups, or organizations to directly or indirectly facilitate exchanges by influencing one or more of the audiences to accept an organization's products. To avoid inconsistencies and to get the most from promotional efforts, marketing managers must be sure that the communications are properly planned, implemented, coordinated, and controlled.

Communication, the basic role of promotion, is defined as a sharing of meaning. This communication process involves various steps. Communication begins with a source, which is a person, group, or organization that has a meaning which it attempts to share with an audience. Initially, the source codes the meaning of the message that is to be communicated. The coding process is the conversion of meaning into a series of signs that are familiar to the audience or receiver. The coded message then is transmitted to the receiver or audience through a medium of transmission, which is the communication channel that carries the coded message. After the audience receives the message, it must be decoded to obtain meaning. This decoding process requires the receiver to convert the signs into concepts and ideas. When the decoded message differs from the coded message, a condition called noise exists. Generally, the receiver supplies feedback to the source, making the communication process circular. Each communication channel has a limit regarding the amount of information it can handle effectively. This limit is called channel capacity.

Since acceptance or adoption of goods, services, and ideas is the long-run purpose of promotion, consideration must be given to the five-step product adoption process. Awareness is the first step in the adoption process. In this stage individuals become aware that the product exists, but they have little information about it and are not concerned about getting more. Individuals enter the interest stage when they are self-motivated to get information about the product's features, uses, advantages, disadvantages, price, and location. During the evaluation stage buyers consider whether the product will satisfy certain criteria that are critical for meeting their specific needs. In the trial stage, individuals use or experience the product for the first time. Finally, people move into the adoption stage when the need arises for that general type of product and they begin using the specific product. Rejection may occur after any stage, including the adoption stage, and can be temporary or permanent.

People tend to use different information sources during different stages of the adoption process. Even though the particular stage of the adoption process may influence the types of information sources used, other factors—such as product characteristics, price, uses, and the characteristics of customers—also affect the types of information sources that buyers use. In addition, when an organization introduces a new product, people do not all begin the adoption process at the same time. Therefore, when designing a promotional campaign, a marketer must consider what adoption process stage a particular target audience is in before developing the message.

A firm's promotion mix consists of the promotion methods used to communicate with customers. Advertising, personal selling, publicity, packaging, and sales promotion are the five ingredients that can be used to make up a firm's promotion mix. Advertising is a paid form of nonpersonal communication about an organization and/or its products that is transmitted to a target audience through a mass medium. Marketers enjoy several benefits when using advertising. Advertising can be an extremely cost-efficient promotional method because it can reach a vast number of people at a low cost per person. In addition, advertising allows the user to repeat the message and can help create a more favorable image of the firm in the minds of the public. On the other hand, advertising has several disadvantages. Its absolute dollar outlay can be quite high, it often does not provide feedback, and its effect on sales is difficult to measure.

Personal selling is a process of informing customers and persuading them to purchase a product through personal communication in an exchange situation. While advertising is aimed at a relatively large target audience, personal selling is aimed at one or several individuals. The cost of reaching one person through personal selling is considerably more than through advertising, but personal selling efforts often can have more impact on customers.

Publicity is, like advertising, a form of nonpersonal communication. With publicity, however, the sponsor does not pay the media costs and is not identified, and the communication is presented as a news story. Publicity must be planned and implemented so that it is compatible with, and supportive of, other elements in the promotion mix.

Packaging may be employed as a promotional device to attract attention and to provide product information. Verbal and nonverbal symbols can inform potential buyers about the product's content, features, uses, advantages, and hazards. A firm can create desirable images and associations by using certain colors, designs, shapes, and textures in packages. When a marketer develops a package that can be reused for other purposes, the package may become a vehicle that promotes the product.

Sales promotion is an activity and/or material that acts as a direct inducement, offering added value or incentive for the product, to resellers, salespersons, or consumers. Frequently, marketers employ sales promotion to improve the effectiveness of other promotion ingredients. Sales promotion also can be used as the primary promotion vehicle, although such use is not common. When marketers use sales promotion, they usually do so to produce immediate, short-run sales increases. Sales promotion methods can be divided into two groups: consumer sales promotion methods and trade sales promotion devices.

The specific promotion mix ingredients employed and the intensity at which they are used by an organization depends on a variety of factors. The size of an organization's promotional resources affects the number and relative intensity of promotional methods. If a company's promotional dollars are limited, the firm is likely to use mainly personal selling. If a company's promotional objective is to create awareness of a new convenience good, the promotion mix is likely to be heavily oriented toward advertising, packaging, sales promotion, and possibly publicity. If the company's objective is to educate consumers about the product features of durable goods, the promotion mix may consist of a large amount of personal selling. In planning a promotion mix, one element that should be considered is whether to use a push policy or a pull policy. If a push policy is used, the producer promotes the product only to the next institution down the marketing channel. A firm that uses a pull policy promotes directly to consumers. The pull policy is designed to pull goods down through the marketing channel by creating demand at the consumer level.

Characteristics of an organization's target market for a product also influence the promotion mix ingredients. If the size of a market is limited and/or a company's customers are concentrated in a small area, personal selling probably will be emphasized. Organizations that sell products in markets consisting of millions of customers (and firms having customers that are highly dispersed across a vast geographic area) often use advertising, packaging, and sales promotion. The distribution of a target market's socioeconomic characteristics such as age, income, or education level may influence the types of promotional techniques that a marketer uses.

Product characteristics also affect the promotion mix ingredients. Generally, promotion mixes for industrial products concentrate on personal selling, while advertising plays a major role in promoting consumer goods. High-priced products require promotion mixes with a great deal of personal selling. For low-priced convenience items, marketers use advertising because the profit margins on many of these items is too low to justify the use of personal selling, and most consumers do not need advice from sales personnel. The stage of the product life cycle also affects marketers' decisions regarding the promotion mix. When a product is marketed through intensive distribution, the firm depends strongly on advertising and packaging. Items distributed through selective distribution vary considerably in terms of the types and amounts of promotion used, while items distributed through exclusive distribution frequently are promoted through a large amount of personal selling. The ways that products are used also can affect the combination of promotional methods employed.

Finally, the costs and availability of promotional methods are major factors to analyze when developing a promotion mix. National advertising and sales promotion efforts require large expenditures. Even though there is an extremely large number of media vehicles in the United States, a firm may not be able to advertise to a certain market because no available advertising medium effectively reaches it.

# True or False Statements

(T) F    1. Coordination of promotional activities is essential to avoid contradictory messages.

T (F)    2. Meaningful communication is achieved through the transmission of any symbols.

(T) F    3. During the encoding process, the source must be careful to avoid signs that have multiple meanings.

T (F)    4. The decoding process performed by the receiver is the source of most noise that arises in the communication process.

(T) F    5. Feedback is the stage in the communication process that makes the process circular.

(T) F    6. Channel capacity is the limit of the volume of information that can be handled effectively through a specific communication channel.

(T) F    7. The basic role of promotion is to communicate.

T (F)    8. A single information source such as mass communication is effective during all stages of the product adoption process.

(T) F    9. Rejection can occur after any stage in the adoption process.

T (F)    10. When an organization introduces a new product, most people begin the adoption process at the same time.

(T) F    11. The five major ingredients that can be included in an organization's promotion mix are advertising, personal selling, publicity, packaging, and sales promotion.

(T) F    12. Advertising is a nonpersonal, paid form of communication that is transmitted by a mass medium.

T (F)    13. Because of relatively high costs, advertising is not cost-efficient.

T (F)    14. Tactile communication is best described as communication through body language.

T (F)    15. Trade sales promotion devices include coupons, free samples, demonstrations, and contests designed to encourage consumer purchases.

T (F)    16. Packaging can perform a promotional function only when used in conjunction with another promotional tool.

(T) F    17. Color is an important component of packaging since people associate certain colors with feelings and connotations.

T (F)    18. Industrial products generally are promoted through a heavy concentration of advertising in the promotion mix.

T (F)    19. Sales promotion and promotion mean about the same thing.

(T) F    20. In making promotion mix decisions, marketers must give consideration not only to the mix ingredients but also to market and product characteristics.

T (F) 21. Distribution methods generally are established after promotion mixes are determined and thus are not an important consideration in establishing promotion mixes.

T (F) 22. If a push policy is used, the producer promotes the product directly to consumers.

(T) F 23. When a company's customers are numerous and highly dispersed, advertising may be a more practical promotional method than personal selling.

T (F) 24. High-priced products require promotion mixes with a great deal of advertising, publicity, and sales promotion.

T (F) 25. Publicity provides an organization with a means of free communication.

T (F) 26. Manufacturers of highly personal products depend heavily on personal selling.

T (F) 27. The stage of the product life cycle has little effect on promotion mix ingredients for a specific product.

(T) F 28. A firm may not be able to advertise to a certain market because no available advertising medium effectively reaches it.

# Multiple-Choice Questions

_e_ 1. According to the text, communication is best defined as which of the following?
a. A transmission of meaning
b. Information transmitted in form or pattern
c. The sending and receiving of information
d. The coding and decoding of information
e. A sharing of meaning

_d_ 2. The coding process is
a. performed by the receiver.
b. often ineffective due to noise.
c. performed by the medium used for transmission.
d. the conversion of meaning into signs representing ideas.
e. the process of message interpretation.

_d_ 3. When coding the meaning into a message, a marketer must do all of the following *except*
a. know what level of language the target market can understand.
b. avoid signs that have several meanings.
c. select a medium of transmission that will reach the target market.

d. include all possible product information.

e. attempt to minimize noise.

*a* 4. An audience is best defined as

a. two or more receivers who decode a message.

b. the component in the communication process responsible for transmitting a message.

c. the major source of noise.

d. the component in the communication p rocess responsible for encoding.

e. people who receive a message.

*b* 5. When the decoded message is different from the coded message,

a. the message was not encoded properly by the source.

b. noise exists.

c. the wrong receivers are reached.

d. an inappropriate medium of transmission was used.

e. it is the source's fault.

*d* 6. Channel capacity is determined by the

a. medium of transmission chosen.

b. intended receiver's prior knowledge.

c. complexity of the information transmitted.

d. least efficient component of the communication process.

e. size of the intended audience

*a* 7. The stage in the adoption process that involves the greatest amount of self-motivation in finding information is the

a. interest stage.

b. awareness stage.

c. adoption stage.

d. evaluation stage.

e. trial stage.

*c* 8. Individuals often seek information, opinions, and reinforcement from personal sources such as friends and relatives during which two product adoption stages?

a. Trial and adoption stages

b. Awareness and interest stages

c. Evaluation and trial stages

d. Interest and evaluation stages

e. Interest and trial stages

*e* 9. Getting immediate feedback and having knowledge of customers' needs are advantages of which promotion mix ingredient?

a. Advertising

b. Publicity

c. Sales promotion

d. Packaging

e. Personal selling

___d___    10. According to the text, advertising is
- a. a process of informing customers and persuading them to purchase products through personal communication.
- b. nonpersonal communication in news story form.
- c. the same thing as sales promotion.
- d. a paid form of nonpersonal communication transmitted through a mass medium.
- e. an activity that acts as a direct inducement, offering added value for the product to consumers.

___e___    11. Kinesic communication is best exemplified by which of the following?
- a. A handshake
- b. The physical distance separating two parties
- c. A spoken word
- d. Written communication
- e. Winking

___b___    12. Proxemic communication involves
- a. hand gestures.
- b. the physical distance separating two parties.
- c. eye movements.
- d. bodily contact.
- e. spoken or written communication.

___e___    13. Which of the following is an activity or material that serves as a direct inducement to resellers, salespersons, or consumers?
- a. Advertising
- b. Personal selling
- c. Packaging
- d. Publicity
- e. Sales promotion

___b___    14. Which of the following is a characteristic of sales promotion?
- a. It is used on a continuous or cyclical basis.
- b. It may be aimed at either final consumers or trade people.
- c. It is used to achieve future, long-run sales increases.
- d. It is a comprehensive area and includes such elements as promotion.
- e. It generally is used as the primary promotion vehicle.

___d___    15. Which of the following is communication transmitted through mass media at no charge?
- a. Advertising
- b. Personal selling
- c. Sales promotion
- d. Publicity
- e. Packaging

_a_     16. If a firm has limited promotional resources, it will mainly use personal selling because
   a. measuring a salesperson's contribution to sales is easy.
   b. personal selling is the most cost-efficient method.
   c. the per unit cost of advertising is higher than the per unit cost of personal selling.
   d. a small firm finds it difficult to obtain publicity.
   e. personal selling supplies the greatest diversification at the lowest price.

_C_     17. A push policy is characterized by
   a. heavy promotional concentration at the level of ultimate consumers.
   b. heavy promotional emphasis at the retail level.
   c. concentration of promotional efforts on the next channel member down the distribution channel.
   d. the manufacturer's supplementing the promotional efforts of all members of the distribution channel.
   e. required compliance with the manufacturer's marketing objectives throughout the distribution channel.

_b_     18. A pull policy is characterized by
   a. producers' domination of the distribution channel.
   b. promotion aimed directly at consumers.
   c. a short distribution channel.
   d. heavy emphasis on personal selling throughout the distribution channel.
   e. heavy promotional emphasis at the wholesale level.

_d_     19. A package that can be reused for other purposes represents
   a. the least expensive form of promotion.
   b. the use of sales promotion.
   c. a form of advertising.
   d. one way in which a package can be used as a promotional tool.
   e. a type of publicity.

_d_     20. If a company's promotional objective is to educate consumers about the features of a home appliance, the promotion mix probably will emphasize
   a. advertising.
   b. sales promotion.
   c. publicity.
   d. personal selling.
   e. packaging.

_A_     21. Organizations that sell convenience products in markets containing millions of customers are most likely to use which of the following promotion mix ingredients?
   a. Advertising, packaging, and sales promotion

b. Personal selling and publicity
c. Advertising, publicity, and sales promotion
d. Personal selling and sales promotion
e. Advertising, packaging, and personal selling

# Programmed Completion Exercises

communicate,
individuals,
groups,
organizations,
influencing

1. The primary role of promotion is to _____ with _____, _____, or _____ to directly or indirectly facilitate exchanges by _____ one or more of the audiences to accept the organization's products.

a sharing of
meaning,
transmission

2. For promotional purposes, a useful approach is to define communication as _____ _____ _____ _____; implicit in this definition is the notion of _____ of information.

planned,
implemented,
controlled

3. To get the most from promotional efforts, a marketing manager must be certain that they are properly _____, _____, and _____.

source, person,
group,
organization

4. Communication begins with a _____, which can be a _____, a _____, or an _____.

source, signs,
ideas, concepts

5. The coding process, sometimes called encoding, requires the _____ to convert the meaning into a series of _____ that represent _____ or _____.

signs, familiar

6. To facilitate the sharing of meaning, the source should use _____ that are _____ to the receiver or audience.

source,
medium,
transmission

7. To share the meaning with the receiver or audience, the _____ selects a _____ of _____ and sends the coded message to the receiver or audience.

decoded, noise

8. When the _____ message is different from what is coded, a condition known as _____ exists.

feedback,
source

9. In the _____ stage, the audience or receiver can be viewed as the _____ of a message directed toward the original source.

limit, channel
capacity

10. Each communication channel possesses a _____ regarding the volume of information that can be handled effectively. This is called _____ _____ .

influence,
encourage,
accept, adopt

11. The long-run purpose of promotion is to _____ and _____ buyers to _____ or _____ goods, services, and ideas.

awareness,
interest,
evaluation, trial,
adoption

12. Although there are several ways to view the product adoption process, one of the more common approaches is to view it as consisting of five stages: _____ , _____ , _____ , _____ , and _____ .

personal
sources,
relatives,
friends,
associates

13. During the evaluation stage, individuals often seek information from _____ _____ such as _____ , _____ , and _____ .

promotion mix

14. The specific combination of promotional methods used by an organization is its _____ _____ .

Advertising,
transmitted,
mass medium

15. _____ is a paid form of nonpersonal communication about an organization and/or its products that is _____ to a target audience through a _____ _____ .

purchase,
personal,
exchange

16. Personal selling is a process of informing customers and persuading them to _____ products through _____ communication in an _____ situation.

inducement,
added,
incentive,
resellers,
salespersons,
consumers

17. Sales promotion is an activity and/or material that acts as a direct _____ , offering _____ value or _____ for the product, to _____ , _____ , or _____ .

news story,

18. Publicity is communication through a _____ _____ , regarding an organization and/or its products,

mass medium,
no charge

that is transmitted through a _____ _____ at

_____ _____ .

size, color,
shape, texture,
graphics

19. When attempting to develop a package that has a large amount of promotional value, the designers must consider _____ , _____ , _____ , _____ , and _____ .

personal selling,
consumer goods

20. Generally, promotion mixes for industrial products are concentrated heavily in _____ _____ , while advertising plays a major role in promoting _____ _____ .

personal selling

21. If the size of the market is quite limited, _____ _____ probably will be emphasized, because it can be quite effective for reaching small numbers of persons.

push policy

22. If a _____ _____ is used, the producer promotes the product only to the next marketing institution down the channel.

pull policy,
pulling,
demand

23. The _____ _____ is directed toward _____ the goods down through the channel by creating _____ at the level of consumers.

# Answers to Objective Questions

*True or False*

| | |
|---|---|
| 1. T | 15. F |
| 2. F | 16. F |
| 3. T | 17. T |
| 4. F | 18. F |
| 5. T | 19. F |
| 6. T | 20. T |
| 7. T | 21. F |
| 8. F | 22. F |
| 9. T | 23. T |
| 10. F | 24. F |
| 11. T | 25. F |
| 12. T | 26. F |
| 13. F | 27. F |
| 14. F | 28. T |

*Multiple-Choice*

| | |
|---|---|
| 1. e | 12. b |
| 2. d | 13. e |
| 3. d | 14. b |
| 4. a | 15. d |
| 5. b | 16. a |
| 6. d | 17. c |
| 7. a | 18. b |
| 8. c | 19. d |
| 9. e | 20. d |
| 10. d | 21. a |
| 11. e | |

# CHAPTER 14

# Advertising and Publicity

## Chapter Summary

Advertising is a paid form of nonpersonal communication that is transmitted to consumers through mass media such as television, radio, newspapers, magazines, direct mail, mass transit vehicles, and outdoor displays. Although business organizations are thought to be the major users of advertising, many types of organizations use it, including government organizations, churches, universities, civic groups, and charitable organizations.

Numerous factors enter into the decision of whether advertising can be an effective ingredient in an organization's promotion mix for a specific product. Products that possess unique, important features are easier to advertise than homogeneous products. The powers of advertising are not limitless. If the generic product category is experiencing a long-term decline, it is less likely that advertising can be used successfully for a particular brand within that generic category. The use of advertising can be effective only when there are sufficient users of the brand in the target market. The size and marketing strength of competitors also will greatly affect the possible success of an advertising campaign. The overall state of the economy and specific business conditions influence the effects of an advertising campaign and the sale of products in general. Advertising is less likely to be effective if an organization is unable or unwilling to spend the amount of money required to undertake an advertising campaign. If the firm is weak in any of the areas of marketing, these weaknesses are obstacles to the successful use of advertising.

Organizations employ advertising in a variety of ways and for many reasons. Advertising is employed to promote goods, services, images, issues, ideas, and people, and it can be classified into two categories—institutional advertising and product advertising. Product advertising often is employed to stimulate demand directly. Examples of product advertising are pioneer advertising (used to stimulate primary demand) and competitive advertising (used to stimulate selective demand). One increasingly popular form of competitive advertising is comparative advertising, which compares two or more specifically identified brands in the same general product class. When marketers advertise to offset or lessen the effects of a competitor's promotional program, they are using defensive advertising. The demand for any product is limited in that persons will consume only so much of it. Therefore, advertising sometimes attempts to enlarge the number of product uses, which, in turn, increases sales. Other uses of advertising include reminder advertising (to remind consumers that the brand is still around), reinforcement advertising (to assure current users they have made the right product choice), and advertising for year-round sales stability. How a firm uses advertising depends on the firm's objectives, resources, and environment.

There are seven major steps in creating an advertising campaign. First, the advertiser should identify and analyze the advertising target. Second, the advertiser should define the advertising objectives, that is, specify what the campaign is intended to accomplish. The third step is developing the advertising platform, which consists of the basic issues or selling points that an advertiser wishes to include in the campaign. The platform provides a base on which to build the message. The next step is to determine the advertising appropriation, that is, the total amount of money allocated for advertising during a specific time period. Fifth, the marketer must develop the media plan by selecting and scheduling the media to be used in the campaign. In the sixth stage the advertiser creates the message through the use of copy and artwork, which are the major components of an advertising message. Copy is the verbal portion and consists of headlines, subheadlines, body copy, and signature; artwork includes the illustrations and the layout or physical arrangement of the advertisement's components. The final phase in the development of an advertising campaign is the evaluation of advertising effectiveness. Evaluations can be performed before the campaign, during it, or after it.

An advertising campaign may be handled by an individual or a few persons within the firm, an advertising department within an organization, or an advertising agency. In very small firms one or two individuals are responsible for performing advertising activities. In certain types of large businesses, and especially in larger retail organizations, advertising departments handle the creation and implementation of advertising campaigns. When an organization uses an advertising agency, the development of the advertising campaign is usually a joint effort of both the firm and the agency. The use of an advertising agency may be advantageous to a firm because an agency can provide highly skilled, objective specialists who have broad experience in the advertising field.

Publicity is communication in news story form, regarding an organization and/or its products, that is transmitted through a mass medium at no charge. Within an organization, publicity is sometimes viewed as a part of public relations. Public relations is a broad set of communication activities employed to create and maintain favorable relations between the organization and its various audiences—customers, employees, stockholders, government officials, and society in general. Compared with advertising, publicity is mainly informative and is lower-keyed and more subdued. An organization does not pay for it. Communication through publicity may have greater credibility among consumers. However, publicity does not provide an opportunity to repeat messages.

Marketers can use different forms of publicity. The most commonly used form of publicity is the news release, which is normally a single page of typewritten copy containing fewer than three hundred words. A feature article is a longer manuscript that normally is prepared for a specific publication. Captioned photographs can be effective for illustrating a new or improved product that has highly visible features. A press conference is a meeting used to announce major news events. Editorials sometimes are sent to newspapers and magazine publishers. Finally, films and tapes sometimes are distributed to broadcast stations.

The selection of the specific types of publicity to be used depends on a variety of factors, including the type of information to be presented, the characteristics of the target audience, the receptivity of media personnel, the importance of the news item to the public, and the amount of information to be presented. Sometimes a marketer uses only a single type of publicity in a promotion mix; in other cases several types of publicity are employed.

Publicity often is used to make people aware of a firm's products, brands, or activities and is used to promote a particular image of a firm. To obtain the maximum benefit from publicity, a firm should create and maintain a systematic and continuous publicity program. Efforts should be made to establish and maintain good working relationships with media personnel. A firm also must establish policies and procedures which will help ensure that publicity releases possess an acceptable level of newsworthiness and that they are well written. Finally, a firm needs some way to measure the effectiveness of its publicity efforts.

Firms also can receive unfavorable publicity from news coverage regarding some negative event. The negative impact of unfavorable publicity can wipe out a firm's favorable image as well as the attitudes of its customers, which take years to build through promotional efforts. The main way to avoid unfavorable publicity is for the organization to reduce the likelihood of negative incidents and events through safety programs, inspections, and effective quality control procedures. In most cases, the best approach for dealing with news coverage of negative events is to expedite the coverage rather than to try to discourage or block it.

The fact that media do not charge for transmitting publicity provides a financial advantage but also contains several limitations. Messages put forth through publicity must be viewed by media personnel as newsworthy, which means that the messages must be timely, of interest to the public, and accurate.

# True or False Statements

T (F)    1. The easiest products to advertise are homogeneous products such as cigarettes, gasoline, and beer.

T (F)    2. Advertising can compensate for most weaknesses in a firm's marketing strategy.

T (F)    3. An advertisement must not mention the name of a competing brand because this is illegal.

T (F)    4. An advertiser sometimes uses advertising to build primary demand, which is demand for a specific brand of product.

(T) F    5. Defensive advertising is used most often by firms in extremely competitive consumer product markets.

(T) F    6. Both reminder and reinforcement advertising are used to prevent a loss in sales or market share.

(T) F    7. Advertising can be used to reduce fluctuations in sales.

T (F)    8. Advertising objectives need not be clear, precise, and measurable because they are only estimates of what an advertiser wants to accomplish.

(T) F    9. A bench mark is used in advertising as a point of reference for defining advertising objectives.

T (F)    10. "Our primary advertising objective is to increase monthly sales from $300,000 to $500,000" is an example of a good advertising objective.

(T) F    11. Even though the long-run goal of an advertiser is to increase sales, not all campaigns are aimed at producing immediate sales.

(T) F    12. Although the advertising platform contains the basic issues, it does not indicate the form in which the issues should be presented.

T (F)    13. The most effective method for determining platform issues is to obtain the opinions of persons within the firm.

T (F)    14. The advertising appropriation for industrial products is large relative to the budget for consumer convenience items.

(T) F    15. The advertising appropriation is the total amount that a marketer allocates for advertising for a specific time period.

(T) F    16. One fault of the percent-of-sales method of setting an advertising budget is that it is based on past or forecasted sales.

T (F)    17. The main problem with using the objective and task approach in setting the advertising appropriation is that it often results in underspending or overspending the firm's resources.

(T) F    18. A marketer usually is concerned about the type and intensity of competitors' advertising.

(T)   F     19. The arbitrary approach to setting an advertising budget uses the opinion of a high-level executive in the firm.

(T)   F     20. Determining the advertising appropriation is an important activity in relation to the advertising campaign.

T   (F)     21. The cost and impact of a television commercial can be compared accurately with the cost and impact of a newspaper advertisement.

(T)   F     22. A cost comparison indicator allows an advertiser to compare the costs of several media vehicles relative to the number of persons reached by each vehicle.

T   (F)     23. The signature is the written portion of an advertisement.

T   (F)     24. Since radio listeners often do not listen attentively, radio copy should be formal and straightforward to attract attention.

T   (F)     25. Television copy should be written so that the visual material overpowers the audio portion of the commercial.

(T)   F     26. The advertising platform is the foundation on which campaign messages are built.

(T)   F     27. The artwork of an advertisement includes the illustrations, the physical arrangement of the illustrations, headline, subheadline, body copy, and signature.

(T)   F     28. The effectiveness of advertising can be evaluated before, during, and after it appears.

(T)   F     29. The major justification for using recognition and recall methods to evaluate advertising effectiveness is that if individuals can remember an advertisement, they are more likely to buy the product.

T   (F)     30. When an organization uses an advertising agency, that agency usually develops the advertising campaign with little help from the firm.

(T)   F     31. An advertising campaign may be handled by one person in the firm.

(T)   F     32. An advertising agency receives much of its compensation through a commission paid by the media rather than from the organization employing its services.

T   (F)     33. Publicity is a paid form of advertising.

(T)   F     34. Publicity is communication that is transmitted through a mass medium at no charge.

T   (F)     35. Publicity releases have identified sponsors.

(T)   F     36. Publicity often is used to make people aware of products, brands, or activities of a firm.

T   (F)     37. A news release is a manuscript of about three thousand words that normally is prepared for a specific publication.

T  Ⓕ    38. A captioned photograph is a form of advertising and not a type of publicity.

Ⓣ  F    39. To obtain the maximum benefit from publicity a firm should try to establish and maintain good relationships with media personnel.

Ⓣ  F    40. The effectiveness of publicity is evaluated on the basis of how many releases are published or broadcasted.

T  Ⓕ    41. The best way to deal with negative publicity is to ignore it.

Ⓣ  F    42. One limitation of publicity is that firms cannot maintain control over the content or timing of the communication.

# Multiple-Choice Questions

*e*    1. What kind of advertising promotes organizational images, ideas, and political issues and candidates?
   a. Product advertising
   b. Governmental advertising
   c. Political advertising
   d. Pioneer advertising
   e. Institutional advertising

*c*    2. Advertising is less likely to be successful when
   a. the product has hidden qualities.
   b. the product possesses unique features.
   c. the generic product category is experiencing a long-term decline.
   d. disposable income is low.
   e. the firm possesses considerable marketing expertise.

*d*    3. Pioneer advertising
   a. compares the product to other similar products.
   b. emphasizes the brand name of the product.
   c. reminds consumers that the brand is still around.
   d. stimulates primary demand.
   e. improves the image of the firm.

*b*    4. Competitive advertising
   a. offsets or lessens the effects of a competitor's promotional campaign.
   b. stimulates selective demand.
   c. reinforces a product's image.
   d. introduces a new product.
   e. stimulates primary demand.

a      5. The type of advertising in which an advertiser mentions the actual names of competitive brands is known as
   a. comparative advertising.
   b. competitive advertising.
   c. selective advertising.
   d. defensive advertising.
   e. pioneer advertising.

a      6. In a business organization in which a sizable proportion of the promotion efforts are aimed at personal selling,
   a. advertising often is employed to improve the effectiveness of sales personnel.
   b. advertising is seldom used.
   c. reminder advertising is used.
   d. advertisements are used to stimulate primary and selective demand.
   e. advertising emphasizes new product uses.

a      7. When an organization advertises to offset or lessen the effects of a competitor's promotional program, it is using
   a. defensive advertising.
   b. competitive advertising.
   c. comparative advertising.
   d. selective advertising.
   e. reinforcement advertising.

b      8. Advertising that shows consumers new ways to use a certain product is employed
   a. to enlarge the geographic market and sell to more people.
   b. to increase sales after the demand for the product has reached its limit.
   c. sparingly, because the demand for competitive brands also increases.
   d. to remind consumers that the brand is still around and that it has certain uses, characteristics, and benefits.
   e. to reduce seasonal fluctuations in sales.

e      9. When advertisers try to increase sales by promoting new uses for a product, they should
   a. advertise established products to remind consumers that the product is still around.
   b. try to assure current users that they have made the right choice and indicate how to get the most from the product.
   c. allocate a sizable proportion of the promotional effort toward personal selling.
   d. adjust the advertising campaign so that it will be aimed only at current users of the product.
   e. attempt to increase demand for the product without increasing the demand for competitive brands.

d    10. Reinforcement advertising is focused on consumers who
      a. have not used the product.
      b. have purchased the product and were dissatisfied.
      c. use another brand of the same product.
      d. already use the advertised brand.
      e. would like to try the advertised brand but are unsure if it will provide satisfaction.

e    11. The advertising target is
      a. the location and geographic distribution of persons.
      b. the distribution of age, income, race, sex, and education level.
      c. consumer's attitudes regarding the purchase and use of a product.
      d. what the advertiser wants to accomplish with the advertising campaign.
      e. the group of people toward whom the advertisements are aimed.

c    12. The first step in the development of an advertising campaign is to
      a. set the advertising budget.
      b. develop the media plan.
      c. identify and analyze the target market.
      d. define the advertising objectives.
      e. create the advertising platform.

d    13. A statement that indicates a firm's current condition or position is commonly known as a
      a. platform.
      b. media plan.
      c. primary objective.
      d. bench mark.
      e. secondary objective.

c    14. Concerning advertising objectives, which of the following statements is *false*?
      a. Advertising objectives that are not clearly defined are seldom successful.
      b. Advertising objectives can be stated in sales terms or in communication terms.
      c. An advertising objective should not be restricted in terms of the time needed to accomplish it.
      d. Precision and measurability are required to allow advertisers to evaluate their campaign.
      e. Not all advertising objectives are aimed at increasing sales.

A    15. An advertising platform consists of
      a. the basic issues or selling points that an advertiser includes in a campaign.
      b. issues that are of little importance to consumers.

c. selling features included in an advertisement.

d. the objectives of the advertising campaign.

e. a survey of consumers' feelings about the product.

___c___ 16. Which of the following is an example of an advertising objective stated in terms of sales?

a. Increase brand awareness.

b. Make consumers' attitudes more favorable.

c. Increase the firm's market share.

d. Increase product awareness.

e. Increase consumers' knowledge of product features.

___c___ 17. The most effective method for determining advertising platform issues is

a. to obtain the opinions of personnel within the firm.

b. to obtain the opinions of individuals in the advertising agency.

c. to obtain consumers' opinions through surveys.

d. to use the trial-and-error method.

e. to consider the firm's past experiences in advertising the product.

___e___ 18. Using the percent-of-sales approach, which of the following industries probably would allocate the greatest proportion of sales to advertising?

a. Insurance

b. Household appliances

c. Radio and television sets

d. Dairy products

e. Tobacco products

___e___ 19. Using the objective and task approach for setting the advertising budget, a marketer would

a. simply multiply the firm's past sales, forecasted sales, or a combination of the two by a standard percentage based on what the firm traditionally has spent on advertising.

b. adjust the amount previously spent on advertising relative to the increase in sales.

c. study the type and intensity of advertising done by competitors and adjust the budget accordingly.

d. request an executive of the firm to set the amount of the appropriation.

e. determine the objectives that the campaign should achieve and then attempt to ascertain how much must be spent to accomplish these objectives.

___b___ 20. The major disadvantage of the percent-of-sales approach for determining the advertising budget is that

a. the marketer usually experiences difficulty in trying to estimate how much money is needed to achieve a certain goal.

b. it is based on the incorrect assumption that sales create advertising rather than that advertising creates sales.

c. it often results in either underspending or overspending the firm's resources.

d. the firm's competitors probably use greater amounts of resources for advertising.

e. it does not take into consideration the sizes and types of audiences that are reached by specific media vehicles.

_d_ 21. Which of the following media presently receives the largest estimated annual advertising expenditures?
a. Magazines
b. Television
c. Radio
d. Newspapers
e. Direct mail

_A_ 22. The media planner's primary goal is to
a. formulate a media plan that allows the advertisements to reach the largest number of persons in the advertising target per dollar spent.
b. decide what type of medium is best for the product to be advertised.
c. decide which specific media vehicles to use.
d. formulate a media plan that allows the advertisements to reach a majority of the advertising target.
e. create a media time schedule.

_e_ 23. If advertisers want to show textures as well as numerous details, they probably would use
a. radio.
b. newspapers.
c. outdoor displays.
d. mass-transit vehicles.
e. magazines.

_A_ 24. The development of the media plan is a crucial stage in the creation of an advertising campaign because
a. its effectiveness determines, to some degree, the effects that the message has on the target market.
b. it is the most expensive step in planning an advertising campaign.
c. it determines the basic content and form of an advertising message.
d. it is a time-consuming task.
e. there is a large amount of media information available.

<u>b</u>    25. AIDA is an acronym that marketers should use when preparing advertising copy and means
   a. action, involvement, desire, and attraction.
   b. attention, interest, desire, and action.
   c. attention, interest, drive, and action.
   d. attraction, interest, desire, and adoption.
   e. action, interest, desire, and adoption.

<u>C</u>    25. AIDA is an acronym that marketers should use when preparing advertising copy and means
   a. action, involvement, desire, and attraction.
   b. attention, interest, desire, and action.
   c. attention, interest, drive, and action.
   d. attraction, interest, desire, and adoption.
   e. action, interest, desire, and adoption.

<u>C</u>    27. The part of an advertisement that links the headline to the body copy is the
   a. signature.
   b. illustration.
   c. subheadline.
   d. artwork.
   e. primary copy.

<u>A</u>    28. When creating a television commercial, the copywriter and the artist combine the copy with the visual material through the use of a
   a. storyboard.
   b. layout.
   c. body copy.
   d. media plan.
   e. parallel script form.

<u>d</u>    29. A consumer jury consists of
   a. persons who have never purchased the advertised product.
   b. consumer advocates who will decide on the safety of the product.
   c. consumers who will report how effective the advertising campaign has been.
   d. consumers who will pretest an advertisement.
   e. consumers who will judge whether the advertisements are misleading.

<u>e</u>    30. Effectiveness during a campaign usually is measured by
   a. post-tests.
   b. pretests.
   c. consumer juries.
   d. paired comparisons.
   e. inquiries.

_e_    31. When evaluating the effectiveness of advertising, subjects may be asked to identify advertisements that they have seen recently, but they are not shown any clues to stimulate their memory. This evaluation technique is known as the
    a.  recognition method.
    b.  post-test method.
    c.  consumer survey.
    d.  aided recall method.
    e.  unaided recall method.

_b_    32. Under the traditional compensation method for advertising agencies, what percent commission is paid by the media?
    a.  10 percent
    b.  15 percent
    c.  20 percent
    d.  33 percent
    e.  25 percent

_d_    33. Publicity
    a.  is transmitted through the media for a fee.
    b.  usually has a sponsor.
    c.  usually is designed to have an immediate impact on sales.
    d.  is transmitted through the mass media at no charge.
    e.  is usually persuasive and informative.

_b_    34. If an advertiser pays $25,000 for a one-page magazine advertisement and that magazine is read by ten million people, how much is the advertiser paying to reach a thousand people?
    a.  $25.00
    b.  $2.50
    c.  $250.00
    d.  $5.00
    e.  $50.00

_c_    35. Publicity is used to
    a.  have an immediate impact on sales.
    b.  be informative and persuasive.
    c.  make people aware of products, brands, or activities of a firm.
    d.  reach a different target market than advertising reaches.
    e.  increase consumers' awareness of a firm as well as persuade them to buy its products.

_c_    36. Which of the following statements concerning the differences between advertising and publicity is *false*?
    a.  Advertising is informative and persuasive; publicity is only informative.
    b.  Advertisements have identified sponsors; publicity releases do not.
    c.  Sponsors pay for publicity but not for advertising.

        d. Advertisements are separated from broadcast programs or editorial portions of print media; publicity releases are part of a program or editorial content.

        e. Media personnel help in preparing advertisements but usually have no part in creating publicity releases.

_d_ 37. Which of the following is *not* a type of publicity?
    a. Press conferences
    b. Films distributed to broadcast stations in the hope that they will be aired
    c. Captioned photographs
    d. Direct mail pamphlets promoting greeting cards and including an order blank
    e. Letters to a newspaper editor

_c_ 38. To obtain the maximum benefit from publicity, a firm should
    a. include various types of publicity in the promotion mix.
    b. spend as much money as possible on publicity.
    c. create and maintain a systematic publicity program.
    d. publish or broadcast as many publicity releases as possible.
    e. block all negative publicity releases.

# Programmed Completion Exercises

paid,
nonpersonal

1. Advertising is a major promotion mix ingredient that is a _____ form of _____ communication and is transmitted to consumers through mass media.

institutional,
product

2. Depending on what is being promoted, advertising can be classified into one of two categories: _____ advertising and _____ advertising.

pioneer,
primary
demand

3. When the product being advertised is a revolutionary innovation and a specific firm is the first to introduce this product, the marketer uses _____ advertising to stimulate _____ _____.

selective,
competitive

4. To develop _____ demand, a firm employs _____ advertising, which points out a brand's uses, features, advantages, and benefits.

Reinforcement

5. _____ advertising is aimed at individuals who already use the advertised brand.

objectives, resources, environment

6. The manner in which a firm uses advertising depends on the firm's _____, _____, and _____.

target, base

7. An advertiser should analyze the advertising _____ to build an information _____ on which to develop the campaign.

Precision, measurability

8. _____ and _____ are required in advertising objectives to allow the advertiser to evaluate the degree to which objectives are accomplished.

how far, what direction

9. The advertising objective should clearly indicate _____ _____ and in _____ _____ the advertiser wishes to move from the bench mark.

sales, communication

10. Advertising objectives usually are stated in _____ terms or in _____ terms.

basic issues, selling points

11. An advertising platform consists of the _____ _____ or _____ _____ that an advertiser wishes to include in the advertising campaign.

consumer research, expensive

12. Even though _____ _____ is the most effective method of determining the platform issues, it is _____.

easy to use, less disruptive, market share

13. The percent-of-sales approach is used often for setting the advertising budget because it is _____ _____ _____ and it is _____ _____ competitively in that it stabilizes the firm's _____ _____ within an industry.

arbitrary approach

14. When using the _____ _____ to set the advertising budget, a high-level executive in the firm states how much can be spent on advertising for a certain time period.

amount, allocated

15. Determining the advertising appropriation is an important activity because it determines the _____ of resources that can be _____ to the advertising campaign.

media plan,
largest number,
per dollar

16. The media planner's primary goal is to formulate a
_____ _____ that allows the advertisements to
reach the _____ _____ of persons in the advertising target _____ _____ spent on media.

Print, broadcast

17. _____ media can be used more effectively than
_____ media when an advertiser wishes to present many
issues or numerous details.

Copy,
headlines,
subheadlines,
body copy,
signature

18. _____ is the written portion of advertisements and includes _____ , _____ , _____
_____ , and _____ .

illustration,
layout

19. Artwork consists of the _____ in the advertisement and
the _____ of the components of the advertisement.

before, during,
after

20. The effectiveness of advertising can be evaluated _____ ,
_____ , and/or _____ the campaign.

recall,
recognition

21. The post-test methods based on memory are called
_____ and _____ tests.

joint effort,
firm, agency

22. When an organization uses an advertising agency, the development of the advertising campaign is usually a _____
_____ of the _____ and the _____ .

news story,
mass medium,
no charge

23. Publicity is communication in _____ _____ form,
regarding an organization and/or its products, that is transmitted
through a _____ _____ at _____
_____ .

informative

24. While advertising messages tend to be informative, persuasive,
or both, publicity messages are mainly _____ .

sponsors

25. Publicity releases do not have identified _____ .

aware

26. Publicity often is used to make people _____ of the products, brands, or activities of a firm.

newsworthy,

27. Messages put forth through publicity must be viewed by media
personnel as _____ , which means that the messages must

timely,
accurate, public

be _____, _____, and of interest to the

_____ .

information,
characteristics,
receptivity,
importance,
amount

28. The selection of the specific types of publicity to be used depends

on the type of _____ to be presented, the _____

of the target audience, the _____ of media personnel, the

_____ of the news item to the public, and the

_____ of information to be presented.

rejected,
newsworthi-
ness, poorly
written

29. A considerable amount of publicity materials are _____

by media personnel because the materials lack _____ or

because they are _____ _____ .

safety
programs,
inspections,
quality control
procedures

30. The main way to avoid unfavorable publicity is for an organi-

zation to reduce the likelihood of negative incidents through

_____ _____, _____, and _____

_____ _____ .

# Answers to Objective Questions

*True or False*

| | | | |
|---|---|---|---|
| 1. | F | 22. | T |
| 2. | F | 23. | F |
| 3. | F | 24. | F |
| 4. | F | 25. | F |
| 5. | T | 26. | T |
| 6. | T | 27. | T |
| 7. | T | 28. | T |
| 8. | F | 29. | T |
| 9. | T | 30. | F |
| 10. | F | 31. | T |
| 11. | T | 32. | T |
| 12. | T | 33. | F |
| 13. | F | 34. | T |
| 14. | F | 35. | F |
| 15. | T | 36. | T |
| 16. | T | 37. | F |
| 17. | F | 38. | F |
| 18. | T | 39. | T |
| 19. | T | 40. | T |
| 20. | T | 41. | F |
| 21. | F | 42. | T |

*Multiple-Choice*

| | | | |
|---|---|---|---|
| 1. | e | 20. | b |
| 2. | c | 21. | d |
| 3. | d | 22. | a |
| 4. | b | 23. | e |
| 5. | a | 24. | a |
| 6. | a | 25. | b |
| 7. | a | 26. | c |
| 8. | b | 27. | c |
| 9. | e | 28. | a |
| 10. | d | 29. | d |
| 11. | e | 30. | e |
| 12. | c | 31. | e |
| 13. | d | 32. | b |
| 14. | c | 33. | d |
| 15. | a | 34. | b |
| 16. | c | 35. | c |
| 17. | c | 36. | c |
| 18. | e | 37. | d |
| 19. | e | 38. | c |

# CHAPTER 15

# Personal Selling and Sales Promotion

## Chapter Summary

Business organizations spend more on personal selling than on any other promotion mix ingredient. Personal selling is defined as a process of informing and persuading customers to purchase products through personal communication in an exchange situation. The specific goals of personal selling usually can be grouped into three general purposes: finding prospects, convincing prospects to buy, and keeping customers satisfied. The exact activities involved in the selling process vary among salespersons and different selling situations. However, many salespersons move through a general process as they sell products. This general selling process consists of seven steps—prospecting and evaluating, preparing, approaching the customer, making the presentation, overcoming objections, closing, and following up.

Most business organizations use different kinds of sales personnel. Salespersons can be classified into three groups based on the functions they perform. The three groups are order getters, order takers, and support salespersons. Order-getting activities often are divided into two categories: current customer sales and new business sales. Order takers seek repeat sales and can be categorized as "inside" order takers and "field" order takers. Support salespersons perform activities such as locating prospects, educating customers, building goodwill, and providing service after the sale. Three common types of support salespersons are missionary, trade, and technical salespersons. Selection of the right type of salespersons is affected by the various attributes of the products, customers, and the kinds of marketing channels.

Management of the sales force requires a diverse set of decisions and activities. Specific areas include: (1) establishing objectives for the sales force, (2) determining its size, (3) recruiting and selecting salespersons, (4) training sales personnel, (5) compensating salespersons, (6) motivating salespersons, (7) creating sales territories, (8) routing and scheduling salespersons, and (9) controlling and evaluating the sales force.

Sales objectives usually are established for the total sales force and for each salesperson. They should be stated in precise, measurable terms, and they should be specific regarding the time period and the geographic areas involved. These objectives tell salespersons what they are to accomplish during a specified time period.

Marketers can use several methods for ascertaining the size of the sales force. The equalized workload method allows the marketing manager to base the sales force size on the condition that each salesperson is assigned a set of accounts that requires about the same amount of sales effort and time. This method requires the dividing up of customers into groups based on size of purchases and the number of sales calls required to service various account sizes. The incremental productivity method states that the marketer should continue to increase the sales force as long as the incremental sales increases are greater than the incremental increases in selling costs.

It is necessary to recruit and select salespersons in order to have and maintain an effective sales force. Recruiting is a process by which the sales manager develops a list of applicants for sales positions. A sales manager usually recruits applicants from several sources: departments within the firm, employment agencies, educational institutions, other organizations' personnel, advertisements, and current employees' recommendation of friends. The process for selecting a sales force varies in complexity from one company to another. An organization's sales management should design a selection procedure that satisfies the company's specific needs.

Salespersons, whether new or experienced, require sales training. When developing a training program, several questions must be considered: Who should be trained? Where and when should the training occur? What should be taught? How should the information be taught?

A compensation plan that attracts, motivates, and holds the most effective salespersons should be developed to maintain a highly productive sales force. The compensation plan should give sales management the desired level of control and provide sales personnel with an acceptable level of freedom, income, and incentive. Sales management should periodically review and evaluate the compensation plan and make necessary adjustments.

Although financial compensation plays an important role in motivating salespersons, a motivational program is necessary to satisfy their nonfinancial needs. Examples of motivational incentives are enjoyable working conditions, power and authority, job security, and an opportunity to excel. Some organizations employ negative motivational measures such as financial penalties, demotions, and even terminations.

Sales management's decisions regarding sales territories can determine the effectiveness of a sales force that must travel. Sales managers must make various territory decisions having to do with size, shape, and routing and scheduling; each of these is affected by many factors.

To control and evaluate the sales force properly, sales management needs information. Information is received through salespersons' reports, customer feedback, and invoices. Once the sales manager has evaluated the salespeople, corrective action must be taken where needed. This may require comprehensive changes in the sales force.

Sales promotion includes all promotional activities and materials other than personal selling, advertising, publicity, and packaging; it is aimed at producing immediate, short-run effects. Marketers use sales promotion to attract new customers, to introduce new products, to increase resellers' inventories, to encourage greater usage among users, to educate consumers regarding product improvements, and for numerous other reasons.

Sales promotion methods can be grouped into two main categories: consumer and trade. Consumer sales promotion techniques encourage consumers to patronize a specific retail store or to purchase a particular product. Trade sales promotion methods stimulate wholesalers and retailers to carry a producer's products and to market these products aggressively. There are a variety of sales promotion methods used by retailers, including coupons, demonstrations, trading stamps, and point of purchase displays. The three most common techniques used to promote new products are free samples, coupons, and money refunds. Four sales promotion methods commonly used to promote established products are premiums, cents-off offers, consumer contests, and consumer sweepstakes. Producers use sales promotion methods to encourage resellers to carry their products and to promote them effectively. These promotion methods include buying allowances, buy-back allowances, counts and recounts, free merchandise, merchandise allowances, cooperative advertising, dealer listings, premiums or push money, sales contests, and dealer loaders.

# True or False Statements

(T) F     1. Business organizations spend more on personal selling than on any other promotion mix ingredient.

T (F)     2. Personal selling usually is the least expensive ingredient in the promotion mix.

(T) F     3. Personal selling provides marketers with their greatest opportunity to adjust a message to satisfy customers' information needs.

(T) F     4. Three general purposes of personal selling are finding prospects, convincing prospects to buy, and keeping customers satisfied.

(T) F     5. The sales presentation provides a salesperson with the greatest opportunity to determine a prospect's specific product needs.

(T) F     6. One of the best ways for a salesperson to overcome objections is to anticipate them.

(T) F     7. Current customer sales are classified under order-getting activities.

T (F)     8. The personal selling process begins with approaching the customer.

(T) F     9. Salespersons who seek repeat sales are classified as order takers.

(T) F     10. Support personnel facilitate the selling function but usually are not involved solely with making sales.

T (F)     11. Trade salespersons usually are employed by manufacturers and assist the producer's customers in selling to their own customers.

(T) F     12. An important function of the technical salesperson is to provide advice to the customer regarding the application of the product.

T (F)     13. One analytical technique used to determine the size of the sales force is the incremental workload method.

(T) F     14. When determining sales force size, a marketing manager will usually use a good deal of subjective judgment.

T (F)     15. Sales objectives usually are established for the entire sales force, not for each salesperson.

(T) F     16. Currently there is no set of general guidelines that a sales manager can use to ensure the recruitment of good sales personnel.

(T) F     17. In training sales personnel, both experienced salespersons and new salespersons must be trained.

T (F)     18. If the straight commission method is used to compensate salespersons, the commission must be based on a single percentage of sales.

(T) F     19. The straight salary compensation method is useful when the firm moves into new sales territories that require developmental work.

T   (F)    20. When deciding on territory size, the sales manager usually attempts to create territories that have different sales potentials.

T   (F)    21. Because several major factors must be considered in designing the shape of sales territories, sales managers seldom employ geometric patterns as guides.

(T)   F    22. A sales manager should develop a systematic approach for motivating salespersons.

(T)   F    23. The dimensions used to measure a salesperson's performance are determined largely by the sales objectives that the sales manager sets for the salesperson.

(T)   F    24. Sales promotion usually is used in conjunction with other promotion mix ingredients.

T   (F)    25. Consumer sales promotion techniques stimulate resellers to carry a product and promote it aggressively.

# Multiple-Choice Questions

__a__    1. Personal selling is an important marketing function because
   a. marketers can "zero-in" on the most promising sales prospects.
   b. it is the most expensive promotion mix ingredient.
   c. it produces more profit than other promotional methods.
   d. it is the least flexible promotion mix ingredient.
   e. it is the main thrust of the marketing field.

__b__    2. Compared with other promotional tools, personal selling is
   a. the least expensive.
   b. the most precise.
   c. less flexible.
   d. usually not used in an organization's total promotion activities.
   e. more often used in conjunction with other promotion mix ingredients.

__d__    3. The most widely used promotional mix ingredient is
   a. publicity.
   b. sales promotion.
   c. advertising.
   d. personal selling.
   e. public relations.

__a__    4. The specific goals of a personal selling effort can be grouped into three general purposes:
   a. to locate prospects, to identify needs of the prospects, and to sell to the prospects.

    b.  to find prospects, to convince prospects to buy, and to educate prospects further.

    c.  to locate prospects, to educate prospects, and to attempt to obtain repeat sales.

    d.  to find prospects, to convince prospects to buy, and to keep customers satisfied.

    e.  to educate consumers, to locate prospects, and to convince prospects to buy.

_c_    5.  In the general selling process, developing a list of potential customers is called

    a.  evaluating.

    b.  preparing.

    c.  prospecting.

    d.  preselling.

    e.  searching.

_a_    6.  The technique in which a salesperson approaches potential customers without their prior consent is known as the

    a.  cold canvass technique.

    b.  repeat contact.

    c.  referral technique.

    d.  blind technique.

    e.  hard sell.

_e_    7.  One of the best ways for a salesperson to overcome a prospect's objections is to

    a.  attract and hold the prospect's attention.

    b.  demonstrate the product to get the prospect more involved with it.

    c.  listen to the prospect's comments and responses.

    d.  fulfill the prospect's needs for information.

    e.  anticipate them and answer them before the prospect has an opportunity to ask.

_d_    8.  During the presentation the salesperson may ask questions based on the assumption that the prospect will buy the product. This is known as a

    a.  follow-up.

    b.  closing.

    c.  cold canvass.

    d.  trial close.

    e.  referral.

_a_    9.  Salespersons can be classified into three groups according to the functions they perform:

    a.  order getters, order takers, and support salespersons.

    b.  order getters, current customer sales, and new customer sales.

     c. past customer sales, current customer sales, and new customer sales.

     d. inside order takers, outside order takers, and support salespersons.

     e. missionary, trade, and technical salespersons.

_a_ 10. Salespersons who facilitate the selling function but usually are not strictly involved only with making sales are known as
     a. support sales personnel.
     b. inside order takers.
     c. outside order takers.
     d. missionary salespersons.
     e. trade salespersons.

_c_ 11. The missionary salesperson's major purpose is to
     a. promote products to potential customers.
     b. perform the order-taking function.
     c. assist the producer's customers in selling to their own customers.
     d. provide advice to customers regarding application of the products.
     e. generate the bulk of the firm's total sales.

_c_ 12. Salespersons who direct much of their effort toward helping customers promote the products are referred to as
     a. technical salespersons.
     b. missionary salespersons.
     c. trade salespersons.
     d. inside salespersons.
     e. outside salespersons.

_b_ 13. Determine the sales force size using the equalized workload method. The average salesperson makes eight hundred calls annually. The company has four hundred Class I customers requiring twenty calls annually and two hundred Class II customers requiring forty calls annually. The company should have
     a. ten salespersons.
     b. twenty salespersons.
     c. twenty-five salespersons.
     d. one hundred salespersons.
     e. sixty salespersons.

_a_ 14. Concerning the incremental productivity method for determining sales force size, which of the following statements is most correct?
     a. A salesperson's workload is a function of the number of sales calls plus travel time between customers.
     b. When using this technique, a marketer must accurately estimate the number of sales calls required to service accounts.

c. The marketer should continue to increase the sales force as long as sales increase.

d. The user must accurately estimate how much sales will increase when an additional salesperson is added.

e. This method's effectiveness depends solely on the marketer's ability to estimate incremental selling expenses.

c  15. Sales goals that call for an increase in the proportion of the firm's sales relative to the total number of products sold by all the businesses in that particular industry are goals based on

   a. volume.
   b. profit.
   c. market share.
   d. sales potential.
   e. total market potential.

b  16. According to the Xerox survey, which of the following training topics is considered most important?

   a. Persuasion skills
   b. Product knowledge
   c. Time and territory management
   d. Business fundamentals
   e. Negotiating skills

e  17. In regard to compensation programs, which of the following statements is most correct?

   a. Most compensation programs place salespersons on an equal basis with each receiving approximately the same pay.
   b. When a straight salary method is used, compensation is determined solely on the basis of sales for a given time period.
   c. If a straight commission method is used, the salesperson is paid a fixed salary plus a commission based on sales volume.
   d. Good compensation programs usually are developed solely on the basis of the product being sold.
   e. Sales compensation programs usually reimburse salespersons for their selling expenses, provide fringe benefits, and deliver the necessary compensation level.

b  18. Sales compensation plans

   a. are easily designed.
   b. should be designed to maintain a productive sales force.
   c. have very little to do with the customer.
   d. pertain only to the income of sales personnel.
   e. are not described by any of these statements.

b  19. One major disadvantage of the straight commission compensation method is that it

   a. results in selling expenses that are directly related to sales revenues.
   b. provides little financial security for salespersons.

c.  provides no incentive for salespersons.

d.  causes fluctuating sales revenue.

e.  results in stable selling expenses during periods of declining sales.

_c_  20. When attempting to determine the size of a territory, the sales manager usually attempts to

a.  create territories that have relatively dissimilar sales potentials but require about the same amount of work.

b.  form territories that are as nearly equal in size as possible.

c.  create territories that have relatively similar sales potentials or territories that require about the same amount of work.

d.  establish territories mainly on the basis of sales potential.

e.  create territories that facilitate the effective distribution and servicing of the product first, and the benefits to the salesperson second.

_d_  21. One major goal of the planner when routing and scheduling a salesperson is to

a.  construct the routes and schedules in such a way that sales potential can be measured easily.

b.  employ symmetrical patterns to maximize the effectiveness of the salesperson.

c.  allow for flexibility in the routes and schedules so that the salesperson can handle special accounts properly.

d.  minimize the salesperson's nonselling time.

e.  minimize selling costs.

_d_  22. An activity and/or material that acts as an inducement, offering added value or incentive for the product, to resellers, salespersons, or consumers is known as

a.  publicity.

b.  advertising.

c.  personal selling.

d.  sales promotion.

e.  personal communication.

_a_  23. The dimensions used to measure a salesperson's performance are determined largely by the

a.  sales objectives

b.  projected sales volume.

c.  desired profit margin.

d.  profit impact point.

e.  the total number of sales calls made.

_e_  24. An example of a sales promotion technique for a new product is

a.  retail coupons.

b.  demonstrations.

c.  premiums.

    d. consumer contests.

    e. free samples.

*b*   25. Sales contests are examples of a sales promotion method aimed at

    a. sales of new products.

    b. resellers.

    c. retail establishments.

    d. sales of established products.

    e. consumers.

# Programmed Completion Exercises

informing, persuading

1. Personal selling is a process of _____ and _____ customers to purchase products through personal communication in an exchange situation.

prospecting, first element

2. Developing a list of potential customers is called _____ and is the _____ _____ in the selling process.

Closing, prospect

3. _____ is the stage in the selling process in which the salesperson asks the _____ to buy the product or products.

order getters, order takers, support

4. Based on the functions they perform, salespersons can be classified into three groups: _____ _____, _____ _____, and _____ salespersons.

creative selling, information

5. The task of obtaining orders is sometimes called _____ _____ because it requires the salesperson to recognize the potential buyers' needs and then to provide them with the necessary _____.

missionary, trade, technical

6. Although there are many kinds of sales support personnel, three common types of support salespeople are _____, _____, and _____ salespersons.

current customers, technical

7. The technical salespeople direct their efforts toward the organization's _____ _____ by providing _____ assistance.

customer,
product,
marketing
channel

8. The types of sales force employed is influenced by the kind of _____ , _____ , and _____ _____ the firm is dealing with.

adjusted,
variations,
markets,
environment

9. The size of the sales force must be _____ from time to time because of _____ in the firm's marketing plans and because of changes in _____ and forces in the marketing _____ .

sales calls,
travel times

10. A salesperson's workload is not just a function of the number of _____ _____ but also is dependent on _____ _____ between customers and the amount of time spent with each account.

management,
success, sales
revenue

11. Effective _____ of the sales force is an important determinant of a firm's _____ because the sales force is directly responsible for generating an organization's primary inputs, namely _____ _____ .

precise,
measurable,
geographic

12. Sales objectives should be stated in _____ , _____ terms and should be specific regarding the time period and _____ areas involved.

volume, market
share, profit

13. Objectives for the entire sales force should be stated in terms of _____ , _____ _____ , or _____ .

recruits,
qualifications

14. To ensure that the recruiting process produces a usable list of _____ , the sales manager should establish a set of _____ that are required to make a good salesperson for the company.

continuous
activity

15. Recruitment should not be sporadic but should be a _____ _____ aimed at reaching the best applicants.

needs,
characteristics,
tasks

16. The selection process should be a systematic procedure that effectively matches applicants' _____ and _____ with the requirements of specific selling _____ .

comprehensive,
refresher,

17. Ordinarily, new sales personnel require _____ training, whereas experienced personnel need _____ courses re-

products

garding established _____ and education about new products.

field, educational institutions, facilities, combination

18. Sales training may be performed in the _____ at _____ _____, in company _____, or in a _____ of these locations.

formulate, administer, attracts, motivates, holds

19. To develop and maintain a highly productive sales force, a business organization must _____ and _____ a compensation plan that _____, _____, and _____ the right types of salespersons for that firm.

sales management, control, freedom, income, incentive

20. A compensation plan should be designed to give _____ _____ the desired level of _____ and to provide sales personnel with an acceptable level of _____, _____, and _____.

selling expenses, fringe benefits

21. Sales compensation programs normally reimburse salespersons for their _____ _____, provide a certain number of _____ _____, and deliver the necessary compensation level.

motivating, motivational, nonfinancial, financial

22. Although financial compensation plays an important role in _____ a salesperson, a _____ program must satisfy the salesperson's _____ needs as well as _____ ones.

size, shape, routing, scheduling

23. When creating sales territories, sales managers make decisions having to do with _____, _____, _____, and _____.

reports, customer feedback, invoices

24. To control and evaluate sales force activities properly, sales management needs information. The sales manager obtains information about salespersons through salespersons' _____, _____ _____, and _____.

criteria, sales objectives

25. The _____ used to measure a salesperson's performance are determined largely by the _____ _____ that the sales manager sets for the salesperson.

generate,
acquires,
resources

26. Effective management of sales activities is critical to an organization because these activities help to _____ dollars, through which the firm _____ its _____.

activity,
material,
inducement,
added value,
incentive,
consumers

27. Sales promotion is an _____ and/or _____ that acts as a direct _____, offering _____ _____ or _____ for the product, to resellers, salespersons, or _____.

supplementary,
advertising,
personal selling

28. Sales promotion efforts do not always play a _____ role; a company sometimes employs _____ and _____ _____ to support sales promotion activities.

attract, new
products

29. Consumer sales promotion techniques can be employed to _____ new customers, to introduce _____ _____, or to promote established products.

trade, money,
merchandise,
gifts

30. Most _____ sales promotion techniques provide incentives to purchase or to perform certain activities based on _____, _____, _____, or promotional assistance.

# Answers to Objective Questions

*True or False*

| | | | |
|---|---|---|---|
| 1. T | 14. T |
| 2. F | 15. F |
| 3. T | 16. T |
| 4. T | 17. T |
| 5. T | 18. F |
| 6. T | 19. T |
| 7. T | 20. F |
| 8. F | 21. F |
| 9. T | 22. T |
| 10. T | 23. T |
| 11. F | 24. T |
| 12. T | 25. F |
| 13. F | |

*Multiple-Choice*

| | | | |
|---|---|---|---|
| 1. a | 14. d |
| 2. b | 15. c |
| 3. d | 16. b |
| 4. d | 17. e |
| 5. c | 18. b |
| 6. a | 19. b |
| 7. e | 20. c |
| 8. d | 21. d |
| 9. a | 22. d |
| 10. a | 23. a |
| 11. c | 24. e |
| 12. c | 25. b |
| 13. b | |

# CHAPTER 16

# Political, Legal, and Regulatory Forces

## Chapter Summary

Political, legal, and regulatory forces influence many aspects of marketing, including product development, branding, packaging, pricing, transporting, storing, wholesaling, retailing, personal selling, advertising, and sales promotion. For purposes of analysis, laws that directly affect marketing practices can be divided into two categories: procompetitive legislation and consumer protection laws. The procompetitive laws were enacted to preserve competition. They include the Sherman Act, the Clayton Act, the Federal Trade Commission Act, the Robinson-Patman Act, and state pricing laws. Consumer protection legislation deals with product safety, product standards, and disclosure of information. Examples are the Pure Food and Drug Act, the Flammable Fabrics Act, and the Cigarette Labeling Act.

Although the provisions of laws provide the legal framework that has the potential to influence many marketing activities, it is the actual interpretations of these provisions by marketers, courts, and regulatory bodies that determine their influence. The interpretations of laws vary over time as the make-up of the courts and regulatory agencies changes. As a result, marketers often require legal assistance to advise them regarding the legality or illegality of certain practices.

Regulatory forces may be governmental or nongovernmental. The goals of most federal regulatory units are to be objective, to maintain a pattern of enforcement, and to be flexible enough to attain the fair enforcement of laws and guidelines.

Although regulatory agencies often are characterized as being independent, in reality they are not. The president of the United States may appoint the commissioners of these regulatory groups and each president can affect the leadership of the agencies to some extent. Moreover, because regulatory commissions are created by Congress, the legislature affects the scope of their regulatory powers. Regulation also is influenced by public opinion.

The Federal Trade Commission (FTC) has, relative to other regulatory agencies, the broadest powers to influence marketing activities. The FTC has no direct power or authority to imprison or fine. However, it can seek civil penalties in the courts for violation of its "cease and desist" orders. Other federal regulatory bodies are the Interstate Commerce Commission, Federal Communications Commission, Environmental Protection Agency, Product Safety Commission, the Food and Drug Administration, the Office of Consumer Affairs, and the Civil Aeronautics Board. In addition to the federal agencies, there are many state and local agencies that regulate such industries as banking, savings and loans, insurance, electricity, natural gas, and liquor. Some state and local agencies also focus on consumers' interests.

In the absence of governmental regulatory forces, some businesses try to regulate themselves, often through trade associations, and often as an indirect result of legal action or proposed legislation. Enforcement of policies and guidelines is the biggest problem facing these self-regulatory units. Group pressure is hard to apply, given that the boycott is considered illegal under the antitrust statutes. The Better Business Bureau and the National Advertising Review Board are examples of two successful self-regulatory bodies.

Legal and regulatory forces influence marketing mix decisions. Product decisions are regulated by numerous laws and regulations. The decision to add products to the firm's product mix by merging is influenced by the provisions in the Sherman Act and the Celler-Kefauver Act. Development of products within the firm is influenced by the patent laws, product safety laws, and regulations of the FDA. Packaging and labeling decisions are affected by the Fair Packaging and Labeling Act. Pricing decisions are influenced by many of the procompetitive laws. The Sherman Act prohibits price fixing; the Federal Trade Commission Act and the Wheeler-Lea Act prohibit deceptive pricing; and the Robinson-Patman Act and the Clayton Act restrict the use of price differences. Distribution decisions are regulated by the Sherman Act. Exclusive dealing contracts and tying contracts are restricted by the Clayton Act. Promotional decisions are constrained by the FTC Act, the Wheeler-Lea Act, and by various governmental agencies.

Generally, marketers try to cope with legal forces either by complying with the demands of legal forces or by trying to influence the creation or change of legal forces. Often, compliance with the laws and regulatory guidelines is difficult because the laws and guidelines are so numerous and vague.

# True or False Statements

T Ⓕ 1. Governmental intervention in our economic system has decreased in recent years.

T Ⓕ 2. When political officials have positive feelings toward particular firms or industries, they are more likely to create and enforce laws that are unfavorable to business organizations.

Ⓣ F 3. Many marketers view political forces as being beyond their control; therefore, they try to adjust to conditions that result from these forces.

Ⓣ F 4. Political forces strongly influence the strength and effectiveness of legal forces.

T Ⓕ 5. The Sherman Act may be categorized as a pricing law.

T Ⓕ 6. The Sherman Act does not apply to U.S. firms operating in foreign commerce.

Ⓣ F 7. The Clayton Act prohibits price discrimination, tying agreements, and interlocking directorates.

T Ⓕ 8. The Federal Trade Commission Act of 1914 specifically prohibits false advertising of foods, drugs, therapeutic devices, and cosmetics.

Ⓣ F 9. Farm cooperatives and labor organizations are exempt from antitrust laws.

Ⓣ F 10. The Robinson-Patman Act originated to control suppliers who were providing chain stores with lower prices than independent stores.

Ⓣ F 11. Consumer protection laws were enacted in part to improve inadequate product standards.

Ⓣ F 12. Unfair trade practices acts are state laws that prohibit wholesalers and retailers from selling below cost or below their cost plus a certain percentage of markup.

Ⓣ F 13. Increased interest in consumer protection has occurred because consumers do not have the time to evaluate all the products they purchase.

T Ⓕ 14. The Wheeler-Lea, Celler-Kefauver, and Consumer Goods Pricing Acts all deal with providing product safety.

T Ⓕ 15. The degree to which business persons understand consumer laws has no influence on the effectiveness of these laws.

T Ⓕ 16. Marketers often make conservative interpretations of laws because the laws are vague and their provisions are always changing.

T Ⓕ 17. All regulatory forces are government sponsored.

T    F    18. The goal of most federal regulatory units is to enforce the laws and guidelines to the letter in order to establish a precedent for business persons to follow in their business activities.

T    F    19. Although regulatory agencies often are characterized as being independent, they are not in reality.

T    F    20. Regulation of business may result in increased prices to consumers and decreased competition.

T    F    21. Although the FTC has no direct power or authority to imprison or fine, it can seek civil penalties up to $10,000 a day for each violation if a cease and desist order is violated.

T    F    22. The Consumer Product Safety Commission can order a firm to make its products conform with established safety standards.

T    F    23. The powers of regulatory units, other than the FTC, generally are limited to specific products, services, and business activities.

T    F    24. Regulatory agencies at the state and local levels enforce specific laws dealing with the production and/or sale of particular goods and services.

T    F    25. Local consumer protection agencies cannot respond as quickly or effectively as federal agencies.

T    F    26. If a firm is planning to add a new product to its product line, the firm must consider whether the new product will violate the patent rights of other firms.

T    F    27. A good way for a firm to expand its product mix is through mergers because there are few regulations regarding the merger of firms.

T    F    28. Marketers may employ price differentials when they do not injure or lessen competition.

T    F    29. Package size is not regulated by law.

T    F    30. An exclusive dealing contract occurs when a reseller agrees to buy all of a specific product from one supplier, thus relinquishing the right to buy from the supplier's competitors.

T    F    31. Any channel structure that tends to restrain trade may be ruled as violating the Sherman Act.

T    F    32. Bait pricing is prohibited by the FTC.

T    F    33. Firms' compliance with consumer laws is aided by the vagueness of the laws.

T    F    34. Court interpretations of laws change over the years, thus making it difficult for marketers to comply with laws.

T    F    35. One reason why marketers at times break consumer laws is that they are not aware of them.

T    F    36. Firms can influence legislation affecting marketing practices by attempting to cooperate with government agencies.

# Multiple-Choice Questions

__C__   1. How do procompetitive laws attempt to ensure free enterprise?
   a. They ensure that consumers can buy quality merchandise.
   b. They regulate the number of firms that compete in a product area.
   c. They attempt to ensure that competition between firms is on an equal basis.
   d. They define competition in clear terms.
   e. They define free enterprise in terms of specific kinds of interaction between firms.

__b__   2. The Sherman Act was created primarily to
   a. establish a means of controlling unfair advertising activities.
   b. prevent businesses from restraining trade and monopolizing markets.
   c. stop the price fixing that was a common tactic of big business at the time.
   d. amend and strengthen the Federal Trade Commission Act.
   e. amend and strengthen the Robinson-Patman Act.

__e__   3. The Clayton Act prohibits all of the following *except*
   a. price discrimination.
   b. tying agreements.
   c. interlocking directorates.
   d. buying stock in another corporation so as to lessen competition or create a monopoly.
   e. actions by labor organizations in restraint of trade.

__a__   4. The Clayton Act
   a. supplements the Sherman Act and prohibits price discrimination, tying contracts, and exclusive agreements.
   b. amends the Robinson-Patman Act and prohibits price discrimination among different purchasers of commodities of like grade and quality when the effect substantially lessens competition.
   c. exempts vertical price fixing from antitrust laws.
   d. supplements the Federal Trade Commission Act and prohibits unfair and deceptive practices regardless of their effects on competition and places advertising of food and drugs under jurisdiction of the FTC.
   e. deals mainly with consumer protection.

__e__   5. The Robinson-Patman Act
   a. prohibits any corporation engaged in commerce from acquiring all or any part of the stock or other share of the capital assets of another corporation when the effect substantially lessens competition or tends to create a monopoly.

b. extends the Miller-Tydings Act to allow the nonsigner's clause to be enforceable in interstate commerce among states that have nonsigner's clauses in their fair trade laws.

c. prohibits contracts, combinations, or conspiracies to restrain trade and designates monopolizing or attempts to monopolize as a misdemeanor.

d. created the Federal Trade Commission, giving it investigatory powers to be used in preventing unfair methods of competition.

e. prohibits price discrimination that lessens competition among wholesalers or retailers and prohibits producers from giving disproportionate services or facilities to large buyers.

___e___  6. Unfair trade practices acts
a. were first enacted in Oregon in 1931.
b. set specific minimum prices.
c. originally applied to intrastate and interstate commerce.
d. were made enforceable in interstate commerce in 1937 with the passage of the Wheeler-Lea Act.
e. currently are not strongly enforced in most states.

___b___  7. Which of the following statements concerning resale price maintenance laws is *false*?
a. They are sometimes called "fair trade laws."
b. They permit retailers to set resale prices of products.
c. They permit manufacturers to set resale prices at which dealers are supposed to sell a firm's products.
d. They are prohibited in interstate commerce.
e. Most resale price maintenance agreements violate the Sherman Act.

___e___  8. Which of the following statements concerning consumer protection legislation is *false*?
a. A number of these laws are aimed at providing consumer safety.
b. The effectiveness of these laws is difficult to determine.
c. Congress has passed several consumer protection laws aimed at disclosing information.
d. The effectiveness of consumer laws is influenced by the strength of their enforcement.
e. Cost is not a significant factor in evaluating the effectiveness of consumer protection laws.

___d___  9. Which of the following is the most correct statement concerning consumer protection legislation?
a. Consumer protection laws have been very effective because of the harsh penalties imposed for failure to comply with provisions.

    b. Under the Consumer Product Safety Act manufacturers are accountable for all "reasonable" safety criteria applicable to their products.

    c. When a manufacturer of a defective product determines that it is defective, the firm must make all "reasonable" attempts to notify the U.S. Justice Department.

    d. Consumer protection laws consist, for the most part, of watered-down statutes that are dependent on the strength of enforcement and court interpretation for their effectiveness.

    e. Consumer protection laws have been in existence only since the 1930s.

*e*   10. Which of the following statements is *false*?

    a. Generally, marketers try to cope with political and legal forces either by complying with their demands or by trying to influence their creation or change.

    b. A few marketers sometimes deal with legal pressures by violating laws and regulatory rules.

    c. It is difficult to comply with all the laws and regulatory guidelines simply because there are so many of them.

    d. Legal compliance is complicated by the vagueness of laws and regulatory guidelines.

    e. Marketers may not know how to comply because the laws change over the years but the interpretations of legal provisions do not change.

*a*   11. Federal regulatory units

    a. when created are usually given power to enforce specific laws.

    b. usually are given little discretion in establishing their own operating rules and in creating regulations to guide certain types of industry practices.

    c. are characterized as being controlled by, but in reality are independent of, the president and Congress.

    d. seldom overlap jurisdictions with regard to specific types of marketing activities.

    e. are little influenced by public opinion.

*a*   12. The Federal Trade Commission

    a. consists of five commissioners, each appointed for a term of seven years by the president with consent of the U.S. Senate.

    b. is set up so that no more than three of the commissioners may be from the same state.

    c. consists of commissioners who are appointed every four years; the commission head, however, is appointed in staggered terms to ensure continuity in the judgment of cases.

    d. was established under the Sherman Act to help strengthen that law.

e. does not vary in its decisions over the years because the laws that give it its powers do not vary, and because of the continuity of experience that staggered terms give.

__c__    13. The Federal Trade Commission
   a. by considering each case on its own merits, establishes guidelines for specific firms.
   b. is intended to be a law-making agency rather than a law enforcement agency, and as such, has little power to enforce its decisions.
   c. has a major goal of providing assistance and information so that business people know how to comply with laws.
   d. seldom tries to explain to business what is considered unfair, deceptive, or illegal but, instead, lets courts determine this.
   e. has the direct power and authority to imprison and can fine up to $10,000 a day for violation of its cease and desist orders.

__d__    14. Which of the following is *not* a federal regulatory force?
   a. The Federal Trade Commission
   b. The Civil Aeronautics Board
   c. The Office of Consumer Affairs
   d. The National Consumer Products Office
   e. The Environmental Protection Agency

__a__    15. The major purpose of the Office of Consumer Affairs is to
   a. handle consumers' complaints and conduct investigations, conferences, and surveys on the problems of consumers, with special emphasis on those with limited incomes—the elderly, the disadvantaged, and other members of minority groups.
   b. review consumer-related programs of the Department of Health, Education and Welfare in terms of their availability and responsiveness to the current needs of consumers.
   c. protect the public against unreasonable risk of injury from any consumer product not covered by other regulatory agencies.
   d. protect consumers by enforcing laws and regulations to prevent distribution of adulterated or misbranded foods, drugs, medical devices, cosmetics, veterinary products, and particularly hazardous consumer products.
   e. enforce laws and guidelines regarding unfair business practices and to take action to stop false and deceptive advertising and labeling.

__a__    16. State regulatory agencies
   a. usually regulate such industries as banking, savings and loans, insurance, electricity, natural gas, and alcohol.
   b. usually act in a consulting role and leave enforcement of specific laws to national regulatory agencies and the governor.

     c. often establish regulations that conflict with the actions of regulatory agencies at the national level since many state governments feel that their authority is being usurped by the federal government.

     d. have no advantages in relation to the national government with regard to consumer protection, leaving this area to the federal government for enforcement.

     e. usually are located in the office of the secretary of state.

*a*    17. Which of the following does *not* describe an advantage of self-regulatory programs?

     a. Many self-regulatory programs do not have the tools or authority to enforce guidelines.

     b. Self-regulatory guidelines are more realistic and operational.

     c. Self-regulatory programs are usually less expensive to establish and implement.

     d. When industries develop self-regulatory programs, the need to expand government bureaucracy is reduced.

*b*    18. The main task of the National Advertising Review Board is to

     a. handle the advertising campaign of the Better Business Bureaus.

     b. screen national advertisements, check for honesty, and process complaints about deceptive advertisements.

     c. replace deceptive advertisements with more informative and honest advertisements.

     d. fine firms that use deceptive advertising.

     e. enforce regulations regarding deceptive trademarks.

*c*    19. Under the patent law, a patent can be in force for

     a. 15 years.

     b. the length of the product life (if less than 20 years).

     c. 3½, 7, and 14 years.

     d. 5 years.

     e. 5, 10, and 15 years.

*e*    20. Which of the following is *not* a criterion by which the National Advertising Review Board evaluates advertisements?

     a. Does it mislead the average consumer?

     b. Does it misuse research data?

     c. Does the advertisement unfairly disparage a competitor's brand?

     d. Is it clear whether the content is a testimonial or a presentation?

     e. Does the advertised product cost too much?

*b*    21. Which of the following types of information is *not* required by the Fair Packaging and Labeling Act?

     a. Number and size of servings, if applicable

     b. Price per unit

    c. Type of product

    d. Name and location of the producer or processor

    e. Net quantity printed on the major display panel in easily readable type

**c** 22. Conspiracies to control prices are prohibited by the

    a. FTC.

    b. NARB.

    c. Sherman Act.

    d. Wheeler-Lea Act.

    e. McGuire Act.

**b** 23. Price differences are ruled as discriminatory and are prohibited if they

    a. increase competition.

    b. lessen competition.

    c. exist because of differences in the costs of selling to various customers.

    d. are charged to customers who are not competitors.

    e. arise because the firm has to cut its price to a particular buyer to meet competitors' prices.

**b** 24. Any channel structure that tends to restrain trade may be ruled as violating the

    a. McGuire Act.

    b. Sherman Act.

    c. Miller-Tydings Act.

    d. Robinson-Patman Act.

    e. Wheeler-Lea Act.

**d** 25. Bait pricing involves

    a. prices that are not lower than regular prices.

    b. free merchandise.

    c. prices that are identical to wholesale prices.

    d. products that are advertised at low prices but can never be found when consumers desire to purchase them.

    e. half-price sales.

**b** 26. Which of the following was *not* given as a reason for why marketers violate laws and guidelines?

    a. Violations occur when the legal forces are so strong that a business firm cannot survive if it operates within the law.

    b. Marketers sometimes intentionally violate laws and guidelines because of the vagueness of some of the provisions.

    c. Marketers break laws to make large profits in the short run because fines are often less than the excess profits made by violating the laws.

d. Marketers sometimes break laws that affect their businesses because they believe enforcement is so inadequate that their chances of being caught are minimal.

e. Marketers break laws and guidelines simply because they are unaware of these laws or rules.

# Programmed Completion Exercises

enactment, interpretation, regulatory agencies

1. Political and legal forces are closely interrelated aspects of the marketing environment because the _____ and _____ of laws and the creation and effectiveness of _____ _____ are determined mainly by persons who occupy government positions.

political forces, influence, political element

2. Many marketers view _____ _____ as being beyond their control, and therefore they try to adjust to conditions that result from these forces. However, some firms attempt to _____ the _____ _____ by helping to elect certain individuals to political offices.

Political, legal forces

3. _____ forces are important to marketers because they strongly influence the strength and effectiveness of _____ _____ .

pricing, advertising, personal selling, distribution, product development, product warranty

4. Legal provisions affect many marketing practices, including _____ , _____ , _____ _____ , _____ , _____ _____ , and _____ _____ and repair policies.

procompetitive, consumer protection laws

5. For purposes of analysis, laws that directly affect marketing practices may be categorized as _____ and _____ _____ .

Sherman Act, restraining trade, monopolizing markets

6. The first procompetitive law, the _____ _____ , was created in 1890 to prevent business from _____ _____ and _____ _____ .

interstate
commerce, U.S.
firms, foreign
commerce

7. The Sherman Act applies to firms operating in _____ _____ and to _____ _____ operating in _____ _____.

Sherman Act,
Clayton Act,
stock, farm
cooperatives,
labor
organizations

8. Partly because of weaknesses in the _____ _____ and partly because of weaknesses in its interpretation, the _____ _____ was passed in 1914. It prohibits price discrimination that is based on tying and exclusive agreements and the acquisition of another company's _____ when the effect may substantially lessen competition or tend to create a monopoly. In addition, interlocking directorates are deemed unlawful, but the act exempts _____ _____ and _____ _____ from antritrust laws.

Federal Trade
Commission
Act

9. The _____ _____ _____ _____ regulates the greatest number of marketing practices.

Wheeler-Lea
Act, deceptive,
false advertising

10. The Federal Trade Commission Act was amended by the _____ _____ _____, which also makes it unlawful to use _____ acts or practices; it specifically prohibits _____ _____ of foods, drugs, therapeutic devices, and cosmetics, and provides penalties for violations and procedures for enforcement.

price
discrimination

11. The Robinson-Patman Act prohibits _____ _____ among different purchasers of commodities of like grade and quality when it substantially lessens competition or creates a monopoly.

safety,
standards,
information
disclosure

12. Many laws and regulatory guidelines that concern marketers deal with product _____, product _____, and _____ _____.

vague,
counseling

13. Many laws and regulations that affect marketing are stated in rather _____ terms, often forcing marketers to resort to legal _____ rather than relying on their own interpretations.

governmental, nongovernmental

14. Regulatory forces may be either _____ or _____, and local, state, or national in character.

objective, enforcement, flexible

15. The goals of most federal regulatory units are to be _____, to maintain a pattern of _____, and to be _____ enough to attain the goals of laws and guidelines.

president

16. Although regulatory agencies often are characterized as being independent, in reality they are not, for several reasons. First, the _____ appoints the commissioners of these regulatory groups, and traditionally commissioners resign when a new president takes office.

Congress, Congress

17. Second, because regulatory commissioners submit legislative proposals to the _____ regarding potential new regulatory powers, _____ controls much of the regulatory power.

five, seven, president, the Senate

18. The Federal Trade Commission consists of _____ members, each appointed for a term of _____ years by the _____ with the advice and consent of _____ _____.

three

19. No more than _____ commissioners may be from the same political party.

assistance, information

20. One major goal of the FTC is to provide _____ and _____ so that businesses will know how to comply with laws.

FTC, complaint, cease and desist

21. The _____ issues a _____ when it has reason to believe that a law has been violated. The FTC can issue a _____ _____ _____ order to stop whatever caused the condition in the first place.

banking, savings and loans, insurance, electricity, natural gas, alcohol

22. Industries that are commonly regulated by state agencies include _____, _____ _____ _____, _____, _____, _____ _____, and _____.

trade
associations,
legal action,
proposed
legislation

23. Firms in a number of industries develop self-regulatory programs through _____ _____ or as an indirect result of _____ _____ or _____ _____ .

National
Advertising
Review Board

24. The _____ _____ _____ _____ screens advertisements to check for honesty and processes complaints about deceptive advertisements.

expensive,
realistic,
reduced

25. The advantages of self-regulatory programs over laws and guidelines are that they are less _____ , their programs are _____ and operational, and the need to expand government bureaucracy is _____ .

number and
size of servings
if applicable

26. The Fair Packaging and Labeling Act requires the following information : (a) type of product, (b) name and location of producer or processor, (c) net quantity printed on the major display panel in easily readable type, and (d) _____ _____ _____ _____ _____ _____ _____ _____ .

vagueness,
large number of
them, change
over the years

27. It is difficult to comply with all the laws and regulatory guidelines because of their _____ and the _____ _____ _____ _____ and because courts' interpretations _____ _____ _____ _____ .

# Answers to Objective Questions

*True or False*

| | | | |
|---|---|---|---|
| 1. | F | 19. | T |
| 2. | F | 20. | T |
| 3. | T | 21. | T |
| 4. | T | 22. | T |
| 5. | F | 23. | T |
| 6. | F | 24. | T |
| 7. | T | 25. | F |
| 8. | F | 26. | T |
| 9. | T | 27. | F |
| 10. | T | 28. | T |
| 11. | T | 29. | F |
| 12. | T | 30. | T |
| 13. | T | 31. | T |
| 14. | F | 32. | T |
| 15. | F | 33. | F |
| 16. | F | 34. | T |
| 17. | F | 35. | T |
| 18. | F | 36. | T |

*Multiple-Choice*

| | | | |
|---|---|---|---|
| 1. | c | 14. | d |
| 2. | b | 15. | a |
| 3. | e | 16. | a |
| 4. | a | 17. | a |
| 5. | e | 18. | b |
| 6. | e | 19. | c |
| 7. | b | 20. | e |
| 8. | e | 21. | b |
| 9. | d | 22. | c |
| 10. | e | 23. | b |
| 11. | a | 24. | b |
| 12. | a | 25. | d |
| 13. | c | 26. | b |

# CHAPTER 17

# Societal and Consumer Forces

## Chapter Summary

The consumer movement is part of the broad societal forces that marketers must deal with. Societal forces include the structure and dynamics of individuals and groups and their issues of concern. Both people and groups want high living standards and a satisfying quality of life. Business is expected to contribute to this. Since marketing activities are a vital part of the total business structure, marketers are responsible for providing what societal members want and minimizing what they do not want.

Various interest groups exert pressure on business, government, and public opinion in order to improve our quality of life. Such issues as racial injustice, human rights, and unethical marketing behavior have led to increased public concern about the role of marketing in society and have placed more pressure on marketers to act responsibly. More and more firms are recognizing that ethical issues and social responsibility must be grounded in the daily decisions of marketers rather than remain abstract ideals. Hence, in order to maintain ethical and socially responsible behavior firms must monitor changes and trends in society's values, even as they attempt to provide people with satisfying marketing mixes. Society does not want faulty or unsafe products, misleading product warranties, or deceptive packages. Marketers, in order to be socially responsible, must deal with three major problems. First, they must determine what society wants and then predict what the long-run effects of their decisions will be. Second, in trying to satisfy the desires of one group, marketers must realize that they may dissatisfy other groups. Third, they must realize that many of the demands of society have costs associated with them.

The consumer movement began in the 1800s. Industry began to grow, and along with this growth came abusive practices. In order to combat abuses, consumers united into consumer groups. The first national group, the Consumers' League, was organized in New York City in 1891. The consumer movement grew rapidly from the mid-1920s through the 1930s. During this period, product-testing organizations were created to provide product information to consumers. The consumer movement was relatively quiet from World War II until the 1960s, when a new surge of interest in consumer issues developed. The emphasis in the 1960s was on consumer rights, including the right of the consumer to safe products, the right to be informed, the right to choose from a variety of products and services at competitive prices, and the right of the consumer to be heard. The consumer movement today is a social movement by which people attempt to defend and exercise their rights as buyers.

Consumer issues fall into one of three general categories: product performance and safety, information disclosure, or environmental protection. The major components of the consumer movement are individual consumer advocates, consumer organizations, consumer laws, and consumer education. These four major forces have facilitated the growth of the consumer movement. Consumer advocates voluntarily take it upon themselves to pursue the rights of consumers. Consumer advocates tell people about fraudulent and deceptive business practices, organize strikes and boycotts, work with businesses to develop programs that benefit consumers, and work with lawmakers to enact consumer protection legislation. Some consumer organizations operate nationally, while others are active at state and local levels. They have contributed to the consumer movement by disseminating consumer information, by urging consumers to get involved, by advising and pressuring lawmakers to enact stronger consumer legislation, by encouraging compliance with and enforcement of existing consumer laws, and by sponsoring consumer education programs.

Consumer education programs contribute to the growth of the consumer movement by preparing consumers to make wiser purchasing decisions. Students in consumer education programs are educated to consider certain factors when buying specific products such as insurance, real estate, automobiles, appliances, furniture, clothes, and food. They learn important features of credit agreements, contracts, and warranties. They study certain consumer protection laws to gain benefits provided by these laws. They become aware of sources of consumer information to allow them to remain well informed in the future.

Marketers have responded in several ways to the many forces that make up the consumer movement. Some have responded with resistance. These marketers view the consumer movement as a definite threat to the free enterprise system. Other marketers are indifferent toward the consumer movement and tend to ignore it. An increasing number of marketers now are viewing the consumer movement as a healthy, positive development for the business community. Firms that are attempting to further consumers' interests are involved in activities such as (1) creating and using internal consumer affairs units and (2) adopting and following the guidelines of codes established by business and trade associations.

# True or False Statements

T   (F)    1. It is impossible to have both a high standard of living and a high quality of life.

T   (F)    2. Various interest groups exert little real pressure on business and government to improve the quality of life.

T   (F)    3. Unsafe products are the fault of consumers because if they did not purchase such products, businesses would not produce them.

(T)  F    4. Ethical issues and social responsibility must be grounded in the daily decisions of marketers rather than in abstract ideals.

(T)  F    5. Marketers have a responsibility to society to help provide what societal members want and to minimize what they do not want.

T   (F)    6. It is enough for marketers to react to things that are wrong; they need not take an aggressive stand to provide products in a responsible manner.

T   (F)    7. If a marketer is satisfying the desires of one or several societal groups, he or she need not be concerned with the problems of other societal groups because it is impossible to please everyone.

(T)  F    8. Determining exactly what society wants and does not want is a difficult task for marketers.

T   (F)    9. The consumer movement began in 1962, when President Kennedy enunciated the basic consumer rights.

(T)  F    10. Some writers in the early twentieth century contributed to the consumer movement by telling people about unsanitary conditions in the meat-packing industry.

T   (F)    11. The consumer movement declined in the 1920s and 1930s as a result of the Depression.

(T)  F    12. The Better Business Bureau is a business-sponsored organization.

(T)  F    13. Being socially responsible means providing a satisfying marketing mix that does not produce adverse effects.

(T)  F    14. The right to be informed refers to the use of false advertising.

T   (F)    15. Being socially responsible means providing society with what it wants, regardless of the cost.

(T)  F    16. Consumerism is involved with product performance and safety, information disclosure, and environmental protection.

(T)  F    17. Individual consumer advocates voluntarily take it upon themselves to pursue the rights of consumers.

T   (F)    18. The general objective of a consumer affairs unit is to improve product specifications.

T  (F)   19. Trade associations that have established codes of ethics also have powers to enforce the codes.

T  (F)   20. Consumer organizations are strictly voluntary groups of private citizens that are organized to promote consumers' interests.

(T)  F   21. Government consumer organizations are regulatory or advisory.

T  (F)   22. Most businesses believe that the present-day consumer movement is a fad.

(T)  F   23. A consumer appeals board is an owner-relations program designed to mediate unsolved customer complaints.

(T)  F   24. Consumer education is an important force in the consumer movement because it prepares consumers to make wiser purchasing decisions.

(T)  F   25. The attitude of businesses toward the consumer movement is increasingly becoming one of active acceptance.

(T)  F   26. The deterioration of the physical environment has contributed to the renewed interest in consumerism.

(T)  F   27. One way a business attempts to handle consumer concerns is by establishing an ethical code.

# Multiple-Choice Questions

___a___  1. One factor that contributes to the high quality of life is
   a. the amount of effort required to achieve a certain living standard.
   b. the unwillingness of marketers to provide products.
   c. political payoffs.
   d. pollution.
   e. legal restrictions on business operations.

___e___  2. All of the following activities have eroded public confidence in marketers *except*
   a. pay-offs.
   b. bribes.
   c. defective products.
   d. cover-ups.
   e. corrective advertising.

___c___  3. Society wants
   a. high living standards.
   b. a high quality of life.
   c. high living standards and a high quality of life.
   d. total utilization of technology.

__a__  4. Which of the following statements about business ethics and social responsibility is *false*?
   a. Ethical issues and social responsibilities by their very nature are abstract ideals.
   b. Firms must monitor changes in society's values in order to maintain ethical behavior.
   c. Marketers must develop control procedures to ensure that unethical employees do not damage the company's public image.
   d. Marketers must aggressively try to provide products in a socially responsible manner.

__e__  5. In order for marketers to be socially responsible they must do all of the following, *except*
   a. determine what product features consumers want.
   b. create clear warranty statements.
   c. establish an efficient distribution system.
   d. provide the product mixes consumers want.
   e. provide product mixes that satisfy all consumer groups.

__c__  6. In order for marketers to be socially responsible, they first must determine what society wants and then
   a. determine what society does not want.
   b. develop products that society wants.
   c. consider what the long-range effects of their decisions will be.
   d. develop products at prices consumers can afford.
   e. develop safe products.

__e__  7. The consumer movement began
   a. in 1962, when President Kennedy stated that consumers have four basic rights.
   b. in 1906, when President Roosevelt influenced the enactment of the Pure Food and Drug Act.
   c. when Ralph Nader battled with General Motors over the Corvair.
   d. after the civil rights movement in the early 1960s.
   e. in the 1800s.

__a__  8. Writers contributed to the consumer movement by
   a. writing about unsanitary conditions in the meat-packing industry.
   b. writing advertisements that would be beneficial to consumers.
   c. outlining the consumer movement, where it began, how it began, and the direction in which it was headed.
   d. writing biographies of well-known consumer advocates.
   e. helping to organize the first consumer league.

*d*        9.  Which of the following statements is most correct?
            a.  The consumer movement began in the eighteenth century as an outgrowth of the abuses resulting from the Industrial Revolution.
            b.  The first consumer league was organized in Boston, Massachusetts.
            c.  Consumer leagues first held meat boycotts and rent strikes to dramatize high prices.
            d.  The consumer movement is a social movement by which people attempt to defend and exercise their rights as buyers.
            e.  Consumer advocates are the major force in the consumer movement today.

*d*       10.  Before the 1960s the consumer movement experienced a period of rapid growth. This period occurred
            a.  from World War II until 1960.
            b.  during the late 1930s and early 1940s.
            c.  in the early 1800s.
            d.  from the mid-1920s to the early 1930s.
            e.  from the Civil War to the 1870s.

*e*       11.  Which of the following is *not* usually a concern of forces in the consumer movement?
            a.  False advertising
            b.  Product safety
            c.  Consumer education
            d.  Pollution
            e.  Equal protection

*c*       12.  Which basic right of consumers involves access to a variety of products and services at competitive prices?
            a.  The right to be heard
            b.  The right to fair prices
            c.  The right to choose
            d.  The right to be informed
            e.  The right to safety

*a*       13.  The consumer movement is concerned about product safety because
            a.  over twenty million people are injured annually as a result of unsafe products.
            b.  unsafe products cost more.
            c.  safe products are too expensive for the average consumer to buy.
            d.  people desire a high standard of living.

*d*       14.  All of the following are major components of the consumer movement *except*
            a.  consumer advocates.

b. consumer organizations.

c. consumer laws.

d. consumer appeals boards.

e. consumer education.

*C*     15. The four basic rights of consumers mentioned in the chapter are the right to be informed, the right to choose, the right to be heard, and

a. the right to fair prices.

b. the right to variety of merchandise.

c. the right to safety.

d. the right of equality.

e. the right of expression.

*a*     16. Consumer advocates

a. voluntarily take it upon themselves to pursue the rights of consumers.

b. usually are lawyers.

c. always work through a supportive consumer organization.

d. work against businesses and for consumers' benefit.

e. have had little influence in encouraging Congress to pass consumer-related laws.

*e*     17. Which of the following is *not* a function of consumer advocates?

a. Organizing consumers to participate in strikes

b. Telling people about fraudulent and deceptive practices

c. Working with business organizations to develop programs that benefit consumers

d. Pressuring lawmakers to enact consumer protection legislation

e. Acting as lawyers for consumers by bringing suits against companies that have produced defective or unsafe products

*e*     18. A consumer advocate who has become well known in recent years is

a. Jody Powell.

b. Betty Ford.

c. George Meany.

d. Bela Abzug.

e. Ralph Nader.

*e*     19. Nader's Raiders consist of

a. lawyers who represent consumers' interests at federal agency hearings.

b. consumers who voluntarily inform other consumers about consumer laws, consumer organizations, and consumer education programs.

c. the automobile workers who were united by Ralph Nader.

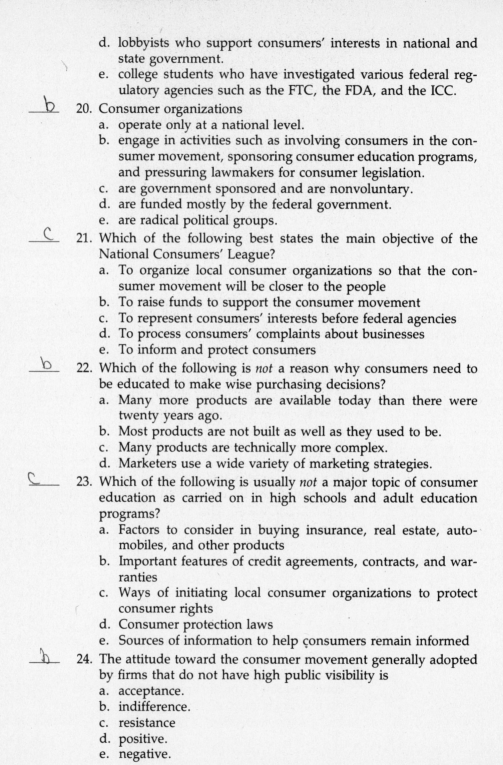

       d. lobbyists who support consumers' interests in national and state government.

       e. college students who have investigated various federal regulatory agencies such as the FTC, the FDA, and the ICC.

**b**    20. Consumer organizations

       a. operate only at a national level.

       b. engage in activities such as involving consumers in the consumer movement, sponsoring consumer education programs, and pressuring lawmakers for consumer legislation.

       c. are government sponsored and are nonvoluntary.

       d. are funded mostly by the federal government.

       e. are radical political groups.

**c**    21. Which of the following best states the main objective of the National Consumers' League?

       a. To organize local consumer organizations so that the consumer movement will be closer to the people

       b. To raise funds to support the consumer movement

       c. To represent consumers' interests before federal agencies

       d. To process consumers' complaints about businesses

       e. To inform and protect consumers

**b**    22. Which of the following is *not* a reason why consumers need to be educated to make wise purchasing decisions?

       a. Many more products are available today than there were twenty years ago.

       b. Most products are not built as well as they used to be.

       c. Many products are technically more complex.

       d. Marketers use a wide variety of marketing strategies.

**c**    23. Which of the following is usually *not* a major topic of consumer education as carried on in high schools and adult education programs?

       a. Factors to consider in buying insurance, real estate, automobiles, and other products

       b. Important features of credit agreements, contracts, and warranties

       c. Ways of initiating local consumer organizations to protect consumer rights

       d. Consumer protection laws

       e. Sources of information to help consumers remain informed

**b**    24. The attitude toward the consumer movement generally adopted by firms that do not have high public visibility is

       a. acceptance.

       b. indifference.

       c. resistance

       d. positive.

       e. negative.

_b_    25. Within the last few years an increasing number of marketers have viewed the consumer movement as
     a. an opposing force that is gradually trying to destroy business.
     b. a positive development for the business community.
     c. a movement that should be ignored.
     d. a definite threat to the free enterprise system.
     e. a threat to the profits of a firm.

_a_    26. Most consumer affairs units within firms
     a. disseminate information to consumers.
     b. act as buffers to present the firm in the best light when a dispute arises.
     c. are minor parts of the overall plan to promote customer satisfaction.
     d. are attempts by big firms to show the public that they are being listened to when, in actuality, they are not.
     e. are usually established to avoid legal action.

_c_    27. The consumer affairs department of a firm
     a. is concerned mainly with the advertising of a firm.
     b. is usually at the bottom of the organization.
     c. tries to improve communication with consumers.
     d. is viewed as unimportant to the firm.
     e. is usually found in the production department.

_d_    28. To improve the "quality of life" a product should *not*
     a. increase leisure time.
     b. help conserve natural resources.
     c. ensure clean air and water.
     d. endanger wildlife.
     e. be durable.

_c_    29. According to the authors' definition of the "quality of life," which of the following products represents an improvement in the quality of life?
     a. The supersonic jet
     b. Gasoline
     c. Solar cells
     d. Aerosol deodorants
     e. Cigarettes

# Programmed Completion Exercises

high living
standard, high
quality of life

1. Persons in our society want not only a _____ _____ _____ but also a _____ _____ _____ _____.

values,
responsibly,
ethically

2. The changing _____ of society have placed more pressure on marketers to act _____ and _____.

Ethical,
responsibility,
daily decisions,
ideals

3. _____ issues and social _____ must be grounded in the _____ _____ of marketers rather than in abstract _____.

react,
aggressive
stand,
responsible

4. Marketers cannot simply _____ to things that are wrong; they must take an _____ _____ to provide products in a socially _____ manner.

lawmakers,
consumer
groups, other
groups

5. Societal members express what they want and what they do not want through _____, _____ _____, and _____ _____.

desires, long-
run effects

6. To be socially responsible, marketers must determine the _____ of society and estimate the _____ _____ of their decisions on society.

in the 1800s

7. The consumer movement began _____ _____ _____.

consumer's
league

8. In New York City, the first _____ _____ was organized in 1891.

rights

9. In his message to Congress in 1962, President Kennedy stated that consumers have four basic _____.

safety

10. The right to _____ protects consumers against the marketing of goods that are hazardous to health or life.

safe, informed,
given a choice,
heard

11. The consumer movement today is a diverse, uncoordinated group of forces that attempts to protect the rights of consumers to be _____, _____, _____ _____ _____, and _____.

product safety,
information
disclosure,
environmental
protection

12. Although the consumer movement focuses upon numerous issues, these issues can be grouped into three areas: _____ _____, _____ _____, and _____ _____.

twenty million

13. Since over _____ _____ people of the United States are injured annually by faulty consumer products, consumers are concerned about improving products to make them safer.

individual
consumer
advocates,
consumer laws,
consumer
education,
consumer
organizations

14. The major forces of the consumer movement are _____ _____ _____, _____ _____, _____ _____, and _____ _____.

Individual
consumer
advocates

15. _____ _____ _____ voluntarily take it upon themselves to pursue the rights of consumers.

Ralph Nader

16. One of the best-known individual consumer advocates is _____ _____. He organized the Center for the Study of Responsive Law, and as a result of his efforts, Congress enacted several consumer-related laws.

voluntary

17. Consumer organizations are either _____ or government-sponsored organizations.

National
Consumers'
League,
Consumer
Federation of
America

18. The two national consumer organizations are the _____ _____ _____ and the _____ _____ _____ _____.

Government

19. _____ consumer organizations are generally regulatory or advisory agencies.

City, county

20. _____ and _____ consumer organizations often are concerned with stopping abuses by local businesses.

purchasing
decisions

21. Consumer education facilitates the consumer movement by preparing consumers to make wiser _____ _____.

consumer
protection laws

22. The four major topics of consumer education are (a) the factors to consider when buying products such as insurance, real estate, automobiles, appliances, furniture, clothes, and food; (b) the important features of credit agreements, contracts, and warranties; (c) sources of consumer information; and (d) _____ _____ _____ .

threat

23. In the early 1960s, some businesses viewed the consumer movement as a _____ to the free enterprise system.

public visibility

24. The attitude of indifference toward the consumer movement could work reasonably well for a firm that did not have high _____ _____ .

increasingly
large

25. An _____ _____ number of marketers view the consumer movement as a healthy, positive development for the business community.

business, trade
associations

26. Firms that are actively involved in furthering consumers' interests are creating and using internal consumer affairs units, and adopting and following the guidelines of consumer codes established by _____ and _____ _____ .

consumers,
responsive,
consumers'
complaints

27. The general objectives of the consumer affairs department are to improve communication with _____ and to make the firm more _____ to _____ _____ .

# Answers to Objective Questions

| *True or False* | | | *Multiple-Choice* | | | |
|---|---|---|---|---|---|---|
| 1. F | 15. F | | 1. a | 16. a | | |
| 2. F | 16. T | | 2. e | 17. e | | |
| 3. F | 17. T | | 3. c | 18. e | | |
| 4. T | 18. F | | 4. a | 19. e | | |
| 5. T | 19. F | | 5. e | 20. b | | |
| 6. F | 20. F | | 6. c | 21. c | | |
| 7. F | 21. T | | 7. e | 22. b | | |
| 8. T | 22. F | | 8. a | 23. c | | |
| 9. F | 23. T | | 9. d | 24. b | | |
| 10. T | 24. T | | 10. d | 25. b | | |
| 11. F | 25. T | | 11. e | 26. a | | |
| 12. T | 26. T | | 12. c | 27. c | | |
| 13. T | 27. T | | 13. a | 28. d | | |
| 14. T | | | 14. d | 29. c | | |
| | | | 15. c | | | |

# CHAPTER 18

# Economic and Technological Forces

## Chapter Summary

Economic and technological forces are strong pervasive forces that affect marketing decisions and activities. Economic forces can be broken down into competitive forces, buying power, spending patterns, willingness to spend, and general economic conditions.

A firm's competitors can be viewed as all firms or, more specifically, those firms in the same geographic area that are marketing products that are similar to or substitutable for its products. The strength of competition in a firm's environment is affected by two factors: the number and size of competitors and the tools of competition. The number of firms within an industry is affected by the ease with which one can start a business in that industry, and by the relationship between the quantity of a specific product wanted by consumers and the amount of this product that can be supplied by producers. A firm often uses competitive tools in order to compete with other firms. Price is one of the competitive tools used most often. Product offerings, distinctive product features, services, gifts, stamps, discounts, and advertising are all used as competitive tools by firms.

Consumer demand forces consist of consumers' buying power, consumers' willingness to purchase, and consumers' spending patterns. Buying power refers to an individual's resources, which give him or her the ability to purchase, qualified by the state of the economy. The three financial sources of buying power are income, credit, and wealth. An individual's income is the amount of money received through wages, rents, investments, pensions, and subsidy payments for a given period of time. This money is used for three purposes—paying taxes, spending, and saving. Disposable income is the portion of an individual's income that is left after taxes have been paid. Discretionary income is the income left after the basic necessities such as food, clothing, and shelter have been purchased. Consumer credit, a second component of buying power, allows individuals to spend future incomes now or in the near future. Consumers' use of credit is affected by the availability of credit, the size of interest charges, credit terms, the amount of future income already committed to past credit agreements, the size of the down payment, and the number of monthly payments. Wealth, the third component of buying power, is an individual's accumulation of past income, natural resources, financial resources, and other assets.

An individual's willingness to spend is related to his or her buying power. Several other factors also influence an individual's willingness to spend: the product's absolute price and its price relative to the price of substitute products; the amount of satisfaction currently received or expected in the future from a product; an individual's expectations about future employment, income levels, prices, family size, and general economic conditions.

Consumer spending patterns indicate the proportion of annual family expenditures or the actual amount of money that is spent on certain kinds of goods and services. There are two types of consumer spending patterns: comprehensive spending patterns and product-specific spending patterns. A comprehensive spending pattern shows the percentages of annual family expenditures that groups of families spend for general classes of goods and services. Product-specific spending patterns indicate the annual dollar amounts spent by families for specific products within a general product class.

The overall state of the economy in our country fluctuates. These fluctuations affect the forces of supply and demand, buying power, willingness to buy, consumer expenditure levels, and the intensity of competitive behavior. These fluctuations follow a pattern that is often called the "business cycle." The various stages of the business cycle include prosperity, recession, depression, and recovery. Inflation and shortages are other factors that may complicate the effects of the business cycle.

Technology is the knowledge of how to accomplish tasks and goals. The effects of technology can be good or bad, depending on how it is applied. Technology results from research performed by business organizations, university personnel, and nonprofit research groups. Technology affects marketing activities in many ways because it has a great impact on consumers and society in general, and also because technological changes directly affect what, how, when, and where products are marketed. Technology has improved our standard of living, but it also has had some undesirable effects, such as polluted air and water. Technology has affected the types of products offered for sale, the communication means by which marketers inform consumers about products, and the mobility of consumers. The use of technology is affected by a firm's ability to use it, by consumers' willingness to buy resulting products, by the potential effects of using it, by the degree to which a business organization is technologically based, and by the extent to which a firm can protect inventions.

# True or False Statements

T (F)    1. There is no relationship between technology and economic forces.

T (F)    2. Marketers can completely control the competitive forces in the environment.

(T) F    3. When supply exceeds demand for a particular product, firms that sell the product generally become more competitive.

T (F)    4. The most commonly used competitive tool is services.

(T) F    5. Income is an important financial source of buying power.

(T) F    6. Disposable income is income that is left after taxes have been paid.

T (F)    7. Discretionary income is equal to disposable income plus the amount paid in taxes.

(T) F    8. Consumer credit increases present buying power at the expense of future buying power.

T (F)    9. Wealth exists only in the form of cash.

(T) F    10. The buying power index is useful for determining buying trends in an area.

(T) F    11. A person's willingness to buy is related to ability to buy.

T (F)    12. A consumer's propensity to spend is not affected by general economic conditions.

(T) F    13. A consumer spending pattern indicates the proportion of annual family expenditures or the actual amount of money that is spent on certain kinds of goods and services.

T (F)    14. Because spending pattern data reflect specific trends, they are the only source of information marketers need for making specific decisions.

T (F)    15. Product-specific spending patterns indicate the percentages of family income allotted to annual expenditures for general classes of goods and services.

T (F)    16. Fluctuations in the economy follow a general two cycle pattern called a prosperity-recession cycle.

(T) F    17. During a recession marketers should consider revising marketing efforts.

(T) F    18. A tax reduction can increase buying power.

(T) F    19. Demarketing is an approach that uses marketing activities to reduce consumption in some markets.

T (F)    20. Demarketing is used during an inflationary period.

T (F)    21. Computers, automobiles, buildings, laser beams, and heart transplants are all considered to be technology.

T  (F)  22. Although technology is used to provide a high standard of living, its use always produces unfavorable effects that also reduce the quality of life for persons in our society.

T  (F)  23. Marketers are not concerned with the effects of technological knowledge on societal members.

(T)  F  24. Technology assessment includes the evaluation of the effects technology has upon society in the long run.

(T)  F  25. We have begun to realize in our society that our standard of living has negatively affected the quality of the environment.

T  (F)  26. Lower-priced products are always seen by the public as being inferior to higher-priced products.

(T)  F  27. Some companies are able to charge more for certain products than their competitors because they are able to provide excellent service and accessibility to parts.

(T)  F  28. The cost of living has doubled since 1967.

T  (F)  29. Citizens of the United States save a higher percentage of disposable income than any other citizenship in the world.

T  (F)  30. Stagflation can occur in any of these forms: inflation-shortage, inflation-recession, inflation-depression, inflation-recession-shortage.

(T)  F  31. Technological processes and materials can often make a product better and lower-priced, thus making it more desirable.

## Multiple-Choice Questions

_a_  1. One major factor that decreases the competition in a firm's environment is the presence of
   a. a small number of firms that control the product's supply.
   b. many large competitors.
   c. other firms that try to match the price.
   d. an easy access to the market.
   e. low demand combined with ample supply.

_d_  2. Competition is greater when
   a. there are few firms in the industry.
   b. demand is greater than supply.
   c. government intervenes.
   d. it is easy for firms to enter the market.

_a_    3. If demand for a particular product is high relative to quantity that can be supplied, then sellers of this product
    a. are not highly competitive.
    b. are competitive.
    c. become more competitive.
    d. can fully utilize the tools of competition.
    e. must consider all firms as competitors.

_c_    4. The most commonly used competitive tool is
    a. services.
    b. product differentiation.
    c. price.
    d. distinctive product features.
    e. personal selling.

_b_    5. One method being used by consumers to fight inflation is
    a. to seek tax loopholes.
    b. to purchase tangible assets, like new homes.
    c. to spend heavily on intangible assets, such as services.
    d. to put all of one's money into the bank.
    e. to travel abroad.

_b_    6. Which of the following is *not* a financial source of buying power for the consumer?
    a. Income
    b. Taxes
    c. Wealth
    d. Credit
    e. Real estate

_a_    7. The buying power index is a weighted index consisting of data on
    a. population, effective buying income, and retail sales.
    b. population, wealth, and consumer credit.
    c. retail sales, gross income, and population distribution.
    d. effective buying income, accumulated wealth, and gross sales.
    e. discretionary income, population distribution, and wealth.

_a_    8. For the purpose of computing buying power, marketers are most interested in
    a. income after taxes.
    b. level of savings.
    c. distribution of income.
    d. disposable credit.
    e. inherited wealth.

_b_    9. Credit allows individuals
    a. to spend present income and to save future income.
    b. to spend future income now or in the near future.

c. to increase future buying power.

d. to decrease present buying power.

e. to delay purchases of expensive and unnecessary items.

_d_ 10. The accumulation of past income, natural resources, and financial resources is

a. discretionary income.

b. credit.

c. disposable income.

d. wealth.

e. real estate.

_c_ 11. In using the buying power index,

a. the lower the index number, the greater the buying power.

b. the higher the index number, the less the buying power.

c. the higher the index number, the greater the buying power.

d. the index number is immaterial to buying power.

e. buying power is unmeasurable.

_a_ 12. Which factor most affects a consumer's propensity to spend?

a. Absolute price

b. Technology

c. Competition

d. Time of day

e. Age

_c_ 13. What kind of spending pattern shows the percentages of family income allotted to the annual expenditures for general classes of goods and services?

a. Product-specific

b. Complete

c. Comprehensive

d. Compound

e. Consumer-specific

_c_ 14. Of the following, which is a type of spending pattern?

a. Complete

b. Compound

c. Product-specific

d. Proportional

e. Classified

_e_ 15. Fluctuations in our economy follow a general pattern that is often called a

a. recession.

b. depression.

c. recovery.

d. family life cycle.

e. business cycle.

___d___  16. The stage of the business cycle in which unemployment is low, aggregate income is high, and buying power is high is the stage of
   a. recession.
   b. recovery.
   c. depression.
   d. prosperity.
   e. inflation.

___c___  17. During a recession, marketers should
   a. reduce their marketing efforts.
   b. stop developing new products.
   c. emphasize the value and utility of products in promotional efforts.
   d. reduce the sales force.
   e. cut out marketing research.

___c___  18. During inflation, consumer buying power
   a. increases if income is constant.
   b. remains constant if income remains the same.
   c. decreases if income remains constant.
   d. increases regardless of income.
   e. decreases if income increases.

___c___  19. Which factor increases consumers' willingness to spend?
   a. A high level of unemployment
   b. A recession economy
   c. Economic prosperity
   d. High interest rates
   e. Wage controls with no price controls

___d___  20. Demarketing, an approach that uses marketing activities to reduce consumption, is used during
   a. a recession.
   b. a depression.
   c. inflation.
   d. shortages.
   e. prosperity.

___e___  21. Technology is
   a. spacecrafts.
   b. computers.
   c. buildings.
   d. laser beams.
   e. know-how.

___b___  22. Which of the following funds over one-half of technological research?
   a. Private individuals
   b. State and federal governments

    c.  Nonprofit research groups
    d.  Universities
    e.  Business organizations

__b__   23. Technological developments
    a.  do not affect business.
    b.  have improved our standard of living.
    c.  have little impact on society.
    d.  seldom change marketing activities.

__e__   24. Business persons may adopt and use technology
    a.  when they want to.
    b.  when consumers want them to.
    c.  when consumers are willing to buy the products.
    d.  when they have the resources to do so.
    e.  when they have the resources to do so and the consumers
        are willing to buy the resulting products.

__d__   25. Technology assessment involves
    a.  analysis of costs to the firm.
    b.  analysis of sales volume.
    c.  analysis of profit probability.
    d.  analysis of effects on the firm, on other business, and on
        society.
    e.  analysis of the effect of demand on competition.


# Programmed Completion Exercises

competitors,
geographic area

1. A business generally views _____ as being those firms in
   the same _____ _____ that are marketing products
   which are similar to or substitutable for the firm's products.

weak

2. When only one or a small number of firms control the amount
   of the product that is available for sale, competition is usually
   _____ .

Buying power

3. _____ _____ refers to the size of the resources that
   give an individual the ability to purchase.

income, credit,
wealth

4. Financial sources of buying power include _____ ,
   _____ , and _____ .

| | |
|---|---|
| discretionary income | 5. Disposable income that is available for spending and saving after an individual has purchased the basic necessities is called _____ _____. |
| increases | 6. As current credit usage _____, current buying power increases. |
| Wealth | 7. _____ is an individual's accumulation of past income, natural resources, and financial resources. |
| willingness to buy | 8. An individual's _____ _____ _____ is somewhat related to his or her ability to buy, in that individuals are usually more willing to buy if they have buying power. |
| increases | 9. When prices are expected to increase in the near future, a person's willingness to buy generally _____. |
| comprehensive spending pattern | 10. A _____ _____ _____ shows the percentages of annual family income allotted to the annual expenditures for general classes of goods and services. |
| product-specific spending pattern | 11. A _____ _____ _____ indicates the annual dollar amounts spent by families for specific products within a general product class. |
| business cycle | 12. Fluctuations in our economy follow a general pattern that is often referred to as the _____ _____. |
| prosperity | 13. During _____, unemployment is low and aggregate income is relatively high, which causes buying power to be high. |
| recession | 14. Promotional efforts would emphasize value and utility during a _____. |
| Technology | 15. _____ is the knowledge of how to accomplish tasks and goals. |
| depression | 16. High unemployment, low wages, minimum disposable income, and consumers' lack of confidence in the economy are characteristic of a _____. |
| demarketing | 17. An approach that is used to reduce consumption through marketing activities is called _____. |

businesses,
universities,
nonprofit
research groups

18. Technology results from research performed by _____,
_____, and _____ _____ _____.

standard of
living

19. Technological developments have definitely improved our
_____ _____ _____.

favorable,
unfavorable

20. Application of technological knowledge has had both
_____ and _____ effects on society.

technology
assessment

21. In some firms today, marketing managers are trying to evaluate
the broader effects of technology by using _____
_____.

production
processes,
materials

22. Technological improvements in _____ _____ and
_____ sometimes allow firms to produce and sell products
that are more durable and lower priced.

capital, land,
labor, technical
skills,
managerial
know-how

23. A particular firm may not have resources such as
_____, _____, _____, _____
_____, or _____ _____ to apply new tech-
nology.

competitors

24. A firm may not apply new technology as long as its
_____ are not attempting to use it.

# Answers to Objective Questions

*True or False*

| | | | |
|---|---|---|---|
| 1. | F | 17. | T |
| 2. | F | 18. | T |
| 3. | T | 19. | T |
| 4. | F | 20. | F |
| 5. | T | 21. | F |
| 6. | T | 22. | F |
| 7. | F | 23. | F |
| 8. | T | 24. | T |
| 9. | F | 25. | T |
| 10. | T | 26. | F |
| 11. | T | 27. | T |
| 12. | F | 28. | T |
| 13. | T | 29. | F |
| 14. | F | 30. | F |
| 15. | F | 31. | T |
| 16. | F | | |

*Multiple-Choice*

| | | | |
|---|---|---|---|
| 1. | a | 14. | c |
| 2. | d | 15. | e |
| 3. | a | 16. | d |
| 4. | c | 17. | c |
| 5. | b | 18. | c |
| 6. | b | 19. | c |
| 7. | a | 20. | d |
| 8. | a | 21. | e |
| 9. | b | 22. | b |
| 10. | d | 23. | b |
| 11. | c | 24. | e |
| 12. | a | 25. | d |
| 13. | c | | |

## CHAPTER 19

# Developing and Controlling Marketing Strategy

## Chapter Summary

The development of a marketing strategy encompasses selecting and analyzing a target market and creating a marketing mix that satisfies people in the target market. A marketing strategy is developed through, and is the result of, strategic marketing planning. The process of strategic marketing planning is based on the establishment of an organization's overall goals, and it must be within the bounds of the organization's opportunities and resources. When the firm's overall goals have been determined and its resources are known, then marketing objectives can be developed. To achieve marketing objectives, an organization must develop a marketing strategy or a set of marketing strategies. A set of marketing strategies is referred to as the organization's marketing program. The strategic marketing planning process is surrounded by environmental forces and is very much affected by them. Environmental forces influence an organization's overall goals and have impact on the creation of a marketing strategy.

In creating a product, price structure, distribution system, and promotional efforts that will satisfy members of a target market, careful consideration must be given to the selection of the target market. The initial step in selecting a target market is to determine the type of market, whether it be a consumer, industrial, or reseller market. According to the marketing concept the final user is the major consideration in determining the type of product to be made.

In selecting a target market a firm can employ a total market approach or a market segmentation approach. When an organization views individual customers within a market as having similar needs for a certain type of product, then a total market approach may be used. A market segmentation approach is used when an organization assumes that submarkets exist with people within each segment sharing one or more similar characteristics. A concentrated segmentation strategy is used when one marketing mix is directed toward one segment. A multisegment strategy is used when several marketing mixes are aimed at several parts of a total market.

The analysis phase occurs both before and after a target market is selected. A marketer's analysis before choosing a target market is likely to be a broad-based investigation assessing the marketing opportunities that each potential target market can provide. After a target market has been selected, the marketer should be concerned with isolating and understanding the behavioral dimensions that influence target market members' purchase decisions and uses of the product.

In developing a marketing mix to satisfy target market members, marketers must make decisions about product, price, distribution, and promotion. The marketing mix should be focused on creating values for all social units involved in an exchange. The marketing mix variables provide four ways to create value. Designing or adjusting the product to create a valued configuration is important because the product is one of the most visible portions of the overall transaction an organization has with a final buyer. The steps involved in setting and adjusting prices also contribute to valuation. The manipulation of price permits a marketer to adjust the marketing strategy to current demand and supply situations, to emphasize quality, or to attain a desired profit level. Consumers manifest strong values about prices, and marketers must fit the price to consumers' expectations. Marketers facilitate exchanges by making products available where they are wanted. Distribution is one of the less flexible variables in the marketing mix; yet the basic method of distribution is very important in establishing the marketing strategy. Changing distribution in the marketing strategy results in commitments to the new distribution structure because most intermediaries do not want to invest resources in selling a product if the distribution task is temporary. Promotion is used for a variety of purposes, and its symbolization aspects contribute to increasing the value of an offering. Promotional techniques are a vital part of a marketing strategy, and decisions about promotional activities are recurrent.

To assess and improve the effectiveness of a marketing strategy, a marketer needs to control it. This requires the marketing manager to establish performance standards for the strategy, to evaluate actual performance, and then to take corrective action to reduce the differences between desired and actual performance. Sales analysis and cost analysis are two general ways of evaluating the actual performance of marketing strategies. With sales analysis, sales figures are used to evaluate a firm's current performance. To provide useful analyses, current sales data must be compared with forecasted sales, with industry sales, with specific competitors' sales, or with costs incurred to achieve the sales volume. Although sales may be measured in several ways, the fundamental unit of measurement is the sales transaction. A sales transaction involves a customer order for a specified quantity of an organization's product sold under specified terms by a particular salesperson on a certain date. A company can use these bits of information about their transactions to analyze sales in terms of dollar volume or market share. Dollar volume sales analysis is a frequently used form of sales analysis because the dollar is a common denominator for describing sales, costs, and profits. A firm's market share is the firm's sales of a product stated as a percent of the entire industry's sales of that product. Whether evaluation is based on sales volume or market share, sales analysis can be performed on aggregate sales figures or on disaggregated data. Aggregate sales analysis provides a marketer with an overview of current sales. Although helpful, aggregate sales analysis does not make the analyst aware of sales variations within the aggregate. To determine such variations, total sales figures usually are broken down by geographic units, salespersons, products, customer types, or a combination of these.

Sales analysis by itself is only a part of evaluating the effectiveness of a marketing strategy. A firm must also perform a cost analysis. With cost analysis, various costs are broken down and classified to determine which costs are associated with specific marketing activities. The first step in determining marketing costs is to examine accounting records. Marketing cost analysis, however, usually requires that some of the costs in natural accounts (rent, for example) be reclassified into marketing function accounts, such as storage, order processing, advertising, and marketing research.

There are three broad categories of marketing costs: direct costs, traceable common costs, and nontraceable common costs. Direct costs are directly attributable to the performance of marketing functions. Traceable common costs can be allocated indirectly to the functions they support. Nontraceable common costs are assignable only on an arbitrary basis. Thus, a cost analysis can include all three cost categories in the cost analysis (the full-cost approach), or it can include direct costs and traceable common costs but exclude nontraceable common costs (the direct-cost approach). Marketers can analyze costs in several ways. They can analyze natural accounts, they can analyze functional accounts, or—to be more precise—they can analyze functional accounts in terms of specific products, geographic areas, or customer groups.

A marketing audit is a systematic examination of the objectives, strategies, organization, and performance of a firm's marketing unit. The scope of a marketing audit may be specific and focus on one or a few marketing activities, or it may be comprehensive and encompass all marketing activities of a company. Like an accounting or financial audit, a marketing audit should be conducted periodically to get the most out of it. Several general guidelines should be considered when performing a marketing audit. Questionnaires should be developed carefully to ensure that the audit is directed at the right issues. To ensure that the audit is systematic, the auditors should develop and follow a step-by-step plan. Auditors should strive to talk to a diverse group of people from many parts of the company. The results of the audit should be set forth in a comprehensive written document. The marketing audit allows an organization to change tactics or to alter day-to-day activities. Several problems may develop, however, in an audit of marketing activities: marketing audits can be expensive in time and money; selecting qualified auditors may be difficult; and marketing audits can disrupt a company's activities.

# True or False Statements

T   F   1. A marketing mix is developed before target markets are selected.

T   F   2. To achieve marketing objectives, an organization must develop a marketing strategy.

T   F   3. The marketing program is a set of strategies that are implemented and used simultaneously.

T   F   4. The strategic marketing planning process is not very much affected by environmental forces.

T   F   5. A marketing strategy should be static so that goals can be implemented better.

T   F   6. A total market approach to selecting and analyzing target markets assumes submarkets exist.

T   F   7. A multisegment strategy is used when several marketing mixes are aimed at several parts of a total market.

T   F   8. The marketing mix should be focused on creating values for all social units involved in an exchange.

T   F   9. Promotion is the most convenient marketing mix variable to change.

T   F   10. The manipulation of price permits a marketer to adjust a marketing strategy to current demand and supply situations.

T   F   11. Distribution systems are restricted to physical goods.

T   F   12. Decisions on promotional activities are nonrecurrent once the marketing program is developed.

T   F   13. Knowing that a shoe store achieved a $750,000 sales volume this year is enough for a manager to determine whether the marketing strategy is effective.

T   F   14. If a firm increased its prices by 10 percent, and its sales volume is 12 percent greater than the previous year, it has experienced a real sales increase in terms of the number of units sold.

T   F   15. The primary reason for using market share analysis is to estimate whether sales changes resulted from the firm's marketing strategy or from uncontrollable environmental forces.

T   F   16. Aggregated sales data provide a marketer with a current overview of sales and give the analyst in-depth insight into sales variations within the aggregate.

T   F   17. If a firm finds that 10 percent of its sales is coming from an area that represents 17 percent of the potential sales for the product, then it can be assumed that the marketing strategy is successful in that geographic unit.

T  F  18. With marketing cost analysis various costs are broken down and classified to determine which costs are associated with specific marketing activities.

T  F  19. Traceable common costs are directly attributable to the performance of marketing functions.

T  F  20. A direct cost approach includes direct costs and traceable common costs, but it does not include nontraceable common costs.

T  F  21. The analysis of natural accounts provides the most precise method of analyzing costs.

T  F  22. A marketing audit is a systematic examination of the objectives, organization, strategy, and performance of a firm's marketing unit.

# Multiple-Choice Questions

_____  1. Organizational resources, overall organizational goals, marketing objectives, and environmental forces all are components of
a. the total marketing environment.
b. the target market.
c. strategic marketing planning.
d. the marketing mix.
e. consumer movement forces.

_____  2. The first step in selecting a target market provides a foundation on which a marketing mix is developed. This first step is
a. deciding who will buy the product.
b. segmenting the market.
c. formulating organizational objectives.
d. determining the type of market.
e. selecting an approach to the market.

_____  3. The central focus in developing a marketing strategy is on
a. the development of marketing objectives to evaluate the effectiveness of the marketing program.
b. developing tactics that will be used from day to day.
c. adjusting and improving performance in order to satisfy consumers' wants.
d. the selection of a target market and the development of a marketing mix.

_____  4. The marketing program is
a. concerned with the implementation of tactics.
b. a way of thinking about all of an organization's activities.

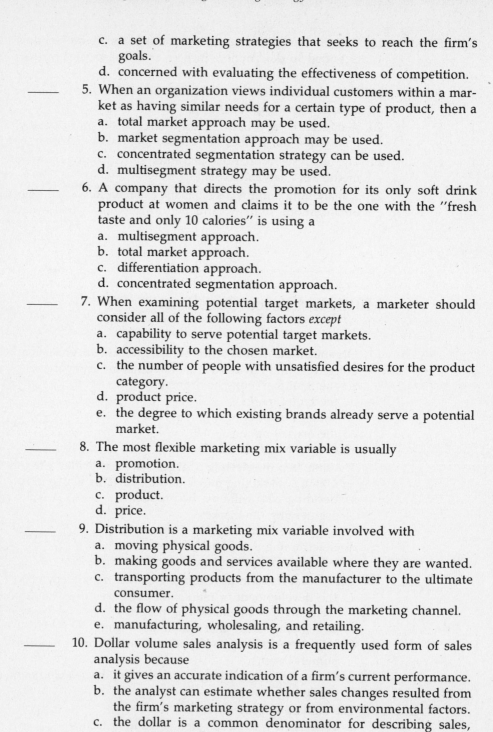

c. a set of marketing strategies that seeks to reach the firm's goals.

d. concerned with evaluating the effectiveness of competition.

5. When an organization views individual customers within a market as having similar needs for a certain type of product, then a
   a. total market approach may be used.
   b. market segmentation approach may be used.
   c. concentrated segmentation strategy can be used.
   d. multisegment strategy may be used.

6. A company that directs the promotion for its only soft drink product at women and claims it to be the one with the "fresh taste and only 10 calories" is using a
   a. multisegment approach.
   b. total market approach.
   c. differentiation approach.
   d. concentrated segmentation approach.

7. When examining potential target markets, a marketer should consider all of the following factors *except*
   a. capability to serve potential target markets.
   b. accessibility to the chosen market.
   c. the number of people with unsatisfied desires for the product category.
   d. product price.
   e. the degree to which existing brands already serve a potential market.

8. The most flexible marketing mix variable is usually
   a. promotion.
   b. distribution.
   c. product.
   d. price.

9. Distribution is a marketing mix variable involved with
   a. moving physical goods.
   b. making goods and services available where they are wanted.
   c. transporting products from the manufacturer to the ultimate consumer.
   d. the flow of physical goods through the marketing channel.
   e. manufacturing, wholesaling, and retailing.

10. Dollar volume sales analysis is a frequently used form of sales analysis because
    a. it gives an accurate indication of a firm's current performance.
    b. the analyst can estimate whether sales changes resulted from the firm's marketing strategy or from environmental factors.
    c. the dollar is a common denominator for describing sales, costs, and profits.

d. it is reliable and inexpensive.

e. inflationary price changes do not affect the analysis.

11. When a company's sales volume increases and its market share stays the same, the marketer can assume that

a. the firm's marketing strategy brought about the sales changes.

b. industry sales increased, and that this was reflected in the firm's sales.

c. the firm's marketing strategy has failed.

d. there has been no real change in dollar volume sales.

12. The *iceberg principle* refers to

a. finding that a large proportion of aggregate sales comes from a small number of products, geographic areas, or customers.

b. disaggregated sales data characteristics.

c. the hidden information that can be extracted from a sales transaction.

d. the inflationary costs hidden in dollar volume sales analysis.

13. When total sales figures are broken down by geographic units, salespersons, products, or customer types, the analyst is evaluating the marketing strategy using

a. segmented markets.

b. aggregated data.

c. the iceberg principle.

d. disaggregated data.

e. the market segmentation approach.

14. Marketing cost analysis usually requires that some of the costs in natural accounts be reclassified into marketing function accounts because

a. marketing function accounts are less complicated and less expensive to use.

b. natural accounts do not explain what functions were performed through the expenditure of funds.

c. natural accounts assign costs on an arbitrary basis.

d. marketing function accounts classify costs into general accounts such as rent, salaries, and utilities.

15. The cost category in which costs are allocated indirectly, using one or several criteria, to the functions they support is called

a. traceable common costs.

b. natural costs.

c. marketing function costs.

d. direct costs.

e. nontraceable common costs.

_____ 16. Changing distribution in the marketing strategy usually results in
   a. changing price.
   b. commitments to new distribution structures.
   c. shortening the channel.
   d. bypassing middlemen.

_____ 17. Which of the following statements about a marketing audit is *false*?
   a. A marketing audit is used to evaluate the effectiveness of an organization's marketing activities.
   b. The audit explores opportunities and alternatives for improving the marketing strategy.
   c. Marketing audits can disrupt a company's activities because employees sometimes fear comprehensive evaluations.
   d. The marketing audit is a control process usually useful only during a crisis.
   e. The audit allows an organization to change tactics or alter day-to-day activities as problems arise.

_____ 18. Which of the following is a specific test of measuring strategy performance?
   a. Dollar volume sales analysis
   b. Auditing
   c. Quality control
   d. Control checks

_____ 19. The discovery that persons who patronize banks do so for two reasons—convenience considerations and financial considerations—should result in what type of market approach?
   a. Total market
   b. Concentration
   c. Multisegment
   d. Single target

_____ 20. What is developed even before the marketing strategy is developed?
   a. The marketing mix
   b. The measurement of performance
   c. The marketing objective
   d. The marketing program

# Programmed Completion Exercises

overall goals,
opportunities,
resources

1. The strategic marketing planning process is based on the establishment of an organization's _____ _____ and on an assessment of the organization's _____ and _____.

type, consumer,
industrial,
reseller,
marketing mix

2. The first step in selecting a target market is to determine the _____ of market, whether it be a _____, _____, or _____ market. That decision provides a foundation on which a _____ _____ is developed.

total market
approach,
submarkets,
share, similar
characteristics

3. When an organization views individual customers within a market as having similar needs for a certain type of product, then a _____ _____ _____ may be used. A market segmentation approach is used when an organization assumes that _____ exist which _____ one or more _____ _____.

product, price,
distribution,
promotion

4. To develop a marketing mix, marketers must make decisions about _____, _____, _____ and _____.

Physical
distribution

5. _____ _____ relates to the physical movement of products and fulfills the logistical function necessary in moving products.

Advertising,
personal selling,
sales
promotion,
packaging,
publicity

6. _____, _____ _____, _____ _____, _____, and _____ are methods of informing and promoting an organization and its products.

Products,
exchange

7. _____ are one of the most visible contacts an organization has with consumers, and they provide values that are necessary in the development of an _____ relationship.

purchasing
power

8. Price is the exchange of something of value, usually _____ _____, for something else of value, usually a product.

Price, demand,
supply

9. _____ is usually the most flexible of all marketing mix variables, and it permits marketers to adjust a marketing strategy to current _____ and _____ situations.

inflexible, long-
term

10. Distribution in the marketing strategy is one of the more _____ variables because distribution arrangements often result in _____ commitments to middlemen.

sales analysis,
cost analysis,
sales volume,
market share,
aggregate,
disaggregated

11. Two general ways of evaluating the actual performance of marketing strategies are _____ _____ and _____ _____. Sales analysis can be based on _____ _____ or _____ _____ and can be performed on _____ sales figures or on _____ data.

marketing cost
analysis, costs,
marketing
activities

12. With _____ _____ _____ various costs are broken down and classified to determine which _____ are associated with _____ _____.

full-cost
approach,
nontraceable
common costs,
arbitrary

13. Proponents of a _____ _____ claim that if an accurate profit picture is desired, all costs must be included in the cost analysis. Opponents of this approach say it does not yield actual costs because _____ _____ _____ have been determined by _____ criteria.

total market

14. Marketing strategy using the _____ _____ approach develops a single marketing mix aimed at all potential customers.

Concentration,
multisegment

15. _____ and _____ approaches are two segmentation strategies.

# Answers to Objective Questions

*True or False*

| | | | |
|---|---|---|---|
| 1. | F | 12. | F |
| 2. | T | 13. | F |
| 3. | T | 14. | T |
| 4. | F | 15. | T |
| 5. | F | 16. | F |
| 6. | F | 17. | F |
| 7. | T | 18. | T |
| 8. | T | 19. | F |
| 9. | F | 20. | T |
| 10. | T | 21. | F |
| 11. | F | 22. | T |

*Multiple-Choice*

| | | | |
|---|---|---|---|
| 1. | c | 11. | b |
| 2. | d | 12. | a |
| 3. | d | 13. | d |
| 4. | c | 14. | b |
| 5. | a | 15. | a |
| 6. | d | 16. | b |
| 7. | d | 17. | d |
| 8. | d | 18. | a |
| 9. | b | 19. | c |
| 10. | c | 20. | c |

# CHAPTER 20

# Industrial Marketing

## Chapter Summary

This chapter discusses the various characteristics of industrial marketing with primary emphasis on the ways in which it differs from marketing to ultimate consumers. In general, industrial buyers are more rational than purchasers of consumer products. They concentrate on obtaining product information and on performing their jobs in ways to help their firms achieve organizational objectives.

Industrial buyers are concerned with obtaining a consistent level of quality at a reasonable price. In turn, the services provided by them are of particular importance to their customers. Some of these include market information, maintaining an inventory, on-time delivery, repair services and replacement parts, and credit. These services may be the primary avenue through which the industrial marketer gains an advantage over competitors.

Industrial transactions have a number of distinguishing features. They are frequently much larger than are consumer sales, they are negotiated less often, and they may involve several individuals or departments in the transaction. Reciprocity, an agreement in which two organizations agree to buy from each other, can be used in a limited number of cases.

Four commonly used methods of industrial buying are description, inspection, sampling, and negotiation. Description is used if the products being purchased are commonly standardized on the basis of characteristics like size, shape, weight, and color. Inspection is relied on if the products are very special or of uncertain condition.

Sampling is used to test large, homogeneous products—like grain—on the basis of a representative sample. Negotiation involves the submission of bids by sellers. Most industrial purchases fall into one of three types: new task purchase, straight rebuy purchase, or modified rebuy purchase.

Industrial demand differs from consumer demand in that industrial demand is (1) derived, (2) inelastic, (3) joint, and (4) more fluctuating. Derived demand refers to the fact that demand for industrial products is ultimately dependent on the demand for consumer products. Inelasticity of demand means that a price increase or decrease will not significantly affect demand for that item. This applies to overall industry demand for a product, however, not to demand for an item produced by an individual supplier. Joint demand occurs when two or more items are used in combination to produce a product. Shortages of such an item jeopardize sales of all the jointly demanded products. Demand fluctuations are brought on by changes in the demand for consumer products, changes in customers' inventory policies, or price changes.

To develop a marketing strategy, an industrial marketer must first select and analyze his or her target market. Most follow a pattern of first determining who and how many potential customers there are, then finding out where they are, and then estimating their purchase potentials.

The Standard Industrial Classification (SIC) System, which was developed by the federal government, categorizes various types of business activities into separate divisions. These are coded and subdivided in order to identify and qualify the characteristics of businesses. Market segments thus result based mainly on the types of products produced and/or handled. Additional information relating to specific firms in industry categories can be found in various government and nongovernment publications.

Once potential customers have been identified and estimates of their purchases have been obtained, the industrial marketer is ready to create a marketing mix that will satisfy customers in a target market. The product component should include an emphasis on services. Industrial customers, even more than ultimate consumers, depend on having prompt delivery and detailed product information regarding purchases. Styling and package design, so long as they are functional, are of less importance. Pricing in industrial markets is affected by legal and economic environmental forces such as the Robinson-Patman Act and federal price controls. Prices are determined by the use of price lists, negotiated contracts, or bidding.

Distribution channels tend to be shorter than for many consumer products, and direct marketing channels are commonly used. Manufacturers' agents and industrial distributors have some advantages as middlemen but also can present problems for the industrial seller.

Several considerations enter into the choice of an industrial marketing channel, such as the availability and costs of intermediaries and the characteristics of the products and customers involved.

Personal selling is stressed in industrial marketing. Buyers need detailed product information, assistance, and service. Advertising plays a complementary role by helping to identify potential customers, by advising customers of new products and brands, and by generally supporting the efforts of sales personnel. Sometimes advertising can stimulate consumer demand and, thus, indirectly stimulate demand for products at the industrial level.

Sales promotion can be important in industrial promotion mixes. There is widespread use of catalogs, trade shows, and trade-type sales promotion methods. Publicity has an importance to industrial marketers similar to the importance it has to consumer product marketers.

# True or False Statements

T    F    1. Ultimate consumers are generally viewed as being more rational than industrial buyers.

T    F    2. Industrial buyers are very much concerned with consistent quality in industrial products.

T    F    3. An industrial buyer often views the price as the amount of investment necessary to obtain a certain level of return or savings.

T    F    4. Industrial sellers may prefer not to sell to customers who place small orders.

T    F    5. When a negotiated contract method is used for industrial buying, sellers are asked to submit bids.

T    F    6. Most industrial purchases can be classified as being one of three types: negotiated, listed, or spontaneous.

T    F    7. Inelasticity of demand means that a change in price results in a significant change in the demand for a product.

T    F    8. The fact that industrial demand is derived from consumer demand may contribute significantly to demand fluctuations.

T    F    9. Industrial marketers have much more information than consumer marketers with which to select and analyze their target markets.

T    F    10. The SIC system divides industrial firms into market segments based on plant capacity and number of employees.

T    F    11. The concept of input-output is one that assumes that the sales of one industry are the purchases of another industry.

T    F    12. After selecting and analyzing the target market, the industrial marketer's next step is to test-market the product in a representative sample of the target market.

T    F    13. The general concepts and methods involved in developing a marketing mix for industrial products are similar in many ways to those involved in marketing to ultimate consumers.

T    F    14. The product ingredients in marketing mixes for industrial products include a greater emphasis on aesthetic values than do consumer marketing mixes.

T    F    15. Industrial marketers depend heavily on sizable repeat purchases from customers.

T    F    16. The Robinson-Patman Act affects consumer goods producers significantly but has little impact on the marketing of industrial products.

T    F    17. The actual price paid by an industrial customer is usually the list price plus shipping charges.

T  F  18. A manufacturers' agent is an independent business person who acquires title to, and possession of, products.

T  F  19. Market information and a well-developed set of customers are among the benefits provided by manufacturers' agents.

T  F  20. Industrial distributors are extremely efficient in putting forth the needed selling activities to local markets, but the costs to the manufacturer are rather high.

T  F  21. All of the industrial channels discussed in the text are equally available, and a producer need only select the one that best fits the firm's needs.

T  F  22. The physical distribution decisions are all geared toward minimizing costs while still maintaining a level of service that will keep customers satisfied.

T  F  23. The relationship between industrial suppliers and buyers is apt to be more independent and self-sufficient compared to relationships that develop in consumer product sales.

T  F  24. Advertising is usually ineffective in the industrial selling context.

T  F  25. Trade publications and direct mail are widely used media because they allow an industrial marketer to reach a precise market and thus avoid wasted coverage.

## Multiple-Choice Questions

_____ 1. Which of the following best explains the behavior of industrial buyers?
   a. They are careless about details in their jobs.
   b. They are characteristically cold, nonfeeling types of people.
   c. They are highly ambitious and may be persuaded to sacrifice integrity for personal gain.
   d. They often seek to fulfill personal goals by helping their firms achieve organizational objectives.
   e. They have social and psychological difficulties in adjusting to their roles as industrial purchasers.

_____ 2. What is the best reason for obtaining a product that meets specifications?
   a. The firm must project an image of quality by always ordering the best materials and components.
   b. Use of an inferior item may produce a product that malfunctions, thus causing the firm to lose customers.
   c. Specifications are government-imposed standards that must be met if the firm is to stay in business.

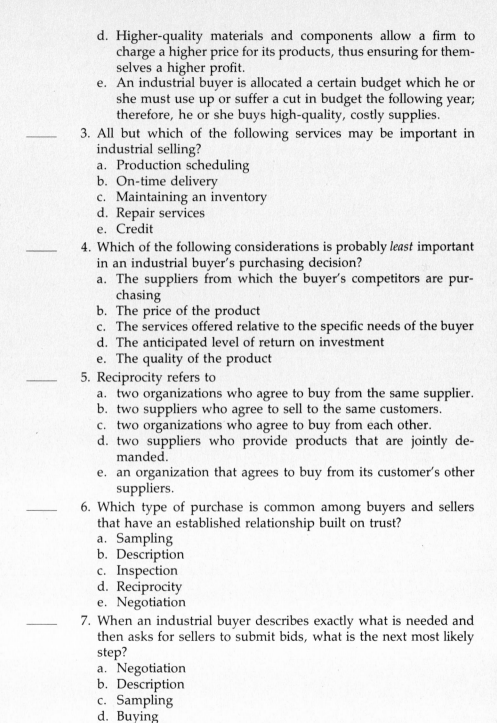

d. Higher-quality materials and components allow a firm to charge a higher price for its products, thus ensuring for themselves a higher profit.

e. An industrial buyer is allocated a certain budget which he or she must use up or suffer a cut in budget the following year; therefore, he or she buys high-quality, costly supplies.

3. All but which of the following services may be important in industrial selling?
   a. Production scheduling
   b. On-time delivery
   c. Maintaining an inventory
   d. Repair services
   e. Credit

4. Which of the following considerations is probably *least* important in an industrial buyer's purchasing decision?
   a. The suppliers from which the buyer's competitors are purchasing
   b. The price of the product
   c. The services offered relative to the specific needs of the buyer
   d. The anticipated level of return on investment
   e. The quality of the product

5. Reciprocity refers to
   a. two organizations who agree to buy from the same supplier.
   b. two suppliers who agree to sell to the same customers.
   c. two organizations who agree to buy from each other.
   d. two suppliers who provide products that are jointly demanded.
   e. an organization that agrees to buy from its customer's other suppliers.

6. Which type of purchase is common among buyers and sellers that have an established relationship built on trust?
   a. Sampling
   b. Description
   c. Inspection
   d. Reciprocity
   e. Negotiation

7. When an industrial buyer describes exactly what is needed and then asks for sellers to submit bids, what is the next most likely step?
   a. Negotiation
   b. Description
   c. Sampling
   d. Buying
   e. Inspection

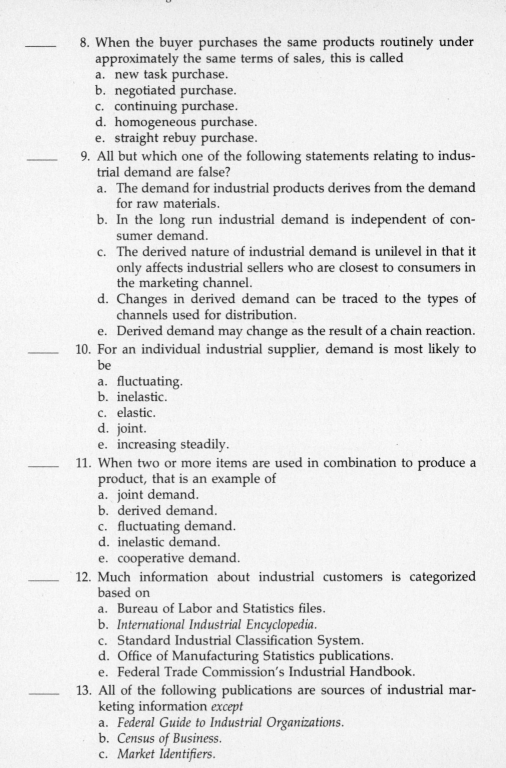

_____ 8. When the buyer purchases the same products routinely under approximately the same terms of sales, this is called
   a. new task purchase.
   b. negotiated purchase.
   c. continuing purchase.
   d. homogeneous purchase.
   e. straight rebuy purchase.

_____ 9. All but which one of the following statements relating to industrial demand are false?
   a. The demand for industrial products derives from the demand for raw materials.
   b. In the long run industrial demand is independent of consumer demand.
   c. The derived nature of industrial demand is unilevel in that it only affects industrial sellers who are closest to consumers in the marketing channel.
   d. Changes in derived demand can be traced to the types of channels used for distribution.
   e. Derived demand may change as the result of a chain reaction.

_____ 10. For an individual industrial supplier, demand is most likely to be
   a. fluctuating.
   b. inelastic.
   c. elastic.
   d. joint.
   e. increasing steadily.

_____ 11. When two or more items are used in combination to produce a product, that is an example of
   a. joint demand.
   b. derived demand.
   c. fluctuating demand.
   d. inelastic demand.
   e. cooperative demand.

_____ 12. Much information about industrial customers is categorized based on
   a. Bureau of Labor and Statistics files.
   b. *International Industrial Encyclopedia.*
   c. Standard Industrial Classification System.
   d. Office of Manufacturing Statistics publications.
   e. Federal Trade Commission's Industrial Handbook.

_____ 13. All of the following publications are sources of industrial marketing information *except*
   a. *Federal Guide to Industrial Organizations.*
   b. *Census of Business.*
   c. *Market Identifiers.*

d. *Survey of Industrial Purchasing Power.*

e. *Census of Manufactures.*

_____ 14. That the sales of one industry are the purchases of other industries is an assumption necessary for

a. input-output analysis.

b. reciprocity.

c. joint demand.

d. matrix economics.

e. inelastic demand.

_____ 15. Which of the following sources does *not* contain information regarding a specific firm, such as name, SIC number, address, and phone numbers?

a. *Census of Business*

b. Commercial industrial directories

c. *Standard and Poor's Register*

d. State industrial directories

e. *Middle Market Directory*

_____ 16. An industrial marketer should select the industrial customers to be included in the target market immediately after

a. determining customers' SIC classifications.

b. consulting government sources for customer information.

c. determining the specific names and locations of potential customers.

d. determining which industries purchase the output of his or her industry.

e. estimating potential customers' purchases.

_____ 17. Compared to industrial marketing mixes, which of the following is *least* likely to be emphasized in consumer selling?

a. Customer satisfaction

b. Pricing

c. On-time delivery

d. Product information

e. Packaging

_____ 18. All but which one of the following statements concerning industrial price lists are true?

a. Industrial marketers base their prices on a series of prices printed on a price sheet or in a catalog.

b. Book prices are not the prices usually paid by customers.

c. The book price is a base price to which charges for customer services are commonly added in order to figure a final price.

d. Functional discounts may be deducted from the list price.

e. The actual price paid by an industrial customer is called net price.

_____ 19. Which of the following is a characteristic of sealed bids?
   a. The amounts of the bids are not made public.
   b. The bids are opened and made public at a designated time.
   c. The bids are made public as sellers submit them.
   d. The bids are only revealed to top management and the board of directors.
   e. The bids can be made public or kept secret at the discretion of the purchasing agent.

_____ 20. Which of the following channels may *not* be used in industrial distribution?
   a. Producer, manufacturers' agent, consumer
   b. Producer, industrial customer
   c. Producer, industrial distributor, industrial customer
   d. Producer, manufacturers' agent, industrial customer
   e. Producer, manufacturers' agent, industrial distributor, industrial customer

_____ 21. Which one of the following is *not* a limitation of manufacturers' agents?
   a. The method of compensation used gives the seller little control over the agent.
   b. Manufacturers' agents usually want to serve only the larger accounts.
   c. They may be reluctant to spend time following up sales.
   d. They often lack the technical knowledge necessary to sell and service certain industrial items.
   e. They do not maintain inventories.

_____ 22. All but which of the following are characteristics of an industrial distributor?
   a. Is an independent business organization
   b. Takes title to products and carries inventories
   c. Does selling at relatively low costs to a manufacturer
   d. Provides credit services to customers
   e. Specializes in items requiring extraordinary selling efforts or unusual handling

_____ 23. Which of the following would be *least* important to an industrial seller of electronic components when choosing a channel of distribution?
   a. Which channels are available
   b. How his or her products are normally purchased
   c. The availability of raw materials
   d. Parts inventory needed in local markets
   e. Amounts of technical assistance needed by customers

_____ 24. Which of the following is *not* one of the ways that industrial salespeople can be characterized?
   a. Outside order taker
   b. Inside order taker
   c. Technical
   d. Missionary
   e. Trade

_____ 25. Which one of the following does *not* characterize industrial advertising?
   a. Industrial marketers seldom use broadcast media.
   b. Trade publications and direct mail are commonly used by industrial marketers.
   c. Industrial marketers can sometimes stimulate demand for their products by stimulating consumer demand.
   d. The content of product advertisements has little detailed information and is highly persuasive in nature.
   e. Industrial marketers attempt to reach a precise group of industrial customers.


# Programmed Completion Exercises

rational

1. Industrial buyers are generally viewed as being more _____ in their purchasing behavior than are ultimate consumers.

quality level, service, price

2. Many of the primary concerns of industrial buyers fall into one of three categories: _____ _____, _____, _____.

specifications

3. In an attempt to maintain a specific level of quality in their products, industrial buyers often buy products based on a set of specified characteristics called _____.

consistent

4. An industrial marketer seeks suppliers that provide industrial products for which the quality level is _____ in order after order.

larger

5. Industrial orders are frequently much _____ than consumer orders.

geographically
concentrated,
limited in
number, large
purchasers

6. Direct selling is most likely to be used by industrial sellers whose customers are _____ _____, _____ _____, and _____ _____.

description,
inspection,
sampling,
negotiation

7. The four most common methods of industrial buying are _____, _____, _____, and _____.

bids

8. When a buyer asks sellers to submit prices for industrial products, he is asking for _____.

new task
purchase,
straight rebuy
purchase,
modified rebuy
purchase

9. Most industrial purchases can be classified as being one of three types: _____ _____ _____, _____ _____ _____, or _____ _____ _____.

inelastic

10. When a price increase or decrease will not significantly affect demand for the item, demand is said to be _____.

Joint demand

11. _____ _____ occurs when two or more items are used in combination to produce a product.

Standard
Industrial
Classification
System,
industrial,
commercial,
financial,
service

12. The _____ _____ _____ _____ was developed by the federal government to classify selected economic characteristics of _____, _____, _____, and _____ organizations.

*Census of
Manufactures*

13. The _____ _____ _____ subdivides manufacturers into five- and seven-digit coded groups.

*Market
Identifiers,
Survey of
Industrial
Purchasing
Power*

14. Industrial market data also appear in nongovernment sources such as Dun and Bradstreet's _____ _____, and in Sales Management's _____ _____ _____ _____ _____.

Input-output
analysis

15. _____ _____ _____ is based on the assumption that the sales of one industry are the purchases of other industries.

*Survey of
Industrial
Purchasing
Power*

16. Compared to most government sources, the data in the

    _____  _____  _____  _____

    _____ are more current because they are updated an-

    nually.

commercial data
company

17. An expedient but expensive approach to identifying and locating

    potential customers is to use a _____ _____

    _____ .

services

18. Compared to consumer marketing mixes, the product ingredi-

    ents of marketing mixes for industrial goods usually include a

    greater emphasis on _____ .

repeat
purchases

19. Many industrial marketers are heavily dependent on

    _____ _____ that are based on long-term relation-

    ships with customers.

on-time
delivery

20. Because industrial customers depend heavily on having products

    available when needed, an important service in the product com-

    ponent of many industrial marketing mixes is _____

    _____ .

less, more,
functional,
styling

21. Compared to research associated with consumer products, in-

    dustrial marketers are more likely to do _____ market

    research and _____ product research directed at

    _____ features rather than _____ .

legal, economic

22. Pricing decisions made by industrial marketers are heavily af-

    fected by _____ and _____ environmental forces.

multiplier

23. An industrial seller can change prices without having to issue

    new catalogs or price sheets by simply changing the

    _____ .

shorter

24. Distribution channels for industrial products tend to be

    _____ than for many consumer products.

direct marketing
channels

25. The most widely used channels in industrial products marketing

    are _____ _____ _____ .

manufacturer's
agent

26. An industrial middleman who does not acquire title to the products and usually does not take possession is a(n) _____ _____.

industrial
distributor

27. An independent business person and middleman who takes title to products and carries an inventory is a(n) _____ _____.

personal selling

28. The promotional ingredient that industrial sellers rely on most is _____ _____.

technical, trade,
missionary,
inside order
taker

29. Industrial salespeople can usually be grouped into four categories: _____, _____, _____, and _____ _____ _____.

interdependent

30. Compared to buyer-seller relationships that develop in consumer product sales, industrial buyers and sellers are more likely to be highly _____.

less

31. Advertising tends to be emphasized _____ in industrial than in consumer product promotion mixes.

print media

32. With respect to media selection, industrial marketers primarily utilize _____ _____.

information,
persuasive

33. Compared with consumer product advertisements, the content of messages in industrial advertisements is more likely to be packed with _____ and is usually less _____ in nature.

catalogs, trade
shows, trade-
type

34. Sales promotion efforts used in industrial marketers' promotion mixes include _____, _____ _____, and _____ sales promotion methods.

# Answers to Objective Questions

| *True or False* | | | | *Multiple-Choice* | | | |
|---|---|---|---|---|---|---|---|
| 1. | F | 14. | F | 1. | d | 14. | a |
| 2. | T | 15. | T | 2. | b | 15. | a |
| 3. | T | 16. | F | 3. | a | 16. | e |
| 4. | T | 17. | F | 4. | a | 17. | c |
| 5. | T | 18. | F | 5. | c | 18. | c |
| 6. | F | 19. | T | 6. | b | 19. | b |
| 7. | F | 20. | F | 7. | a | 20. | a |
| 8. | T | 21. | F | 8. | e | 21. | d |
| 9. | T | 22. | T | 9. | e | 22. | e |
| 10. | F | 23. | F | 10. | c | 23. | c |
| 11. | T | 24. | F | 11. | a | 24. | a |
| 12. | F | 25. | T | 12. | c | 25. | d |
| 13. | T | | | 13. | a | | |

## CHAPTER 21

# Nonbusiness Marketing

## Chapter Summary

Nonbusiness marketing embraces marketing activities that are conducted by individuals and organizations to attain some goal other
than usual business goals like profit, market share, and return on
investment. Marketing concepts and methods used by businesses are
also applicable to marketing activities in nonbusiness situations. Organizational and individual goals determine whether an organization
is business or nonbusiness. Marketing is a social activity, however,
and the gaining of acceptance of a nonbusiness product (whether
values, ideas, concepts, services, or goods) requires the performance
of marketing activities.

Nonbusiness exchange activities can be described as a form of
marketing. Charitable organizations and social causes are major nonbusiness marketers in this country. The beneficiaries of a nonbusiness
organization are its clients, its members, and the general public,
while the main beneficiaries of a business are the owners or stockholders. Nonbusiness organizations need to adopt the essence of the
marketing concept. Sometimes their goals and clients are difficult to
define, and the planning of marketing activities and the implementation of the marketing concept may therefore require more coordination and refinement of goals than are required in businesses. The
public or target markets served will reflect the organization's unique
philosophy and mission.

In some cases, nonbusiness organizations may be controversial
because of environmental forces. Opposing organizations may evolve

to resist the success of a movement or a social cause. Marketing attempts to provide a body of knowledge and concepts to help further an organization's goals. Personal judgment, however, must be used in deciding whether to approve or disapprove of an organization's goals.

A marketing strategy involves defining a target market and creating and maintaining a marketing mix. It is often difficult for a nonbusiness organization to think in terms of the needs, perceptions, or preferences of its market or public. Often this is because the organization assumes it already knows what the public needs or wants. Moreover, the target market and target public are difficult to determine for many nonbusinesses. In nonbusiness organizations, the direct consumers of the product are called client publics, and indirect consumers are called general publics. The techniques and approaches to segmenting and defining markets that are used in business situations, however, are applicable in nonbusiness situations.

The marketing mix for nonbusiness organizations includes decisions about product, price, promotion, and distribution. Nonbusiness organizations typically deal with ideas or services rather than with goods. Price amounts to the value placed on the items involved in an exchange; often it is not a financial value that is exchanged, but rather a complicated intangible value. In fact, pricing strategy often places public and client welfare before the matching of costs with revenues. Distribution usually is examined in terms of the way it relates to decisions about product and promotion, since it affects the way a nonbusiness product will be made available to clients. A very short channel—nonbusiness organization to client—is typical. Promotion is an important variable in nonbusiness situations because it is needed to facilitate exchanges. Sales promotion, advertising, publicity, and personal selling activities are used widely by nonbusiness organizations to communicate with their target markets.

Control of marketing activities in nonbusiness organizations uses information obtained in the marketing audit to determine if goals are being achieved. Controlling involves a complete inventory of what activities are being performed and a readiness to adjust or to correct deviations from standards. It may be difficult to control nonbusiness marketing activities, however, because it is often difficult to determine if the goals of nonbusiness organizations are being achieved.

# True or False Statements

T  F  1. Most concepts and techniques used to manage marketing activities for profit-oriented organizations are not applicable in nonbusiness situations.

T  F  2. The most obvious characteristic distinguishing nonbusiness organizations from businesses is the lack of the profit incentive.

T  F  3. The definition of nonbusiness marketing embraces a set of individual and organizational activities conducted to achieve some goal other than ordinary business goals like profit, market share, and return on investment.

T  F  4. The nonbusiness organization is often designed to benefit a wider spectrum of clients; sometimes this may be the public at large.

T  F  5. The planning of nonbusiness marketing strategies requires less refinement and coordination of goals than the planning of business strategies.

T  F  6. Goal orientation is similar in nonbusiness and business organizations.

T  F  7. Planned Parenthood is an example of a nonprofit agency that uses nonbusiness marketing.

T  F  8. In a nonbusiness situation, negotiation and persuasion activities often are conducted without any awareness of the role of marketing in transactions.

T  F  9. Even though the identity of the owners may be unclear in a nonbusiness organization, this actually aids in the direct-line accountability.

T  F  10. In the nonbusiness environment the importance of distribution channels is to develop the availability of products.

T  F  11. Marketing is a function of society; therefore it should direct its activities away from any organization questioned by society.

T  F  12. Obtaining market information is not as important in marketing political candidates as it is in marketing activities for businesses, which need marketing information in order to avoid launching products that fail.

T  F  13. The opportunity cost for a nonbusiness organization is the time one donates to a cause; thus, other choices are forgone.

T  F  14. The exchange transactions and the purpose of an organization have little impact upon the marketing objectives of a nonbusiness enterprise.

T  F  15. A marketing objective for a charitable organization could be the feeling of satisfaction that comes from participating in the solution of social problems or from promoting a social cause.

T   F    16. It is much more difficult to describe what is provided by a service-oriented organization than to describe what is provided by a product-oriented organization.

T   F    17. Nonbusiness organizations do not need to develop a pricing strategy because they lack a profit incentive.

T   F    18. Developing a marketing channel to coordinate and facilitate the flow of nonbusiness products to clients is a necessary task in nonbusiness marketing.

T   F    19. The marketing of health services includes such marketing activities as the determination of health needs of clients, the construction of a distribution system to make services available to the target market, obtaining financial support, and altering the values and behavior of the public.

T   F    20. The technique of personal selling is used by many nonbusiness organizations, even though it may not be called personal selling.

T   F    21. The consummation of exchanges never takes place in the performance of nonbusiness marketing activities because of the intangible nature of most social products.

## Multiple-Choice Questions

_____    1. Nonbusiness marketing includes all of the following *except*
   a. the accomplishment of some goal other than profit.
   b. activities aimed at facilitating and expediting exchanges.
   c. marketing activities conducted by individuals and organizations.
   d. lack of a profit incentive.
   e. direct accountability to an owner.

_____    2. In a nonbusiness marketing situation,
   a. the individuals involved are often unaware of the role marketing plays in transactions.
   b. the consummation of exchanges does not occur.
   c. the division of labor and specialization of labor are not required.
   d. the target market is easy to define.

_____    3. Which of the following does *not* use nonprofit-oriented marketing?
   a. A private university
   b. The National Highway Safety Council
   c. Regional planning commissions
   d. Commercial banks
   e. The Catholic Church

_____ 4. Nonbusiness organizations are gradually switching to the marketing concept that planning should be guided by
   a. the thinking of the board of trustees.
   b. clients, members, or the publics being served.
   c. a professional planner's intuition.
   d. what has always worked in the past.

_____ 5. Nonbusiness organizations serve their constituents in order to achieve
   a. maximum profit.
   b. the goal outlined by society.
   c. the goals established by the donors.
   d. some social or environmental goal.
   e. the breakeven point of expenses.

_____ 6. Which one of the following statements about the marketing of political candidates is *false*?
   a. Opinion surveys are a widely accepted and frequently used marketing research activity.
   b. Market segmentation concepts become very important when resources are limited.
   c. The modification of the candidate's values to satisfy the target public does not represent an exchange transaction.
   d. Obtaining market information to avoid defeat is just as important to the candidates as it is to businesses that try to avoid launching products that fail.

_____ 7. The direct consumer of the product of a nonbusiness organization is referred to as
   a. the client public.
   b. the general public
   c. the target public
   d. the public at large
   e. consumer public

_____ 8. Which of the following is *not* an example of personal selling in a nonbusiness environment?
   a. The recruitment of new members by volunteers
   b. The use of volunteer work in soliciting donations
   c. The use of a contest to attract donations
   d. The use of a special event for fundraising
   e. The shipping of material to the national headquarters

_____ 9. The most obvious product in a political candidate's marketing campaign is
   a. political issues.
   b. the candidate.
   c. a political party.
   d. the campaign theme.

10. Distribution in nonbusiness marketing involves
    a. showing the organization's interest in the area.
    b. facilitating the product.
    c. being located near trustees.
    d. providing credibility.
    e. making the product available to clients.

11. In nonbusiness organizations, developing a channel of distribution often leads to a(n)
    a. extended channel.
    b. long channel.
    c. vertical channel.
    d. very short channel.
    e. horizontal channel.

12. The value of the benefit that is forgone by choosing one alternative over another is called
    a. economic cost.
    b. social cost.
    c. opportunity cost.
    d. marginal cost.
    e. variable cost.

13. Which of the following is *not* an example of the goals of a nonbusiness organization?
    a. Providing religious values and services
    b. Ensuring protection and security
    c. Obtaining financial contributions
    d. Providing time and support
    e. Promoting goods for the purpose of financial gain

14. Which one of the following statements is *false*?
    a. Nonbusiness organizations may have goals that are opposed by members of society.
    b. Marketing as a field of study attempts to make value judgments about what a nonbusiness organization's goals should be.
    c. One nonbusiness organization may emerge in order to oppose a social cause or a movement that another organization is trying to market to the public.
    d. Nonbusiness organizations exist to serve clients.

15. Planned Parenthood must develop a marketing strategy that includes many marketing variables so as to satisfy many needs. Which of the following is the most complete group of variables that should be used?
    a. Books, materials, and brochures
    b. Ideas, clinical services, and goods
    c. A concept of planning births and child care
    d. Birth control pills and devices

16. Which one of the following concepts is ordinarily *not* associated with nonbusiness organizations?
    a. Profit
    b. Negotiation
    c. Persuasion
    d. Marketing objectives

17. In order to have the most effective impact on a community a nonbusiness organization such as Planned Parenthood needs
    a. a large board of directors.
    b. considerable government aid.
    c. good public relations and public support.
    d. extensive medical connections.
    e. the approval of every member of society.

18. The marketing of political candidates places heavy emphasis on what variable in the marketing mix?
    a. Price
    b. Promotion
    c. Distribution
    d. Product
    e. All elements of the marketing mix

19. In applying the marketing concept to nonbusiness organizations the text is essentially stating that
    a. all organizations are really the same although their products differ.
    b. promotional activities are easier for nonbusiness organizations to develop because the public has more interest in the commodity being offered.
    c. goods and services are easier for nonbusiness organizations to market because there is no real competition for them to contend with.
    d. the development of a product should be influenced by the clients receiving or using it.

## Programmed Completion Exercises

Charitable organizations, social causes

1. _____ _____ and supporters of _____ _____ are examples of nonbusiness marketers in the United States.

desired response

2. The marketing objective of nonbusiness organizations is to obtain a _____ _____ from a target market.

target market,
marketing mix

3. The two steps in developing a nonbusiness marketing strategy are defining a _____ _____ and then creating and maintaining a _____ _____.

client publics,
general publics

4. In nonbusiness organizations, the direct consumers of the product are called _____ _____, and indirect consumers are called _____ _____.

value, thing

5. Opportunity cost may be, for example, the price paid, and price is the _____ of the _____ that is given up by choosing one alternative rather than another.

target public

6. A _____ _____ is broadly defined as a collective of individuals who have an interest in, or a concern about, an organization, a product, or a social cause.

deviations,
standards

7. To control nonbusiness marketing activities, it is necessary to inventory what activities are performed and to be prepared to correct _____ from _____.

clients,
members,
general public

8. The beneficiaries of a nonbusiness organization are its _____, _____, or the _____ _____, while the chief beneficiaries of a business enterprise are the owners or stockholders.

Opposing
organizations,
combat, success

9. _____ _____ in some cases may develop to _____ the _____ of a movement, social cause, or goal of a nonbusiness organization.

intangible,
opportunity
costs, financial
contributions,
donation

10. Values received from the target market could be _____ values, _____ _____, _____, the _____ of goods or services, or some other type of exchange.

ideas, services,
goods

11. The nonbusiness product takes the form of _____ and _____ more often than the form of _____.

product,
promotion

12. The marketing mix variable of distribution usually is examined in nonbusiness organizations as it relates to decisions about _____ and _____.

short

13. The typical marketing channel of a nonbusiness organization is _____ and is made up of the organization and the client.

profit, market share

14. Nonbusiness marketing includes exchange activities performed by individuals and organizations to accomplish some goal other than _____, _____ _____, or return on investment.

planning, implementation

15. The _____ of nonbusiness marketing activities and the _____ of the marketing concept may require more coordination and refinement of goals than are required in businesses.

exchange, objectives

16. The nature of the _____ and the goals of the nonbusiness organization will shape the organization's marketing _____.

Advertising, publicity, personal selling, sales promotion

17. _____, _____, _____ _____, and _____ _____ are widely used by nonbusiness organizations to communicate with clients and the public.

promotion, funds

18. The concept of _____ is used when nonbusinesses attempt to obtain _____, communicate ideas, or persuade clients.

Advertising, publicity

19. _____ and _____ are used widely in nonbusiness marketing to communicate with clients and the public.

marketing strategy

20. Control is an activity in analyzing and verifying whether the _____ _____ and organizational goals have been reached.

individuals, groups, organizations, negotiation, persuasion

21. An exchange situation exists when _____, _____, or _____ possess values they are willing to give up in an exchange relationship, usually facilitated through _____ and _____.

marketing audit

22. Control of marketing activities in nonbusiness organizations focuses on using information obtained in the _____ _____ to make sure that goals are achieved.

goods, ideas,
services

23. In nonbusiness organizations, distribution is not involved as much with the movement of ＿＿＿＿＿ as it is with the communication of ＿＿＿＿＿ and the delivery of ＿＿＿＿＿.

goals

24. It may be difficult to control nonbusiness activities because it is hard to determine whether ＿＿＿＿＿ are being met.

personal selling

25. Churches and charities use ＿＿＿＿＿ ＿＿＿＿＿ when they send volunteers to recruit members or request donations.

## Answers to Objective Questions

| *True or False* | | | *Multiple-Choice* | |
|---|---|---|---|---|
| 1. F | 12. F | | 1. e | 11. d |
| 2. T | 13. T | | 2. a | 12. c |
| 3. T | 14. F | | 3. d | 13. e |
| 4. T | 15. T | | 4. b | 14. b |
| 5. F | 16. T | | 5. d | 15. b |
| 6. T | 17. F | | 6. c | 16. a |
| 7. T | 18. T | | 7. a | 17. c |
| 8. T | 19. T | | 8. e | 18. e |
| 9. F | 20. T | | 9. b | 19. d |
| 10. T | 21. F | | 10. e | |
| 11. F | | | | |

# CHAPTER 22

# International Marketing

## Chapter Summary

The management of international marketing activities requires an understanding of marketing concepts and a grasp of the environmental complexities of foreign countries. International marketing is marketing activities performed across national boundaries. The planning and control of marketing activities across national boundaries can be significantly different from marketing within national boundaries. The development of integrated multinational marketing strategies requires a more detailed marketing intelligence effort, and most businesses have to adjust their marketing strategies and redesign their organizational structures in order to compete effectively in international markets.

The term *multinational enterprise* refers to the organizational aspects of firms that have operations or subsidiaries located in many countries to achieve a common goal. Although the United States remains the single largest force among multinationals, other countries are expanding in influence. The growth of multinational firms has occurred as businesses have become more sensitive to national customs, to labor relations practices, and to governments' desires for capital, tax revenues, employment, technical skills, foreign exchange, and access to new products from abroad. The level of international marketing varies widely, ranging from casual or accidental exporting, to active exporting, to full-scale international marketing involvement. Foreign opportunities should be assessed as potential target markets;

the marketing mix should be designed to serve the foreign market if an international marketing commitment is made.

International marketing intelligence involves analyzing markets in terms of the culture, institutions, and behavior of potential buyers. Moreover, a detailed analysis of the environment is necessary when entering foreign markets. The marketing mix is an important part of the international marketing strategy; making and implementing the marketing mix decisions is the final step. Five possible strategies for adapting product and promotion for international markets are (1) using the same product and promotion worldwide; (2) adapting promotion only; (3) adapting the product only; (4) adapting both the product and promotion; and (5) inventing new products. Businesses must consider the problems of distribution between countries as well as distribution within a foreign country. Several approaches are possible in developing a distribution channel across national boundaries. Pricing decisions are affected by many factors, such as research costs, transportation costs, tariffs, and other marketing management expenses. A cost-plus approach is probably the most typical pricing method. The price of a product across national boundaries is also a function of foreign currency exchange rates.

The standardization of an international marketing mix makes a firm more efficient in international marketing. The potential economic payoffs for a standardized product, price, distribution, or promotion are great. However, differences in legal and political systems, economic development, and social institutions make standardization difficult. The degree of similarity in environmental and market conditions determines the feasibility of standardization.

There are different levels on which the multinational firm can be involved in international marketing. Exporting represents the lowest level of commitment to international marketing and is the most flexible approach to use. Licensing is an attractive alternative to direct investments when the political stability of the foreign country is questionable or when resources are not available for direct investments. Joint ventures are often a political necessity because of nationalism and governmental restrictions on foreign ownership. Direct ownership represents the highest level of commitment to international marketing, but it involves the greatest risk and uncertainty. A foreign subsidiary or division usually requires a sizable investment in facilities, distribution system, research expenditures, and management costs. One of the greatest advantages of having a foreign subsidiary or division, however, is that the development of nationals as managers provides a crosscultural approach.

# True or False Statements

T  F  1. What complicates the marketing task in foreign countries is the fact that the environment—particularly the cultural environment—often consists of elements that are unfamiliar to, and perhaps not even recognized by, marketing executives.

T  F  2. International marketing entails marketing activities that are performed in a controlled foreign market environment.

T  F  3. The term *multinational enterprise* refers to the organizational aspects of firms that have operations or subsidiaries located in many countries.

T  F  4. Direct ownership of foreign subsidiaries represents the greatest commitment and includes the smallest risk in international marketing.

T  F  5. Germany has become the single largest force among multinationals in recent years.

T  F  6. Attempts by firms to make large bribes or payments to influence government decisions should be viewed as a viable alternative in conducting international marketing.

T  F  7. Environmental differences that exist among and within the many nations have no effects upon marketing activities.

T  F  8. The degree of commitment that is required to maintain a position in the foreign market will determine modifications or the extent to which the marketing mix must be redesigned.

T  F  9. When products are introduced into one nation from another, acceptance is far more likely if there are similarities between the two cultures.

T  F  10. Mass marketing technology is an ideal way to create the jobs needed in developing countries because it enables the absorption of their rapidly expanding labor forces.

T  F  11. The export of technology with strategic importance to the United States may require Defense Department approval.

T  F  12. Opportunities for international marketers are limited mainly to countries with high incomes.

T  F  13. Aggregate GNP and GNP per capita provide measures of the standard of living.

T  F  14. Multinational firms indicate that, if possible, it is highly desirable to have nonstandardization in brand labeling and packaging.

T  F  15. When the function that a product serves in a foreign market changes, then both the product and its promotion need to be altered.

T    F     16. An understanding of the cultural environment in a given market will, in turn, help in understanding the buying motives and habits of consumers in foreign markets.

T    F     17. The competitive approach to international pricing is probably the most typical pricing method.

T    F     18. The sale of the same product in different markets to exploit demand or competitive differences is called dumping.

T    F     19. Joint ventures are often a political necessity because of nationalism and governmental restrictions on foreign ownership.

T    F     20. Sometimes a firm's foreign price may be lower than its domestic price.

T    F     21. International marketing intelligence involves the analysis of markets and environments.

T    F     22. Marketers should recognize that marketing activities can have a disruptive effect on the social institutions of a society.

T    F     23. According to a survey of General Foods, Coca-Cola, and Procter and Gamble, standardization can be accomplished on a wide regional basis.

# Multiple-Choice Questions

_____  1. All of the following are needed to support international marketing *except*
   a. worldwide transportation.
   b. techniques to analyze different environments.
   c. worldwide communications systems.
   d. homogenizing of global cultures.
   e. techniques to determine foreign market potentials.

_____  2. What is the expansion of marketing to foreign markets usually associated with?
   a. A corporate strategy of long-term growth and increase in profits
   b. A desire for more power
   c. The lessening of tariff laws
   d. A change in the foreign political environment

_____  3. Which one of the following statements is *false*?
   a. The dynamics of international marketing intelligence influence the development of the marketing strategy.
   b. International marketing involves marketing activities that are performed in controlled foreign market environments.

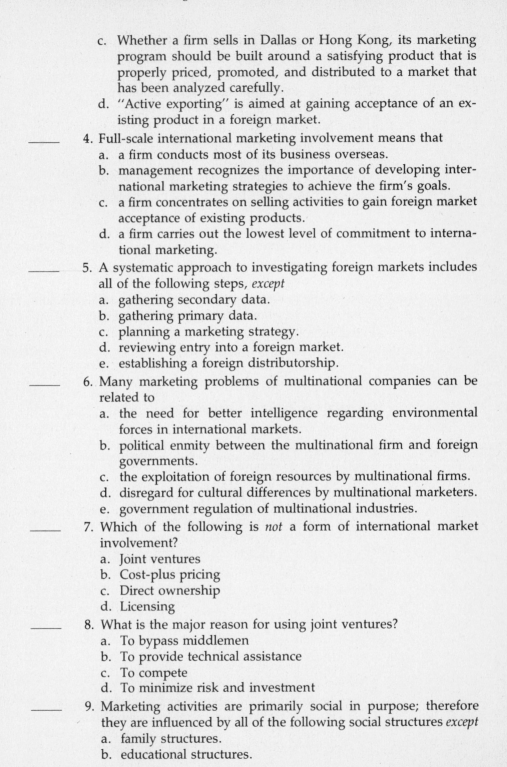

   c. Whether a firm sells in Dallas or Hong Kong, its marketing program should be built around a satisfying product that is properly priced, promoted, and distributed to a market that has been analyzed carefully.

   d. "Active exporting" is aimed at gaining acceptance of an existing product in a foreign market.

4. Full-scale international marketing involvement means that
   a. a firm conducts most of its business overseas.
   b. management recognizes the importance of developing international marketing strategies to achieve the firm's goals.
   c. a firm concentrates on selling activities to gain foreign market acceptance of existing products.
   d. a firm carries out the lowest level of commitment to international marketing.

5. A systematic approach to investigating foreign markets includes all of the following steps, *except*
   a. gathering secondary data.
   b. gathering primary data.
   c. planning a marketing strategy.
   d. reviewing entry into a foreign market.
   e. establishing a foreign distributorship.

6. Many marketing problems of multinational companies can be related to
   a. the need for better intelligence regarding environmental forces in international markets.
   b. political enmity between the multinational firm and foreign governments.
   c. the exploitation of foreign resources by multinational firms.
   d. disregard for cultural differences by multinational marketers.
   e. government regulation of multinational industries.

7. Which of the following is *not* a form of international market involvement?
   a. Joint ventures
   b. Cost-plus pricing
   c. Direct ownership
   d. Licensing

8. What is the major reason for using joint ventures?
   a. To bypass middlemen
   b. To provide technical assistance
   c. To compete
   d. To minimize risk and investment

9. Marketing activities are primarily social in purpose; therefore they are influenced by all of the following social structures *except*
   a. family structures.
   b. educational structures.

c. health and recreational structures.
d. trade channel structures.
e. religious structures.

10. Which of the following statements is *false*?
   a. In foreign markets, just as in the United States, consumers' buying habits are a major factor in shaping distribution channels.
   b. Distribution alternatives are determined by the existence of retail institutions and wholesalers that perform marketing functions between and among nations.
   c. The sales of the same product in different distribution channels at different prices is called squeezing.
   d. Products that require information about servicing need to be controlled in the distribution process.

11. Which of the following statements about technological forces is *false*?
   a. Much of the technology used in industrialized areas is well suited for developing countries.
   b. Mass marketing technology is too complex to be of much use in developing countries.
   c. Mass marketing technology is too expensive to create the jobs needed in developing countries.
   d. Export of strategically important technology from the United States may require Defense Department approval.

12. Dumping is a pricing practice used in foreign markets to
   a. charge the same price in different markets.
   b. stabilize the prices of products.
   c. get rid of surplus production.
   d. charge a lower price in foreign markets.

13. What is the lowest level of involvement in international marketing?
   a. Casual or accidental exporting
   b. Active exporting
   c. Licensing
   d. Joint venture

14. What is the greatest disadvantage of a joint venture in a foreign country?
   a. Loss of standardization
   b. Political uncertainty
   c. Increase in tariffs
   d. Product planning

15. What is a primary reason for licensing agreements?
   a. To minimize insurance expenses
   b. To avoid export agents

c. To exchange mangement techniques and minimize risks

d. To bypass middlemen

16. A major shortcoming of secondary data is

a. its high costs.

b. its overabundance.

c. that too much detailed information results.

d. the nonfeasibility of translating it.

e. the unreliability of some of it.

17. Which of the following is *not* a possible strategy for adapting product and promotion across national boundaries?

a. Keeping product and promotion the same worldwide

b. Adapt promotion only

c. Invent new products

d. Adapt product only

18. Foreign marketing opportunities should be investigated through the use of

a. the firm's data bank.

b. export bank marketing research.

c. international marketing intelligence.

d. market review and control.

19. Standardization of international marketing mixes

a. is not desirable, since uniformity of brands, packages, and labeling ignores cultural differences.

b. would result in competitive disadvantages.

c. would increase the expense of international marketing.

d. depends on the degree of similarity among environmental and market conditions.

20. A society's culture, as defined by the text, does *not* pertain to

a. attitudes toward heterosexual relationships.

b. common eating habits.

c. average age of males in urban centers.

d. the manner in which people express pleasure.

# Programmed Completion Exercises

accidental,
active, full-scale

1. The level of involvement in international marketing varies widely from casual or _____ exporting, to _____ exporting, to _____ commitment.

markets,
environments

2. International marketing intelligence involves analyzing foreign _____ and _____.

economic    3. Producers, wholesalers, retailers, buyers, and other organizations that produce, distribute, and purchase products are among the _____ institutions operating in foreign markets.

standardization    4. The degree of similarity of environmental and market conditions in different countries determines the feasibility of _____ .

Licensing    5. _____ is an alternative to direct investments when the political stability of the foreign country is questionable or when funds are not available for direct investment.

divisions, subsidiaries, risk    6. Direct ownership of foreign _____ or _____ involves the greatest _____ possible in international marketing.

secondary    7. The shortcomings of _____ data in international marketing intelligence include unavailability of detailed data, unreliability of some data, and the comparability and currency of available data.

social    8. Marketing activities are primarily _____ in purpose and are structured by institutions.

distribution    9. The existence of retail institutions and wholesalers that perform marketing functions between and within nations determines _____ alternatives.

pricing    10. Transportation costs, taxes, tariffs, research expenditures, and other management costs affect _____ decisions in foreign markets.

Exporting, flexible    11. _____ represents the lowest level of involvement in international marketing and is the most _____ approach to use.

Active    12. _____ exporting recognizes that foreign markets exist, but little effort is made to consider foreign markets in the overall marketing strategy.

International marketing

13. _____ _____ involves the performance of marketing activities across national boundaries.

multinational, customs, employment, technical, products

14. The growth of _____ firms has occurred as they have become more sensitive to national _____, to labor relations, and to governments' desires for capital, tax revenues, _____, _____ skills, foreign exchange, and access to new _____ from abroad.

Cultural

15. _____ aspects of the environment that are important to international marketing are customs, taboos, morals, beliefs, and knowledge.

political

16. The international _____ practice of payoffs and bribes is entrenched deeply in many foreign governments.

adaptation, standardization

17. The choice between _____ and _____ of an international marketing mix is considered only when there is a potential foreign market opportunity to justify the involvement.

invention

18. Product _____ is often the most expensive strategy affecting international product and promotion decisions.

regional

19. Standardization of the international marketing mix is highly desirable, but most evidence indicates that it is restricted to a _____ standardization.

multinational enterprise

20. The _____ _____ refers to the organizational aspects of firms that have operations or subsidiaries located in many countries in order to achieve a common goal.

technology, strategic importance

21. The export of _____ with _____ _____ to the United States may require Defense Department approval.

market potential

22. Aggregate measures of foreign _____ _____ are provided by such measures as overall buying power, credit, per capita GNP, and income distribution.

political, legal

23. The _____ and _____ system—including national laws, regulatory bodies, courts, and national pressure groups—all have great impact on international marketing.

Promotional

24. _____ adaptation is a low-cost modification compared with the engineering and production redevelopment costs of physically changing products.

dumping

25. The sale of a product in foreign markets at lower prices, when all costs have not been allocated, is called _____.

## Answers to Objective Questions

*True or False*

| | |
|---|---|
| 1. T | 13. T |
| 2. F | 14. F |
| 3. T | 15. T |
| 4. F | 16. T |
| 5. F | 17. F |
| 6. F | 18. F |
| 7. F | 19. T |
| 8. T | 20. T |
| 9. T | 21. T |
| 10. F | 22. T |
| 11. T | 23. T |
| 12. F | |

*Multiple-Choice*

| | |
|---|---|
| 1. d | 11. a |
| 2. a | 12. d |
| 3. b | 13. a |
| 4. b | 14. b |
| 5. e | 15. c |
| 6. a | 16. e |
| 7. b | 17. a |
| 8. d | 18. c |
| 9. d | 19. d |
| 10. c | 20. c |